KU-413-148

Rogue Warrior of the
SAS

LT-COL 'PADDY' BLAIR MAYNE
DSO (3 BARS), CROIX DE GUERRE, LÉGION D'HONNEUR

WHO DARES WINS

Roy Bradford and Martin Dillon

Foreword by
COL DAVID STIRLING, DSO, OBE

JOHN MURRAY

THE SAS BADGE (*see title-page*) was designed in the Western Desert by Cpl Tait, MM, in 1941. It comprises the sword 'Excalibur', winged on a shield. The light blue wings and background to the motto scroll and the dark blue shield were attributed to the Oxford & Cambridge University boat crews, in which several of the SAS had served. The motto on a three-part scroll WHO DARES WINS was in black thread, as well as black detail on the sword and centre of the wings – the whole badge bordered in red thread. (A brass version was also issued, but in a crude casting.) Following the badge being worn on a variety of head-dress, a white beret was adopted, but soon changed to the sand-coloured one. This beret was worn until 1944, when members of the SAS were ordered to wear the maroon beret of the Airborne Forces. This was not always adhered to, many still favouring the sand-coloured, a notable person being Paddy Mayne, CO of 1 SAS.

© Roy Bradford and Martin Dillon 1987
Foreword © David Stirling 1987

First published 1987
by John Murray (Publishers) Ltd
50 Albemarle Street, London W1X 4BD

Reprinted 1987, 1988

All rights reserved
Unauthorised duplication
contravenes applicable laws

Typeset by Goodfellow & Egan Ltd, Cambridge
Printed and bound in Great Britain
at the Bath Press, Avon

British Library Cataloguing in Publication Data

Bradford, Roy
Rogue warrior of the SAS : Lt-Colonel
'Paddy' Blair Mayne, DSO (3 Bars),
Croix de Guerre, Légion d'honneur.
1. Mayne, Robert Blair 2. Great Britain,
Army. Special Air Service Regiment——
Biography
I. Title II. Dillon, Martin
356'.167'0924   D760.S6

ISBN 0-7195-4430-0

Contents

Foreword by Col David Stirling, DSO, OBE   xii

1 'Paddy's done it!'   1
2 Early Years of a Viking   8
3 War and 11 Commando   16
4 Birth of the SAS   26
5 Joint Operations   37
6 El Alamein   47
7 A Proper Establishment   60
8 Special Raiding Squadron, SAS   70
9 Italy: Bagnara and Termoli   81
10 Retraining for France   91
11 TITANIC and its Lessons   98
12 The Garstin 'Stick'   108
13 Operation GAIN   115
14 Operation KIPLING   126
15 Brave and Brilliant Exploits   132
16 A Different Role in Germany   146
17 The Fourth DSO   163
18 'Blue-Pencil Idiots'   183

19 Final Days of the War 198
20 Norway and Disbandment 210
21 Home Again 216
22 Fish out of Water 229
APPENDIX 1: SAS personnel who took part in raids on Axis airfields in North Africa, 1941–2 236
APPENDIX 2: Operation HOWARD personnel in Germany, 6–29 April 1945 238
Selected Bibliography 245
Index 246

Illustrations

(Between pages 114 and 115)

1 Paddy's first rugby international, Belfast, 1937
2 Paddy, Duncan Macrae and Frank Mellish during British Lions'
   Tour of South Africa, 1938
3 Springbok killed on the night of the Pietermaritzburg ball
4 A dejected Paddy after first abortive parachute drop in the
   Desert at Tamimi, Nov. 1941
5 Paddy, the Desert Raider, near Kabrit, 1942
6 Paddy and Raymond Shorter sampling dates near Kufra
7 Members of 'B' Squadron, 1 SAS, at the entrance to an
   abandoned underground fort at Bir Zalten, Nov. 1942
8 Col David Stirling, DSO, OBE
9 RSM Bob Bennett, BEM, MM
10 Brig Mike Calvert, DSO*
11 Malcolm Pleydell in the Desert, 1942
12 Capt Mike Sadler, MC, a brilliant navigator
13 Capt Bill Fraser, MC
14 Capt Alex Muirhead, MC
15 Sgt Reg Seekings, DCM, MM and Sgt Johnny Cooper, DCM, on
    leave in Cairo, 1941
16 Paddy and comrades, Nahariya, Palestine, May 1943
17 Men of 3 Troop, Special Raiding Squadron, 1 SAS, Cape
    Murro di Porco, Sicily, July 1943
18 Paddy, Maj John Tonkin, MC, and comrades, Cape Murro di
    Porco, Sicily, July 1943

19   Harry Poat, Tony Marsh, Phil Gunn relaxing after fighting after Bagnara
20   Paddy on an American LCI prior to Termoli landing, 1943
21   Carnage at Termoli, Oct. 1943
22   Officers of 'C' Squadron in the 'cage', Fairford, Glos
23   Maj Mike Blackman, MC
24   Cpl 'Billy' Hull
25   Lt John Scott, MM, and Sgt J. Edwards
26   German tracked tricycle, after SAS ambush
27   Paddy on leave in Scotland, 1944
28   A KIPLING patrol makes contact with Gen Patton's forward elements at Courtenay, near Lyons, Aug. 1944
29   The KIPLING patrol shortly before the fire-fight with German SS troops at Les Ormes
30   Mrs Hanbury with SAS troops at Hylands, Chelmsford, 1944
31   Tanks of Canadian 4 Armoured Division heading for Oldenburg
32   Maj Harry Poat's jeep patrols in the forest beyond Lorup, April 1945
33   Members of 'D' Squadron, 1 SAS, before entering U-boat base at Kiel, May 1945
34   Paddy with Maj Roy Farran, DSO, MC, Stavanger airport, May/June 1945
35   Paddy, Tony Marsh and John Tonkin in a captured enemy speedboat, Bergen harbour, June 1945
36   Paddy with his niece, Margaret, at Mount Pleasant, Newtownards, shortly before the war
37   Paddy's funeral procession to Movilla Churchyard, Newtownards, Dec. 1955

ENDPAPERS

Front: Members of 'B' Squadron, 1 SAS, at Bir Zalten, North African Desert, 1942
Rear: Willys jeeps of the victorious SAS making their way through Bergen, Norway, at the end of the war (Bob Bennett behind wheel of nearest jeep)

SOURCES OF ILLUSTRATIONS

Plates 1, 2, 3, 4, 5, 6, 19, 21, 26, 27, 30, 31, 32, 36, 37: Mayne family; front endpaper, 7, 16, 17, 18, 33, 34, 35: John Tonkin; 8: David Stirling; 9, rear endpaper: Bob Bennett; 10: Mike Calvert; 11: Malcolm Pleydell; 12: Mike Sadler; 13: Bill Fraser; 14: Alex Muirhead; 15: Reg Seekings; 20, 22, 28, 29: Derrick Harrison; 23: Mike Blackman; 24: William Hull; 25: John Scott.

MAPS

1 North African Desert, 1941–3   p. 35
2 Assault operations by Special Raiding Squadron, 1 SAS,
   in Sicily and Italy, 1943   73
3 Typical SAS dropping zone in France, 1944   109
4 SAS operational bases in France, 1944   122
5 SAS operations in NW Germany, 1945   151
6 Lt Philip Schlee's map of the scene in which Paddy
   gained his fourth DSO   171
7 Maj Harry Poat's map, sent to Paddy, to indicate the
   ambush of SAS troops by the Germans on the road to
   Nienburg, April 1945   201

Acknowledgements

The authors wish to acknowledge their debt to the many individuals who contributed to this book. Although the events related go back almost fifty years we are fortunate that so many of those who played, fought and drank with Paddy Blair Mayne are still alive to tell the tale. All of them gave most generously of their time in long conversations, in letters from as far away as New Zealand and in providing papers and photographs (many previously unpublished).

Most of those concerned feature in the text, where their experiences speak for themselves. From the list of many brave and distinguished soldiers we single out one for special mention: Col David Stirling, DSO, OBE, 'father' of the SAS and President of the SAS Regimental Association, who has kindly written the Foreword. His approval opened all doors, in a sense, and made our task considerably easier; for all his invaluable help we are deeply grateful.

That does not lessen our sense of gratitude to his and Paddy's comrades-in-arms in the SAS for their tireless, willing and ever-patient assistance. We thank: Maj J. E. Almonds, MM; Leslie C. Bateman; RSM Bob Bennett, BEM, MM; Brig Michael Blackman, OBE, MC; Jim Brough, MM; C. J. Bryan, CMG, CVO, OBE, MC; John Byrne, DCM; Brig J. M. (Mike) Calvert, DSO*; Roy Close, CBE; Dr David Surrey Dane; Lt-Col David Danger, MBE, MM; Gordon Davidson; Lt W. A. Deakins; Derrick Harrison, MC; Col Pat Hart, OBE; William (Billy) Hull; G.

Hutchinson; Dave Kershaw, MM; J. Keith Killby; Maj-Gen David Lloyd Owen, CB, DSO, OBE, MC; Very Rev Dr Fraser McClusky, MC, MA, BD; Dr Alex Muirhead, MC; Dr Malcolm Pleydell; John Randall; Maj Pat Riley, DCM; Ian Robinson; Mike Sadler, MC; Philip Schlee; the late John Scott, MM; Sandy Scratchley; Reg Seekings, DCM, MM; Lt-Col I. F. ('Tanky') Smith, MBE, Secretary of the SAS Regimental Association, who placed the Official SAS records at our disposal; Maj John Tonkin, MC; Ian Wellsted, OBE; Frederick ('Chalky') White, DCM, MM; John Wiseman, MC.

We are indebted also to Harold and Jessie Taylor, custodians of the Commando Museum at Lamlash, Arran; Rev George Cromey, H. R. McKibbin and J. A. E. Siggins, who were team-mates with Paddy in Irish international rugby matches; Col Mervyn Dennison, Desmond Marrinan, Mr & Mrs George Matthews, Jack Midgeley and Sir Robert Porter for their reminiscences of Paddy after the war; and, especially, Ted Griffiths, DFC, who began as Paddy's teacher and became his life-long friend.

Above all, we must pay tribute and grateful thanks to the inestimable part played by the Mayne family. Douglas Mayne, Paddy's younger brother, and his sister, Frances – Mrs Frances Mayne Elliott – were ungrudging in their efforts to provide guidance and information. They gave us their confidence and opened to us all the family papers and records. They gave us insights into the character of their exceptional brother which we could have obtained from no one else. We trust that they and their family are satisfied that we have done him and his comrades justice.

Finally, we wish to point out that the responsibility for errors of fact, serious omissions or unattributed expressions of opinion rests with the authors alone.

RB : MD
1987

Foreword

By Colonel David Stirling, DSO, OBE

The remarkable feats of Lt-Colonel Robert ('Paddy') Blair Mayne inevitably attract the adjective 'legendary' but the use of this word is a reminder of the danger of his audacious exploits and wild escapades becoming the source of apocryphal stories passed on by people who scarcely knew him, if at all.

More than forty years have passed since those days in the Western Desert when Paddy first made his name, and if his deeds then and later in Sicily, Italy, France and Germany were to be chronicled then it was essential to tap the memories, still astonishingly fresh and vivid, of those who served with him.

The merit of *Rogue Warrior of the SAS* is that the authors, Roy Bradford and Martin Dillon, do justice to Paddy Mayne's career as a soldier and place him unquestionably where he belongs – among the outstanding military heroes of the Second World War. In addition to his personal gallantry, his achievements in battle and his superb leadership of the Regiment (see footnote, p. xiv) undoubtedly made inevitable the establishment of the SAS as a permanent part of the British Defence Forces.

It is always hard to pin down the qualities that go to make up an exceptional man and Paddy could be exasperatingly elusive because his character was such a mixture of contrasting attributes. On the one hand there was his great capacity for friendship: his compassion and gentleness displayed during the war in his deep concern for the welfare of all his men and expressing itself in peacetime in his voluntary work with juvenile delinquents and boys' clubs and as a regular prison visitor; his love of the countryside and the attention he lavished on his rose garden; and his essentially happy family life. Qualities like these would seem to demonstrate his belief in God. On the other hand, there was a reverse side to his character which revealed itself in outbursts of satanic ferocity.

Let me give one example. In mounting our attacks in the Western Desert I believe it was necessary to be ruthless because one of our main purposes was to cause the enemy to withdraw troops from the front line to defend installations in their rear. On one of his early operations Paddy was brilliantly successful but he pushed ruthlessness to the point of callousness.

His temperament and moods made him a difficult subordinate. He had, I suppose, something in common with Hotspur, the young Harry Percy – quick-tempered, audacious and vigorous in action but not one who took kindly to being thwarted, frustrated or crossed in any way.

I think I found the clue to Paddy's moods in my own experience as a painter manqué. One evening in our Mess at Kabrit, Paddy and I were talking about our families and about life before the war. I was describing to him how determined I had been for some years to become a professional artist and how for many months I had worked in the studio of a great French critic and teacher in Paris. I told him how bitterly I felt it when I finally realised that although I had, according to my teacher, the creative talent to conceive original work, I lacked the drawing discipline and therefore my painting would never achieve real merit. The frustration was so great that it drove me to compensate by tackling the most exacting physical goal I could set myself – the climbing of Mount Everest (in the event, the declaration of war interrupted my training after six months in the Alps and seven months in the Canadian and American Rockies).

It was the look in Paddy's eyes in response to this confession rather than what he said (which was incoherent), which convinced me beyond doubt that he realised he was himself suffering from extreme frustration. A creative urge within the inner recesses of his subconscious mind was constantly seeking expression without achieving it; as there was no outlet for his creative energy, it got bottled up to an intolerable level and this led to some of his heavy drinking bouts in an attempt to open the closed door; and this frustration explained at least some of his violent acts and his black moods. Among its positive effects it also explained Paddy's astonishing intuition and inspiration in battle.

Paddy was a complex man and in deciding to write about him Roy Bradford and Martin Dillon set themselves a daunting task. It is greatly to their credit that they have succeeded in presenting a rounded portrait and, in doing so, have offered an illuminating insight into an exceptional individual who in operation after operation in different theatres of war stretched himself to the uttermost extent of his physical and mental resources, not once, as any man might have done, but time after time.

But at what cost to himself? The well-documented evidence in this book enables the reader to comprehend sympathetically the heavy toll exacted in the long run by the relentless demands Paddy imposed on himself.

*On the occasion of opening the new barracks (Stirling Lines) at Hereford in June 1984 Col David Stirling pointed out to the many visitors present: 'I have always felt uneasy in being known as the founder of the Regiment. To ease my conscience I would like it to be recognised that I have five co-founders: Jock Lewes and Paddy Blair Mayne of the original 'L' Detachment, SAS; Georges Berge, whose unit of Free French joined the SAS in January 1942; Brian Franks, who re-established 21 SAS Regiment after the SAS had been disbanded at the end of the Second World War; and John Woodhouse, who created the modern 22 SAS Regiment during the Malay campaign by restoring to the Regiment its original philosophy.'

I

'Paddy's done it!'

IT was 14 December 1941, one week after the Japanese attack on Pearl Harbor. The United States had joined the Allies in the war against the Axis Powers, Germany and Italy. On the outskirts of Moscow, in a temperature of minus 30°C, the Russians had launched a fierce counter-offensive on the frozen and exhausted German army.

In the North African Desert the military advantage which had see-sawed across Libya for a year and which twice had brought Rommel to the borders of Egypt now saw him falling back again – back to the defensive position of El Agheila, half-way between Cairo and Tripoli, from which he had launched his first, devastating advance in April 1941. Rommel's retreat had been conducted with his usual masterly grasp of Panzer movement. He still held Benghazi but his main forces, at El Agheila, were entrenched in an area of soft sand and salt pans at the southernmost point of the Gulf of Sirte which extended inland from the coast for many miles. Few tracks led through it. In the past it had proved, if properly held, almost impregnable.

The night of 14 December was windy and, as usual, once the sun had gone down, bitterly cold. The Cairo moonlight chart, prepared by a Forward Company of the Royal Engineers, shows that moonrise was not until 01.00 hrs. Tamet, one of Rommel's forward air bases on the coastal road, almost midway between El Agheila and Tripoli, had closed down for the night. Guards were on duty. Inside one of the wooden huts which served as the officers' mess about thirty German and Italian pilots were talking, drinking and playing cards. They had no cause for concern. They were a long way, 250 miles, behind the fighting and Rommel was in charge. The mess was snugly blacked out, a fire brightly burning. Against the danger of air attack their planes had been widely dispersed around the perimeter of the airfield and they would have plenty of advance warning of approaching bombers. But the threat was to come from a very different quarter, a threat for which they were completely unprepared.

With a crash, the door of the hut burst open. Framed in it stood a giant of a man in khaki battle gear, a sandy-coloured beard under an officer's battered peaked cap. It was their first and, for many of them, their last glimpse of Lieutenant Robert ('Paddy') Blair Mayne of the Special Air Service (SAS). The tommy-gun clutched to his right side spoke. The talk and laughter turned to shouts, screams and gasps of horror. Burst after burst he fired. There were fifty rounds in the drum. Within seconds the hut was littered with dead and dying. As the wounded tried to crawl for cover, any cover, a final burst blew out the lights. Only the firelight now played on the bloody bodies. Then Paddy Mayne was gone. For him the night's work had only just begun.

Outside, the five other men in the party he commanded – a sergeant and four privates – stopped in their tracks and waited for what was bound to come. One of the two surviving witnesses of the Tamet raid, a private then, later Sergeant Reg Seekings, recalls what happened next: 'As soon as Paddy cut loose, Chalky White and I dived for cover, cover being one of the other huts he had told us to check on. We dived behind it. In a matter of minutes the whole place went mad – everything they had, including tracer. The next few seconds seemed to be funny. They had fixed lines of fire about a couple of feet from the ground. We had to either jump over or crawl under them. One man, Chesworth, came slithering over to us on all fours. I can still see him getting to his feet, pulling in his arse as the tracer ripped past his pack, missing him by inches. On a signal from Paddy we got to hell out of it.'

Swiftly they were swallowed up in the black night of the surrounding desert. About half a mile away the six men met up again and held what Seekings calls a 'confab'. His sergeant had for some time been unenthusiastic about the whole exercise. It was the first of its kind ever undertaken by the SAS and no one knew what to expect. Three hours earlier they had been dropped by the trucks of the Long Range Desert Group (LRDG) to make the raid on foot. After an hour and a half, heavily laden with equipment, they still had no evidence that they were nearing their objective. Had they been heading in the wrong direction? The sergeant was in favour of calling it off. Otherwise they could be late for the return rendezvous with the LRDG, and be left stranded. Jalo oasis, their base in the south which they had left six days previously, was 350 miles away. Only Seekings' own unshakeable insistence that he could sniff the scent of high-octane petrol on the night-wind had convinced his leader that they were heading roughly in the direction of the airfield. After almost another hour stumbling across stony terrain, fatigue and hope deferred brought renewed doubts. Suddenly they struck a concrete post, which turned out to be a boundary marker at the end of a runway. Joyous relief. They crept forward, fatigue now forgotten. Despite their keen night-sight, developed over months of training, visibility was no more than twenty or thirty yards! Still no aircraft could be seen. Then the dim silhouette of several huts loomed ahead. Paddy had directed the men to spread out and check. Without warning several Italians came out of the nearest hut. It was the one from which issued sounds of life and laughter and which Paddy had chosen for himself.

That attack had been made twenty minutes before. It was now past 22.00 hrs. Time was getting tight. They were due back at the rendezvous by midnight. The firing on the airfield was gradually dying down.

The sergeant reckoned that all the guards would now be on full alert. To attempt to co-ordinate separate actions in the darkness would be almost impossible. Others reasoned that the enemy would assume that, having done their work, the raiders had decamped for good. Paddy Mayne listened. He had taken the voices. Now he made his decision. If there had ever been doubt in his mind as to what course to take, it had not shown. They would return to the airfield. It was nearly an hour since they had left it. The gunfire had ceased. Tamet was once again silent and dark. But for Seekings the smell of high-octane fuel was stronger than ever. Now, even after forty-five years, he still hates the smell, and anything that resembles it, like women's nail varnish remover. They retraced their steps heading for an area away from the huts. The sky had lightened only a little. By crouching down they had a better chance of spotting outlines against it. On the edge of the airfield they came upon their first aircraft, an Italian CR42, a two-seater biplane similar to a Gloster, used for both interception and observation.

It was a moment not to be forgotten. 'I thought Paddy had gone mad as he dived into the cockpit,' Seekings recalls. 'He ripped the dashboard completely out. How he did it I shall never know. I don't think any of us before had been so excited. Our first aircraft! Not any of us acted the true Englishman.'

A bomb was left on the wing. Then they spotted a second plane about a hundred yards away. 'Christ! Another,' said Private Hawkins. It became clear that the aircraft were all parked on the perimeter. They continued their hazardous mystery tour, dealing with whatever they came across – planes, supply dumps, telephone poles. The explosive they used had been devised specially by Jock Lewes, the SAS expert. What looked like a lump of black putty was a stinking mixture of plastic, engine oil and thermite to provide the incendiary element. The bombs were activated by a time-pencil. As the capsule was squeezed, acid started eating through a copper wire which, when severed, released the detonator. The timing was regulated by the wire thickness.

During their time on the airfield they were left surprisingly undisturbed. Seekings remembers the odd movement here and there, but not enough seriously to interfere with their operation. Bomb dumps were underground, down several steps. With the 500-lb bombs the nose cap was unscrewed and the charge stuck to the detonator. Petrol was simpler. Once the cans in the centre ignited, it would go up. After an hour's steady progress, during which they had almost circled the entire field, the sergeant again voiced concern about the time factor. Paddy Mayne ordered him to return with the three others and tell the LRDG to wait. He and Seekings took the three remaining bombs. On the sea-front they spied more huts. A swift recce proved them empty. Then they discovered another row of German planes, Stukas. Soon they had no bombs left, so they smashed the instrument panel.

'I could not shift it,' Seekings said, 'so I smashed it with my revolver. As I jumped down my lanyard caught and I was helpless until Paddy freed me.'

On the edge of the airfield, they rested under a bush and had a smoke. Paddy produced a flask. 'Drop of whiskey?' To Seekings' surprise, knowing his officer, there was more water than whiskey.

It was well over an hour now since they had planted the first bomb. Would the explosive work? How soon? It was the first time it had been used in an operation. For Lieutenant Blair Mayne it was also a first time, his first as commander in sole charge. One can only imagine the tension, and his anxieties, for he was not given to expressing them. Had he made a mistake? Attacked the mess too soon? For Seekings and the others he had been, up to then, an unknown quantity. 'He was dubious. I mean in those days he was very scruffy. Nothing fitted. Had a hell of a temper, especially when drinking. He didn't mix. We used to say, with his ginger beard, he looked like Jesus Christ. All the way to Tamet we were wondering.' Earlier that year Seekings had taken part in a raid on Bardia with 7 Commando. He had started out with the Cambridgeshire Territorials, and had as much battle experience as his officer.

Their waiting was cut short. Something was happening. They saw men coming towards them. They got moving quickly. Hardly had they gone fifty yards when the first bomb went up. They stopped to look. Then another went up, too near them. They ran for it. At a safe distance they stopped to watch and count the explosions. It was not possible to distinguish between planes and dumps. The sky lit up with flaming debris. Then there was a 'terrific roar' as the petrol and bomb dumps went up. Men were running around all over the place. Constant machine-gun fire. The Germans and Italians, whom they had identified as occupying different areas on the airfield, appeared in the general confusion to be firing at each other. As Paddy Mayne himself noted in his all-too-brief report, dictated later: 'The guards were slack and, when alarmed, wasted many rounds in misdirected fire.' For the two observers all this was a gloriously heart-warming sight.

Many miles out in the desert, waiting anxiously at his LRDG rendezvous point, Captain David Stirling, the commander of the Special Air Service, had been anxiously scanning the horizon: 23.00 hrs, the time for Mayne's attack, came and went; 23.30 hrs, still nothing. Stirling himself had just come back from an abortive raid on nearby Sirte, arriving to find it empty of aircraft. It was beginning to look like a total failure for the SAS. Then, suddenly, all his doubts and fears were dissolved. A great flash lit up the western sky, followed by explosion after explosion. Stirling had never heard such sweet thunder. Up to then there had been nothing but failure. All that was changed, changed utterly. His ideas had at last been vindicated. Paddy Mayne, the old bastard, had done it!

'We got cracking then,' Seekings remembers vividly. 'Our LRDG lads were flashing lights at a few minute intervals. We packed our compass away. A light flashed to our right. Next thing we knew we were off our course. We turned towards it, but it was soon obvious that the enemy were flashing lights as well. We had an alternative signal – blasts on a whistle. We blew it and were answered nearby, much to our relief.

'I was gasping for a drink. We had no water with us and Paddy had set a cracking pace. Sergeant Jacko [Jackson, a Rhodesian with the LRDG] gave me a water-bottle, one of the big type the Rhodesians had. I took a long drink from it. As I took it from my lips I could not get my wind. Too late I realised it was neat rum. In a matter of minutes I was three parts in the blind. I staggered to my truck and fell off to sleep in spite of the rough going. I awoke to the sound of hammering and cursing – the steering had broken and the fitter was doing his best to put it right. Jacko had got a fire going and a brew on. I think it was Mike Sadler, the navigator, trying to tell him we were only a few yards from Sirte, to which Jacko replied he did not give a hell. If we were only a few yards away, he still intended to have a brew.

'It was Mike's first patrol as navigator. We had to rendezvous miles out into the desert with the other half of the patrol [i.e. with Stirling's group]. In spite of the rough going and darkness, he made it dead on. A marvellous performance he was to repeat often. In mending the truck we had been forced to dismantle the brakes and therefore could not stop. When we sighted the patrol we had to coast towards them. They started firing everything. We almost died of shock thinking they had mistaken us for the enemy, but luckily they were firing into the air giving us a royal welcome. They had seen the fires and explosions in the distance.'

Such was the first SAS raid on Tamet. It was the beginning of a devastatingly new form of warfare; and the first, most searching examination of Lieutenant Robert ('Paddy') Blair Mayne. Up to then his fellow soldiers and comrades had been wondering what kind of stuff their strange and aloof companion was made of. After Tamet they knew. But neither they nor even those closest to him in his own family even guessed at how much more there still was to know.

2

Early Years of a Viking

R OBERT BLAIR MAYNE was born on 11 January 1915,
five months after the start of the First World War. He was
christened Robert Blair after a cousin of his mother, Captain
Robert Blair of 5 Battalion, The Border Regiment, who was
killed the following year in the act of winning the DSO – a
singular presage of the future. His younger brother, Douglas,
born in 1919, was named after Field Marshal Sir Douglas Haig.
Already the local paper, the *Newtownards Chronicle*, was carrying
lists of casualties from Flanders. In that week of 9 January the
largest advertisement offered 'Officers' Khaki Uniforms'. A
column called 'From the Firing Line' quoted letters from
Newtownards soldiers writing home. Ulster had paused in its
fight against Home Rule for Ireland to direct its energies
elsewhere. Thousands of men had shown their loyalty by
rallying to the Union Jack. The same issue of the *Newtownards
Chronicle* contains a report of Sir Edward Carson, the Ulster
Unionist leader (who later became First Lord of the Admiralty),
reviewing troops of the local North Down Battalion of the Ulster
Volunteer Force. Twelve months later they were blown to pieces
at Thiepval, on the Somme.

But neither war nor its rumours – the *Newtownards Chronicle*
also carried an account of the sinking of the two German
battle-cruisers, *Gneisenau* and *Scharnhorst*, off the Falkland
Islands as well as, much nearer home, a German bombardment
of Scarborough and Hartlepool – interfered much with the

comfortable life of the Mayne family. Blair's father, William Mayne, now with six young children and debarred from war service by childhood polio, looked after the family wine and grocery business. The most prosperous shop in town, catering for the carriage trade – such as that of the Marquess of Londonderry, who lived nearby at Mount Stewart – it had been established by William's grandfather, also William, a miller and a Justice of the Peace who, a hundred years before, had married Frances O'Neill, a daughter of local gentry. By then the Mayne family, originally from Scotland, had been established in the Strangford peninsula of County Down for nearly a hundred years, since the birth of John Echlin Mayne in 1781.

It was around 1847 that William, the JP, purchased Mount Pleasant, a property on the outskirts of Newtownards. Rebuilt in 1802, it is now listed as a historic building, and originally it had been the manse of First Newtownards Presbyterian Church, whose Minister had taken part in the 1798 rebellion of the United Irishmen. The house is still in the possession of the Mayne family with, in the older part, the rifle-slits through which the young Blair used to poke his first air-gun.

Blair's father William had inherited Mount Pleasant from his father, Thomas, and Blair himself was the first of his generation to be born there. He had two older brothers, Thomas and William, and three sisters, Molly, Barbara and Frances, as well as the youngest child, Douglas, born four years later. It was a close-knit, self-contained family, typically Presbyterian in that its affluence was without show or pretentions. Dinner was at midday, followed by high-tea at six. There were two indoor servants and a general handy-man.

Transport was by wagonette driven by Blair's mother, and ponytraps, with, in the early 1920s, the first motor-car, a Lee-Francis. Besides the carriage horses there were hunters. In his younger days William – he was married at twenty-four – went out regularly with the North Down Harriers. There are stories of how he had been scolded by his own father, Thomas, for not dressing properly for the hunt. This meticulousness in dress was later very marked in the grandson, Blair, during his army days.

William Mayne had many interests. As a young man he had been a champion racing cyclist. He bred and raced pigeons. In the walled garden, the fruit-trees were his special care. He pruned and grafted apples, pears and figs, and won many prizes at the local Show which was the main social event of the year. In this he was following in the footsteps of his grandfather. In the possession of the family is an ornate testimonial to him, signed in copperplate by most of the Victorian dignitaries of the town. Dated 8 December 1892 it is inscribed 'Newtownards Horticultural and Showjumping Society, addressed to William Mayne Esquire, celebrating forty summers since he and others laid the foundation of the Society'. Sixty years later his great-grandson was to continue the tradition by growing flowering shrubs, but during the 1920s, with so many animals around the house, there was no trouble in filling a boy's day. Besides the horses and a cow to provide their own milk, there were pigeons, poultry, rabbits, pigs and several dogs – terriers and always Airedales, William Mayne's favourite breed. His daughter Frances recalls houses in trees, a special Mayne game played with hockey sticks and croquet balls, and the boys sleeping in tents on the lawn. Nor was the household regime in any sense strict or puritanical. On Sundays the children were allowed to do as they pleased, unusual for an Ulster Presbyterian family. Mother took the children to church. Their memory is that their father did not normally accompany them. His Sunday mornings were usually spent with his terriers, killing rats at the hunt kennels.

Mrs Mayne, born Margaret Boyle Vance, was a strong determined woman, deferring to but certainly not dominated by her energetic husband. Her family originally came from Cumberland and there were still strong family links there. Her grandfather, Gilbert Vance, a linen merchant in Belfast, was also a partner in Blair & Vance, the company which owned the Hematite Iron Works in the town of Parton. The iron works was not successful and, after Margaret's birth, they moved from their fine house in Holywood, near Belfast, to Movilla House, a more modest dwelling in Newtownards. She was one of eleven children. In seeking to trace the genes that went to the shaping of her son, Blair, the influence of her only brother, Gilbert, is possibly significant. He was the black sheep, the wild one, hard-living, hard-drinking. He sailed for Canada and did not return. Margaret Vance was left with her four sisters. Her surviving children agree that, in her eyes, her daughters took second place. Frances, the third youngest child, recalls how on the Sunday walk to church, when she wanted to take her mother's hand, it was to one of the boys that the sought-after favour was granted. Thomas, the first-born son, and Blair were favourites, until tragedy struck in 1937.

Tom appears to have been moulded from the same clay as his uncle Gilbert. Unsettled, undisciplined, he ran away from two boarding schools. His father took him into the shop but the off-licence attached to the grocery proved a fatal temptation. He was banned from the business on several occasions for drunkenness, once for a period lasting three months during which time he constructed a large rockery at Mount Pleasant. The size of the stones bears witness still to the effort which the work must have entailed. As his brother Douglas said, he was strong and fond of shooting; but, at the age of thirty-two, on that same rockery when, one can only assume, his mind was unbalanced by drink – and possibly after another furious row with his long-suffering father – he turned a shot-gun against himself. The trauma profoundly affected the whole family, but hit the mother hardest. In the words of her daughter, she withdrew into herself and her social life was reduced to a minimum. From then on her affection was concentrated solely on Blair, and in his life the influence of his mother became more and more potent. He idolised her. Malcolm Pleydell-Bouverie, a medical officer who knew him well and served with him in the SAS during the long desert campaign, says that Blair Mayne 'had with his mother almost a spiritual relationship'. Certainly they were unusually close. When he was playing rugby, it was his mother, not his father, who used to accompany him in the car to watch the game, and who drove home with him. Sigmund Freud has said, 'The boy who is his mother's favourite will go through life like a conqueror.' In a remarkably literal way the dictum held good for Blair Mayne, although there were other aspects of his life where the fierce maternal devotion was possibly less happy in its effect.

There were the exclusions and alliances between siblings that occur in every large family, but by all accounts Paddy Mayne's childhood was reasonably happy and contented. The father, immersed in his business and leisure activities, was a man of regular habits. Douglas, the youngest son, remembers him as very gentle, despite a mercurial temper. He recalls driving his father on Thursdays up to Belfast to the old-established Linenhall Library, where a selection of books for the coming week was carefully chosen. After the library there was the Turkish bath, and lunch in Thompson's restaurant with his cronies, often fellow racing-pigeon enthusiasts. All the Mayne family were 'great readers' to quote their own words, and 'an odd lot'. In this way they seek to describe a distinctive family trait, an 'odd-man-out', prickly quality, an individual self-sufficiency and shyness, which was especially noticeable in Blair. Unusually, they did not go on annual family holidays, an almost universal custom in Ulster at the time. Father and Mother used to take the waters at the spas of Droitwich or Harrogate in England.

The children were taken for day picnics to neighbouring beaches or they planned their own expeditions. Once they spent a week in a seaside cottage at Portaferry, a dozen miles away on Strangford Lough. His sister remembers that Blair, though a keen swimmer, 'read the whole time'. Among his reading matter was the *Strand Magazine* to which his father subscribed. The addiction to books remained with him all his life.

While his two elder sisters were sent to boarding school in Dublin, Blair was kept at home in Newtownards. He attended Miss Brown's Lady School which was situated on the Town Square. There, at the age of six, he first came to public attention when he climbed out through a skylight out on to the roof. His sister, Frances, recalls the fearful excitement as he waved to the knot of spectators below. Later he went to the local Grammar School, Regent House. 'A tall gangly boy,' he was popular with his companions, according to one of his teachers, ex-Squadron Leader Ted Griffiths, who later became a close friend: 'Everybody liked Blair, he was quiet, modest and by no means aggressive. His bent was literary rather than mathematical and he was enthusiastic about all forms of sport.' His copy of Charles Letts' School-Boy's Diary for the year 1931 is meticulously filled with results of rugby games, and a list of the books he read: John Buchan, Ian Hay, Anthony Hope, Dickens, Kipling, J. B. Priestley and Sir Walter Scott all score Good or Excellent in the column headed Remarks. There are the usual banalities about the rain and frequent mentions of having 'a really good bathe'.

He goes to the cinema about once a week: *King of Jazz, Journey's End, Raffles*. There is only one mention of a girl on 9 October: 'At Moffet's. She has finished with me.' A blighted romance? No, Miss Moffet was his dentist. Soon Blair was captaining the school rugby team. It is recorded too that, at the age of thirteen, he could drive a golf ball further than most adults – the nearby golf course crowns the hill of Scrabo, which overlooks the family home. This was the first inkling of the exceptional physical strength which marked him in manhood.

Ted Griffiths coached him in Latin, which he had failed in the Higher Certificate examination. Then, after leaving school, Blair was apprenticed to a solicitor in Newtownards. As part of his training, he attended lectures in the Law Faculty at Queen's University, Belfast. It was at university that he emerged as a sportsman of international class. At the age of eighteen he was captain of the Newtownards rugby team. By twenty-one he was Irish Universities' Heavyweight Boxing Champion. The first of six caps for Ireland came in 1937, against Wales. George Cromey, who was then the outstanding Irish fly-half, played with him in all his internationals and accompanied him in the British Lions side which toured South Africa in 1938. He was well placed to observe Blair, a second-row forward, in action; and confirms Mayne's reputation as a hard player, almost indestructible, as someone who retaliated only when attacked, yet did so with such ferocity that he was liable to floor several of the opposing scrum. In that first game against Wales Mayne was involved in fisticuffs. 'It was great to have Blair around,' George Cromey remarks. 'I can't ever remember him initiating any kind of rough stuff on the rugby field, but he could look after us when things were going wrong.'

After the Lions' tour, one of the Morkels, a family celebrated in Springbok history, described Mayne as 'The finest all-round forward I have ever seen and magnificently built for the part. In staying power he has to be seen to be believed.' Sammy Walker, a fellow Ulsterman and the Lions' captain, saw him as 'quiet, soft-spoken, self-effacing off the field, but in the heat of a match he could be frightening. He was the toughest and strongest man I have ever known. Jamie Clinch, a tough man himself and one of the great Irish international players, once confided in me that the only man he ever feared on a rugby field was Blair Mayne.'

The sharp contrasts, the chiaroscuro in the Mayne make-up, were beginning to appear. With the shyness went a propensity for schoolboy pranks. In Pietermaritzburg there was a grand dinner and ball for the visiting Lions. The ladies wore their most dazzling gowns, and the men were in evening dress. It was the kind of social occasion which Blair Mayne always avoided. Since schooldays he had never been at ease in mixed company other than that of his family; and at university none of his friends remembers seeing him 'chatting up' a girl. At the Saturday night 'hops', the informal dances at Queen's where the lusty and romantic young mixed and matched, he had never been seen on the dance floor. He was usually present, but would spend the evening among the males up at the bar. On the night of the Pietermaritzburg ball, he disappeared after dinner. The excuse he made later was that he did not wish to desert some new-found Afrikaner friends who were not in proper dress. It was late next morning when he strode through the hotel lobby, an extraordinary apparition, his dress-suit torn and filthy as though he had been scrambling through ditches and thorn-bushes. Across his broad back was slung a bloodstained buck. Sammy Walker awoke to find Mayne standing over him and the springbok lying across the bed. Mayne had gone game-hunting with his Afrikaner friends and brought back a souvenir for his captain. In his history of Irish rugby, Sean Diffley gives an estimate of Mayne, on and off the field:

'Mayne was a Viking, a throwback to the ancient days of towering warriors, gentle and charming when in repose, but fierce and dangerous when aroused – and a "hyphenated" nuisance when he had a "couple of jars". His fierce dark physical outbursts may well have been the stuff of legend, but they were not always fun to those immediately concerned, and they were a great cause of worry to his friends. There was the case of the Irish player for instance, who, in 1939, was thrown out of the window of the Swansea Hotel by Mayne during the post-match celebrations. Witnesses were thankful that it was a ground floor window and that the player came to no harm, and it was not simply high jinks either that caused the incident, but the result of Mayne brooding darkly on something that is now long forgotten.'

This is confirmed by a South African player who records that Mayne regarded the playing of the game as more important than the result, but also that he loved the physical contact of play.

3
War and 11 Commando

IN 1938 came the Munich crisis. Britain was now preparing for war. Blair Mayne was already a member of the Queen's University Officer Training Corps, yet he took the fateful step in the most slap-happy, unconsidered way. Ted Griffiths was with him when he produced a couple of army application forms, and recalls: 'Blair said what about having a crack at this? We were drinking two or three bottles of stout one Saturday which were in the digs. He went on, we'll fill one of these forms up, which we did with a very scratchy and blotchy pen. Blair was wearing a sports jacket with a very capacious pocket; he stuffed the forms in the pocket and away he went. I never thought any more about it. The following Saturday, he was in Dublin, playing – I think it was in an international trial. He pulled the forms out, thought he would post them, shoved them into one of Jury's [hotel] envelopes, no stamp and away they went.'

The forms must have reached their destination because both gentlemen were called for an interview. That was in December 1938. The following February Blair Mayne was commissioned in 5 Light Anti-Artillery Territorial Regiment, Newtownards, even though the Queen's University Officer Training Corps had assessed him as 'unpromising material for a combat regiment, undisciplined, unruly and generally unreliable'. When war was declared in 1939 he was called up. 5 Light Anti-Artillery Battery was sent to Egypt without him and he spent a frustrating few months hanging around Belfast. In April 1940 he transferred to the Royal Ulster Rifles, then volunteered for the Royal Cameronians in Scotland.

A letter home from the Cameronians Depot reflects his restlessness at that time: 'I am getting fed up playing about here. I might as well be back in Ballymena [Royal Ulster Rifles Depot in Northern Ireland]. I'll give it another week or so, and if it doesn't brighten up, I'll have to try something else.'

He was sent to England on courses and was still playing rugby, on one occasion at Twickenham for the Army against the Empire, both sides being largely made up of internationalists.

His writing is often like that of a schoolboy who has to fill the statutory pages for his parents. His pen is running out of ink. He is writing in bed and enumerates all the times he has to get in and out to fetch paper or switch off the wireless. 'I think I must be the best person at padding,' he says. Time and again occurs the phrase 'nothing much happening'. This does not necessarily reflect the actual state of affairs, since it recurs throughout his military career. He keeps up a desultory correspondence with his brother, Douglas, his sisters and his parents. To his mother he writes of how much he treasures her letters. He enjoins his sisters to 'take care of Mother', and to make sure that she does not go 'raking around Belfast'.

After another spell, still chafing at the bit, he was accepted by 11 Scottish Commando. This proved to be the beginning of the metamorphosis of Mayne, the undisciplined and unreliable, into a professional soldier. The duality in his nature was always there. 'Paddy' Mayne – as he came inevitably to be dubbed off-duty – was a different animal from the officer he later became. On operations he was strict on discipline, avoided all alcohol, was serious about his responsibilities and, above all, totally reliable. The basic qualities of leadership that had been developed on the playing field were already there: never ask your man to do something you cannot do or have not done yourself; the need for the training that brings fitness, the fitness that extends a man's capacity and enables mind and body to cope with a crisis – a crisis that affects not just yourself, but those in your charge; above all the ability to inspire confidence.

Paddy Mayne did inspire confidence. It was not just his physical frame – he was six foot, three inches tall – which impressed, but what many described as 'his deadly calm' in moments of danger. The elements were there. Time and experience would temper them to a unique degree.

11 Commando, 'The Scottish', was based at Lamlash, on the Isle of Arran off the west coast of Scotland. The climate and the mountains, the cliffs and the beaches, were all testing. To the normal routine of PT, training in a variety of weapons, map-reading, cross-country marches, initiative tests, and exercises by night and day, was added another range of specialist skills: swimming in full kit, rock climbing, unarmed combat, the use of explosives, a knowledge of transport beyond that required of the ordinary regimental soldier. The schemes undertaken by the Commandos stretched endurance to the limit. In a letter written to his mother late in 1940, and headed 'Sunday Night, Machrie Bay', Blair Mayne records the first day of such a scheme:

'We left Lamlash about two o'clock and walked over here, about seventeen miles. For the first four miles there were odd showers. They didn't hinder us much since we quickly dried, but after it wasn't so good as the final shower lasted for the last thirteen miles, and there was a regular gale blowing off the sea into our faces.

'I waded through a river the other night and I don't think it was any wetter! This book [the letter was written on blotched sheets torn from a squared notebook] was in my pocket and is still wet. We got in here about seven o'clock and then started to find somewhere to sleep. We were carrying nothing except some food, we would not demean ourselves by carrying blankets. It is a smallish hamlet, eight or nine houses and I started going to them to find somewhere for my twenty-five men to dry their clothes. They were all decent, one old lady reminded me of you. I knocked at the door and the girl who opened it seemed scared. I think at first she thought I was a Jerry parachutist, though Father Christmas would have been more like the thing, what with all the equipment I had on. At any rate, I told her who we were, that we intended sleeping out and wondered if she could get some clothes dried.

'She rose to her feet. "You'll not stop outside as long as I've a bed in the house," she declared, and then went into a huddle with her two daughters and her clatter of children and then announced that she could take six. To cut a long story short, I am sitting in borrowed pajamas and an overcoat made for a much smaller man than myself, so much so that when one of my lads saw me he said "Let Burton dress you!"' [The slogan of a British mass-tailoring firm.]

On one occasion, which is recalled by Gerald Bryan, Blair Mayne marched his Troop, No 7, off the end of a pier into deep icy water. He then marched in after them. It was a proof of discipline, like that of Zulu chiefs who ordered their Impi warriors over cliffs. But in this case the commander was soundly berated by indignant landladies, who looked after the soldiers in their care like mothers.

With the Commando he began to feel at home. He wrote to his mother: 'I like this place [Landour in Lamlash] – we are very comfortable here and the mess is fine. I don't live in the mess as I think I told you. Five of us are in a small parlour house, only for sleeping of course. I prefer it. We keep a fire going, have a gramophone, and there is always a pot of tea made in the evening. I think this is the sort of place I'll live in. No women about it, and clothes lying all over the place, dirty teacups on the floor, wet boots in the oven, a rugby jersey over one armchair and your feet on the fender, a perfect existence. We have lots of labour-saving devices also, e.g. the coal is in very large lumps. To split it we just fire a revolver shot into it, it cracks it wonderfully.'

11 Commando wore glengarry bonnets with a black hackle so that it was often referred to as 'The Hackle'. It was first formed at Galashiels in the Borders, all the men being volunteers from Scottish, English and Irish Regiments. Blair Mayne joined with his friend Eoin McGonigal. They had been together since the Royal Ulster Rifles. The Commando training was tough because, of course, they were the élite troops, the aggressive part of the Service from 1940 to 1943, when the war was still primarily a defensive one. Colonel Tommy MacPherson recalls how more nights were spent out on the hills than in bed. 'At the

end,' he said, 'we felt there was nothing we could not undertake.'

Blair Mayne shared his agreeable billet on Arran with four others, including Captain Gerald Bryan, who was to lose a leg in the Litani River action in Syria. On Old Year's Night, 1941, he and three of the others went out with some girls to celebrate at the local hotel. Blair was not interested in that kind of Hogmanay party and remained in the billet alone. Bryan returned in the early hours to turn out the guard, the normal routine for the officer in charge. Blair was still alone. From his appearance he had clearly seen the New Year well and truly in. Truculently he held out a jug to Bryan, 'Get me some water.' Bryan demurred, 'Look, Blair, I've been out and about for the last bloody hour. Get your own water.' Whereupon Blair 'picked me up and hit me one hell of a blow on the face that knocked me against the wall. I managed to get up and get out as quickly as possible. I was hardly out of the door, when he loosed off in my direction a full magazine of the .45 revolver he always kept by him.

'We decided it was prudent not to return to the billet that night. We got back next morning and found three things. Blair was sitting there, surrounded by thirty-six small bottles of cherry brandy, one side of beef, one leg of lamb and two loaves. All the windows were shot out. He was sober. We said, "Blair, where the hell did you get all this stuff? Get up that track into the hills and hide the lot." We discovered later that he had nipped over to Brigade HQ and purloined the lot. But that morning he just stared at my bruised and swollen face with genuine concern. "Who hit you?" he asked. "Just you tell me and I'll sort the bugger out."

Bryan is convinced that Blair had no recollection of the night before. They just managed to get the windows replaced before the police arrived to interview the Duty Officer about the shooting. The whole affair was successfully hushed up.

Bryan recalled how, a few months later, in Cyprus, Lieutenant-Colonel Richard Pedder, the Commanding Officer, turned to Blair one night in the mess and said, 'By the way, I know who broke into Brigade HQ on New Year's Eve and stole the drink.' 'Do you?', replied Blair, with what Bryan describes as his sweet lovely smile. 'I wish you'd tell us, because it was a great mystery at the time!' Apparently Pedder stamped angrily away. Blair Mayne did not always get on with his superiors. His ways were not their ways.

Bryan also tells how, in the billet at Lamlash, a favourite game was for Blair to stand in the middle of the room and the other four would advance from the corners and try to get him down. They never succeeded and it could become very rough – shooting at Landour was not confined to splitting lumps of coal. The only person who was able to control Blair when he cut loose was Eoin McGonigal. McGonigal had been known to point a revolver at him and say, 'I'll shoot you, Blair.' Blair would stop because, according to Bryan, he knew that McGonigal meant it. The present owners confirm that the walls of Landour are still marked with bullets. Mayne was a 'terrific shot' with both revolver and Thompson machine-gun. He and McGonigal ran the Commando shooting courses during their four months in Arran.

11 Commando embarked in Lamlash Bay in December 1940 for what was to have been their first operation – the 'snatch' of the island of Pantelleria, midway between Sicily and North Africa, a heavily fortified base with underground aircraft hangars. Winston Churchill himself, the Prime Minister, had pressed for this operation codenamed WORKSHOP, and Admiral Keyes, Director of Combined Operations, had been eager to mount the assault; but there were delays and postponements and by January 1941 the Luftwaffe, which had moved in strength into Sicily, was about to enjoy a period of air-supremacy in the central Mediterranean: this would enable it to inflict damage on convoys bound for Malta and to bomb Malta itself day and night. The initiative had been lost and the operation was cancelled much to the vexation of Admiral Keyes and the chagrin of the Commandos.

Dinner that Christmas was of venison shot by permission of the Duke of Montrose. They embarked again at midnight on 31 January 1941 and sailed round the Cape to the Bitter Lakes and the neighbouring base of Kabrit, at the southern end of the Suez Canal. After desert training, the whole force of 11 Commando moved its base to Cyprus. In a letter to his father, dated 2 June, Mayne reports: 'Everything going fine. Sunbathing and eating fruit all day. We have had the odd bit of fun, but nothing really exciting. I have a fine bed at the moment, mattress and springs and everything. I'll be getting soft but I expect to leave here very shortly.'

The following day, the whole of 11 Commando, nearly 400-strong, embarked for Syria and the perilous Litani River raid. This action was Blair Mayne's first real taste of hard fighting. 11 Commando formed part of Layforce, a group commanded by Brigadier Robert Laycock, whose original task had been to seize the strategic island of Rhodes. But German successes in Cyrenaica and in the Balkans had put paid to that. The Commandos of Layforce were being used in large-scale raids on enemy centres along the North African coast, none of them successful.

One operation which did, however, achieve a measure of success was mounted not against Rommel's rear but against the Germans and the Vichy French in Syria. Marshal Pétain and his deputy, Admiral Darlan, were still supporting the Axis powers. Churchill had been urging action in the eastern Mediterranean to counter the German thrust through Greece. Through navigational error by some of the landing craft, many of the Commandos were put ashore in the thick of the enemy defences. Their CO, Colonel Pedder, and about half of the other officers, and 120 men, were all killed. In a letter to his brother from Kabrit, dated 15 July 1941, Paddy Mayne looks back on the operation and describes it in, for him, unusual detail:

'I have left the Scottish Commando now – it was not the same when the CO got written off. Nearly a year I was with it and I liked it well, but I think Commandos are finished out here.

'We did a good piece of work when we landed behind the French lines at the Litani River. We were fired on as we landed, but got off the beach with a couple of casualties. Then we saw a lot of men and transport about 600 yards up the road. I couldn't understand it as they seemed to be firing the wrong way, but might have been Aussies [there were Australians in the Allied force advancing north through Palestine]. There was quite a lot of cover – kind of hayfield – I crawled up to thirty yards or so and heard them talking French. So I started whaling grenades at them and my men opened fire. After about five minutes, up went a white flag. There were about forty of them – two machine-guns and a mortar – a nice bag to start with. We had only a couple of men hurt. They had been firing at McGonigal's crowd who had landed further north. We left those prisoners and pushed on McGunn, a Cameronian, was in charge of my forward section and he got stuck, so we went round him. I had about fifteen men.

'It got hilly and hard going and Frenchies all over the place. Eventually, we came to a path which we followed and came on a dozen mules and one knew that there must be something somewhere and we came on it just around the corner. About thirty of those fellows sitting twenty yards away. I was round first with my revolver, and the sergeant had a tommy-gun – were they surprised! I called on them to "jettez-vous à la planche" but they seemed to be a bit slow on the uptake. One of them lifted a rifle and I'm afraid that he hadn't time to be sorry. This was a sort of HQ place, typewriters, ammunition, revolvers, bombs and, more to the point, beer and food. We had been going about six hours and we were ready for it.

'While we were dining the phone rang. We didn't answer but followed the wire and got another bull – four machine-guns, two light machine-guns, two mortars and fifty more prisoners. We lost only two men (sounds like a German communiqué). It was a long time since I had a day like it. Eventually, about eight hours later, we came back through the Aussie lines. We were rather tired so the prisoner laddies kindly carried the booty and equipment. The rest of the story can keep until I see you. I am getting rather tired of this country (Egypt). The job is not bad, but I can't stand the natives!'

After the Litani raid the Commando returned to Cyprus. There Mayne was involved in another escapade. One night he ran amok with a rifle and bayonet and chased everybody out of the mess including the new Commanding Officer, Colonel Geoffrey Keyes, promoted at the age of twenty-four to the rank of Acting Lieutenant-Colonel, who had taken over after Pedder's death. Later there was to be a more serious incident. The

Commando had moved back to the base at Kabrit on the canal. Preparations were in train for the famous attempt by Keyes to abduct Rommel from his rear headquarters, 250 miles behind the lines. It was planned to land by submarine. Mayne was not included in the raiding party. Douglas Mayne, Blair's brother, confirms that before the raid there was a mess night at Kabrit: 'Blair and Eoin McGonigal were playing chess together. Perhaps it was regarded as inappropriate for them to be playing chess on a mess night, but according to Blair the manner in which Keyes, the Commanding Officer, approached them was asking for trouble.'

There was trouble indeed. Blair Mayne rose from the chess table and knocked his CO unconscious. He was instantly placed under close arrest. Precisely what sparked off the incident we can never know. There was clearly an antipathy between the two men. Nor can the incident in Cyprus have helped. No Commanding Officer likes to be driven out of his mess at bayonet point by a subaltern, and clearly Keyes had been very tolerant of that insubordination. Perhaps Mayne was nursing a resentment because he had not been chosen for the Rommel raid. In temperament and background, he and Keyes were poles apart. Son of Admiral of the Fleet Lord Keyes of Zeebrugge, and educated at Eton and Sandhurst, Geoffrey Keyes was a regular soldier in the Scots Greys and his recreations were those appropriate to the cavalry – hunting, show-jumping, polo. Unlike Paddy, he was a sociable young man who enjoyed mixed company, parties and dancing. What he had in common with Paddy was courage. He had already been awarded the Croix de Guerre for service in Norway, the MC for his part in the Litani River action and he was to receive a posthumous VC after being killed leading the abortive raid on the German HQ in Libya, thought to be those of Rommel but in fact used by his quartermaster and staff and visited only occasionally by Rommel.

Paddy had already been mentioned in dispatches for his courage at Litani. But he always had, quite irrationally, a social chip on his shoulder. He instinctively recoiled from what he regarded as the 'snooty' public school type. Yet when roused or in his cups he made no distinction of persons. He was as likely to knock down a NCO as a superior officer. His next Commanding Officer, David Stirling, was well aware of this.

4
Birth of the SAS

DAVID STIRLING, a young Scots Guards subaltern, was born in 1915. His idea for the SAS was shining in its simplicity, and was his alone. It was he who followed it through with the persistence, diplomatic cunning and imaginative energy which overcame the outworn thinking (or lack of it), the jealous vested interests: in his own words, the 'fossilised shit' which from time immemorial has clogged the middle echelons of military command.

It was a help that the Stirlings were a well-known Scottish family, distinguished in war and peace. David's father, Brigadier-General Archibald Stirling of Keir, had been a MP and Deputy Lieutenant of Perthshire. His cousin, Lord Lovat, head of Clan Fraser, was the son of the man who raised the famous Lovat Scouts in the Boer War. His brother, Peter, was in the British Embassy in Cairo.

David Stirling, who had been in 8 Commando, had come to Suez with Layforce. He had taken part in several large-scale Commando raids against enemy targets along the Cyrenaican Coast. As none of these had been successful, Stirling, with time on his hands, wrestled with the problem. Big raids by sea always tended to sacrifice the one great essential element – that of surprise. On the initiative of another officer, Jock Lewes, therefore, Lewes and Stirling began experimenting at jumping with some accidentally acquired parachutes and an old borrowed Valencia bomber. Stirling injured his back, and during two months in hospital had time 'to evaluate the factors which would justify the creating of a special service unit to carry on the Commando role, and amass a case to present to the Commander-in-Chief [Auchinleck], in favour of such a unit'. Economy of effort and surprise: his idea comprised both. Highly trained specialised small units would drop by parachute under cover of darkness, far behind enemy lines. Unseen, unsuspected even, they would plant time-bombs on aircraft, railways, petrol dumps – anything which they could usefully blow up. Before the first bomb exploded, they would have faded away. Instead of a full frontal assault he would substitute concealed insinuation, leaving no marks – until the devastating consummation.

There was only one way to avoid getting bogged down in the whole ascending hierarchy of 'fossilised shit'. He went straight to the top and gate-crashed the office of the Deputy Chief of Staff, Middle East Forces, Major-General Neil Ritchie. Stirling's idea had, by good luck, found its time. It was July 1941. Churchill was pressing Auchinleck to engage in any kind of guerrilla attack short of a set-piece offensive in order to divert German attention and supplies, however briefly, from the enormous operations in Russia. Ritchie was aware of this.

Ritchie studied the pencil-written memo which the tall and intense young subaltern had thrust into his hand, insisting that the business he had come on was 'vital'. According to Stirling a quick read-through was enough to convince Ritchie that here was the kind of plan they so much needed. It was new, and it was daring. Never had so much been offered for so little. Churchill would relish it.

Three days later, Stirling was summoned to GHQ to see Auchinleck, who had Ritchie with him. Discussion was to the point, decision was swift, and Stirling got what he wanted. He could recruit six officers, and sixty NCOs and men, from the ranks of the disbanded Layforce, now in the depot at Geneifa, on the Bitter Lake. As he had particularly requested, he would report direct to the Commander-in-Chief. He would start preparing and training at once for the first operation he had proposed, an attack on the airfields at Tamimi and Gazala, about 150 miles behind the German lines. The attack was to take place the night before the major offensive, planned for November. He had three months. Stirling was promoted to Captain with immediate effect and his force would be known as 'L' Detachment, Special Air Service. Auchinleck explained that the Special Air Service was non-existent. It was merely a name given to a bogus formation of dummy gliders and installations meant to deceive the enemy into thinking that British paratroops had arrived in strength to reinforce 8 Army. Special Air Service, or SAS, was a classic piece of what would now be called dis-information.

Stirling lost no time in recruiting. He held a meeting in a large tent at Geneifa and was overwhelmed with volunteers whom he interviewed individually. Among the first were NCOs from the Commandos, Bennett, Cooper, Lilley, Rose and Seekings, all of whom were highly trained soldiers who later won decorations. Eoin McGonigal was one of the officers. No doubt it was he who suggested his friend Paddy Mayne. Mayne, of course, had been under close arrest for some weeks since striking his Commanding Officer. It was a tribute to Mayne's reputation after the Litani raid, and perhaps to Stirling's personality, that the Ulsterman was permitted to hear Stirling's proposition.

David Stirling himself has told of that first encounter: 'I went to see him. He was gravely suspicious, very suspicious of me initially. However I told him what I was up to and I could see he was becoming extremely responsive. After half an hour or so he committed himself to come and join me. It wasn't because by joining me he got out of prison, it was because he wanted to. The SAS was something that he'd been dreaming about. However, I had to make a deal with him, that this Commanding Officer wasn't for hitting. He undertook that, I thought slightly reluctantly, but he always kept his word.'

It was as a result of Stirling's growing influence in high places that there was no more talk of a court-martial.

By August the SAS base had been established at Kabrit, a village in the Canal Zone, about a hundred miles from Cairo. The new camp was a depressing place, with no relief from desert heat and flies. Three tents and a three-tonner truck represented their total resources. The 'Q' branch was being totally uncooperative – there would be a long delay in supplies of any kind. But there were ways of circumventing that and, if need be, of bulldozing the 'fossilised shit'.

Bob Bennett, then a Corporal, later to be RSM of the SAS Regiment, was detailed to carry out the first raid. This was on a neighbouring New Zealand camp and it took place stealthily by night. The New Zealanders lived well and had no trouble with supplies. That night they were out on an exercise. The SAS three-tonner made four trips back to Kabrit. By the time the last 'consignment' was unloaded, the SAS had fifteen new tents, tables, chairs, lamps, washbasin, kitchen utensils, as well as a piano, a bar, wicker chairs, a long mess-table and even a woven grass carpet. It was an unconventional buccaneering form of existence, dear to the heart of Blair Mayne.

But when it came to work Stirling demanded the highest standards in both discipline and physical fitness. Battle training at Kabrit was in the hands of army PT intructors who, in the workouts, gave no quarter. Cleanliness, turn-out and behaviour were of Brigade of Guards standard. Keep the tough-guy stuff for the enemy, insisted Stirling.

In charge of overall training was an Australian, Jock Lewes, an Oxford rowing Blue who had joined the Welsh Guards. With an honours degree in science he had the right kind of organised mind to tackle the new problems faced by the SAS. He had invented the bomb which bore his name.

The regime was strict and thorough. Canal crossings, night marches, map-reading, firing practice – much the same basic routine as the Commandos on Arran. What was extra was a parachute course. With no help forthcoming from Ringway, the parachute school in England, much had to be improvised. Initially there were jumping platforms about fifteen feet high. When it proved too difficult to have moving platforms so that the trainees could practise forward and backward rolls down an incline, Stirling decided to make do with the men jumping off trucks which would be moving at 30 mph. This took such a toll in casualties that it was soon abandoned. Paddy Mayne, however, survived that episode. Despite his bulk – he weighed 15½ stone (217 lb) – he was extraordinarily agile and very quick on his feet. The boxing ring had proved its value.

The first series of live parachute jumps proved disastrous. Initially all went well with Stirling leading the way. On the third run the parachutes of the first two men out failed to open. The rest were stopped just in time. Stirling had been watching the tragedy. A faulty clip was identified. Bob Bennett recalls the shock of that disaster: 'It was the worst twenty-four hours any of us had ever spent. We sat in our tents, smoking one fag after another and tried not to think of it, but we did. Next day every man jumped, Captain Stirling first. No one backed out. It was then I realised I was with a great bunch of chaps.' However, it was a light-hearted bet that really convinced the army top brass that the SAS were on the right track. An RAF Group Captain had been sceptical about the ability of Stirling's men to get on to airfields undetected. Heliopolis, the main Cairo airfield, was chosen as a test. 'I don't mind you warning them,' said Stirling. 'Tell them we'll be paying a visit around the end of October.'

Forty men took part in the exercise, in four independent groups. The target was ninety miles across barren rocky desert. They marched by night and lay hidden by day to avoid reconnaissance planes sent out to foil them. Blair Mayne's group covered their thirty miles the first night easily and camouflaged down to try and sleep by day under hessian sacks. The heat was intense, and each man had only four pints of water. After two days and three nights their thirst was acute. Bob Bennett says that all he could see that last long day under his sack in the desert was a tap of delicious running water.

There was another incident during that march, he recalls. Private Chesworth had been constantly complaining. 'He was whingeing the whole day. Paddy had had enough. We were on a rocky feature called the "Big Flea", about four hundred feet up. He lifted Chesworth with one hand and held him over the cliff. "Another word out of you and that's your lot," he said. There was no more moaning after that!'

When night fell they made the last few miles to the aerodrome. Entering it proved child's play. Silently they cut through the wire and moved around the planes, sticking labels in lieu of bombs on forty-five of them. Unmolested, they slipped away again. All four groups were successful. Most of the aircraft bore several labels. As a dress rehearsal for the first SAS operation it could not have been better.

That first operation now took place precisely as set out by Stirling in his first meeting with Auchinleck. Two nights before the British offensive, planned for 18 November 1941, two groups of SAS would be dropped ten miles inland of the Axis advance airfields at Tamimi and Gazala, on the coast west of Tobruk. They were used by the latest German fighters, the Me109F, recently arrived in large numbers to give added punch to the Luftwaffe. Having planted their bombs on the aircraft, the SAS would rendezvous forty-five miles away with the trucks of the Long Range Desert Group which would take them across the desert to Siwa Oasis. There were high hopes of wiping out Rommel's entire fighter force, but the raid went badly wrong. All occasions seemed to inform against them. No moon, and gale-force winds. Stirling was advised to call off the operation, but decided that cancellation would be bad for morale, and went ahead.

Five planes took off. In charge of Section 4 was Blair Mayne. He later told how the plane went bucketing across the sky, through thick cloud, rain and lightning. Navigational calculations were useless – it was impossible for the aircrew to guess the force of the gusts battering them. They were two hours in the air. Mayne's party jumped but were scattered all over the place. He himself landed hard, and was dragged a long way over the rocky ground before he could release his harness. Badly bruised, and with a broken toe, he set about collecting his party together. Wandering around in the dark, flashing their torches, eventually and amazingly all eleven found each other, then began the three-hour search for the containers with the arms and supplies. Only four packs were found – the total bag comprising two tommy-guns, sixteen bombs, fourteen bottles of water, food intended for four men and four blankets. Two of the party were too badly injured to continue. They were given three bottles of water with some rations. Mayne and the others shook hands with these two and wished them luck. He was still determined to press on to Tamimi, with the Lewes bombs they still had. They walked for three and a half hours at night and laid up in a wadi. Sergeant MacDonald was sent out on a recce, to locate the coast and the airfield, about six miles north. Then with nightfall the rain came. The heavens opened. Within minutes the wadi became a lake. They scrambled to higher ground but kit was lost and damaged, the detonators ruined. Seekings says: 'Paddy wanted to attack the place on his own with grenades, but we managed to talk him out of it'; and Bennett adds: 'The harder things got the calmer Paddy got, but even he realised that it was no go – we were non-operational. We tried to keep some of the rain out – we had only three blankets for nine men. It was better than nothing so with constant wringing out of the blankets and the odd sip at the "old rum stakes" we managed to survive, so we made for the rendezvous where the LRDG was to pick us up. A thirty-six-hour march brought us to the approximate position. By this time we were exhausted and lay down. Seekings said he thought he saw a light in the distance. No one seemed to take much notice and Sergeant Kershaw said it was not a light but a star low on the horizon. Paddy had us up at daylight and walking again. Then a truck appeared – one of the LRDG patrol! The first thing to greet us were cigarettes. It was the finest fag I've ever tasted – all ours had been ruined by the rains.'

Of the sixty-four men taking part, only four officers – Stirling, Mayne, Jock Lewes and Bill Fraser – and eighteen men reached the rendezvous. One plane was shot down. Another, they learnt later, had been 'talked down' on to an enemy airfield by an English-speaking German. Many were taken prisoner. Eoin McGonigal was badly injured and died the same day.

Paddy wrote to his sister Frances: 'I am getting very tired of this country, especially since Eoin landed a loser, it was all right when there was someone you could talk about home with.' It is one of the rare moments of depression revealed in his letters. From all points of view the operation was a complete failure. Both Stirling and Mayne knew that the situation was critical. The sceptics and 'knockers' back at GHQ would have had their doubts confirmed.

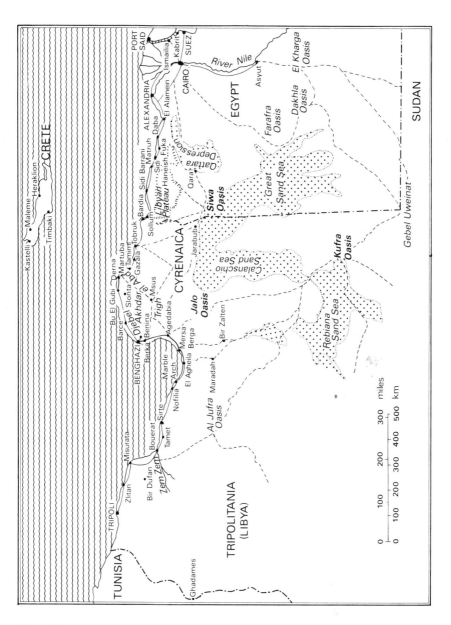

Fig 1 North African Desert, 1941–3

Like the beginner who falls off his horse, Stirling knew that he must mount again at once. What was left of his force was flown back from Siwa Oasis to Kabrit in order to fetch more men and supplies. He himself set off for 8 Army HQ to see what he could salvage. He was lucky. At that moment the High Command was fully occupied with Rommel's dash to the Egyptian frontier. He had two brief meetings with Generals Cunningham and Ritchie, both shortly to be sacked. They had little time for Stirling's concerns but the net result was that he was given a free hand and the help he needed. 'L' Detachment, SAS, was sent to the oasis of Jalo, 200 miles deep in the Sahara on a vertical line approximately midway between Benghazi and Tobruk. It was well away from the coastal areas along which the main battle between 8 Army and Rommel's Panzers had been surging to and fro. It was in British hands and already stationed there was a squadron of the LRDG. For the SAS it was the perfect base from which to plan and launch their attacks.

5
Joint Operations

WHO DARES WINS

STIRLING wasted no time in setting up his first joint operation with the LRDG. On 8 December 1941, just two weeks after the disastrous drop at Tamimi, he and Paddy, with nine men, set off for Tamet and Sirte.

Rommel had by this time retreated before the CRUSADER offensive and was installed at El Agheila. The SAS party had seven trucks loaded with explosives, guns, petrol, food, water, spares, camouflage nets, sand mats, spades, all the impedimenta required. The trucks were painted pink and light green, a combination that blended into the terrain. The LRDG commander was Captain Holliman with Captain Mike Sadler navigating. At Sirte, Stirling and Sergeant Brough dropped off, only to find the airfield being evacuated. Mayne and his group continued for another thirty miles to make that first raid at Tamet of 14 December 1941. Mayne's official report, typewritten, but with the map reference filled in in pencil and the dates in ink in his own hand, records the bare facts:

The following damage was done on or in the vicinity of the aerodrome:
(a) Bombs were placed on 14 aircraft.
(b) 10 aircraft were damaged by having instrument panels destroyed.
(c) Bomb and petrol dumps were blown up.

    (d) Reconnaissance was made down to the seafront but only empty huts were found.

    (e) Several telephone poles were blown up.

    (f) Some Italians were followed, and the hut they came out of was attacked by sub-machine gun and pistol fire and bombs were placed on and around it. There appeared to be roughly thirty inhabitants. Damage inflicted unknown.

The last section of the report is vintage Mayne. Never embroider. Always underplay. For his part in the raid he was awarded a DSO. Tamet was not only a vindication of the SAS. It was the bench-mark against which future levels of achievement would be measured, the brilliant opening night that inspired confidence in future performances – and a long run.

Determined to reinforce success, and gambling that the enemy would not expect a return visit so soon, Stirling and Mayne set off again two weeks later for a repeat raid on Tamet and Sirte. Again Mayne with five men attacked Tamet on 27 December. They motored to about three miles from the airfield and simply walked in. 'It always fascinates me,' Bob Bennett has commented, 'the number of times these airfields were done, you'd have thought they'd have been like a fortress. But no, a bit of wire and a couple of machine-gun posts – we never had much trouble getting on to them.'

On this occasion they sprinted between the planes which were tucked among trees, Savoia bombers then being used against Malta, wings twelve feet up. They were about fifty yards apart; and the bombs were simply lobbed up. The time pencils were set for thirty minutes. But the first went off prematurely while they were still on the airfield. There are two accounts, both by Paddy Mayne. The first is his official report:

> The Italian guards were more vigilant than a fortnight previously and were sited in groups of seven or eight round the drome. The attacking party were engaged as they left the drome and although silhouetted by burning planes had no casualties, grenades being used to break through the encircling cordon.

The tone of his letter to his sister Frances is rather different:

Everything went OK except that as we were coming out after leaving our bombs we were challenged. I answered 'Friendt' [sic] but they didn't believe me and started firing. That was rather a mistake for them as I don't like being fired at.

Bennett recalls Paddy lobbing grenades at the Italians before dashing off into the darkness, the blackness of which was intensified by the lurid bonfires flaming behind them. Sergeant MacDonald and Private White were separated from the rest in the rush but were picked up later. Bennett also recalls Paddy saying: ' "What am I doing here messing about on such low pay? I could earn much more working for the Germans, couldn't I?" "I suppose you could," I said. God knows what he meant by it. He had this twist about him.'

The whole party managed somehow to contact the LRDG and celebrated Christmas belatedly on 28 December, with 'plenty of beer and pudding' and two gazelles which they shot and roasted.

The bag on the second Tamet raid was twenty-seven aircraft, three lorries, two trailers carrying spare aircraft parts and several petrol dumps. Stirling, who had been baulked in his attempts to bomb the planes on Sirte airfield, was already planning ahead. The Germans, having been driven out of Benghazi, would be forced to use the major port of Bouerat, 350 miles to the west. The SAS commander was given permission to attack Bouerat with its fuel tankers and supply ships on the night of 23 January 1942. Since Jock Lewes had been killed at the time of the last Tamet/Sirte raids, there was only one experienced officer to train the new SAS volunteers at Kabrit. Paddy Mayne did not take kindly to the news that he was going to be left behind. His mood was one of resentful insubordination. Stirling tells how he began what he could only describe as a massive sulk in his tent. There, having constructed for himself a huge bed and laid in a stock of Penguin paperbacks and a sufficiency of whiskey, he remained incommunicado for several days. Eventually, on Stirling's return and after a furious row which did much to clear the air, normal relations were restored. What it underlined, though, was that for Mayne it was action or nothing.

The Bouerat raid, although the harbour had been empty of shipping, resulted in the destruction of eighteen petrol bowsers and four food dumps. But while the SAS party was en route from Jalo Oasis, Rommel had launched a series of lightning counter attacks, driving 8 Army back at a speed which reached 15 mph. By 6 February, he was back at the Gazala line, just west of Tobruk, the position he had abandoned two months before.

Stirling's efforts, therefore, were now concentrated on attacking Rommel's supply lines. On 15 March a large-scale operation was launched involving separate attacks on Benghazi harbour and the neighbouring airfields. Mayne's party – consisting of himself, now promoted to Captain, Corporals Rose and Bennett and Private Byrne – was allocated the airfield known as Berka Satellite. From Siwa they reached the Djebel Akhdar, the mountainous escarpment overlooking the Benghazi plain, in three days. The foothills were wooded and fertile with ravines, well suited as lying-up places for the SAS as they waited to attack at night. The wadi they found was concealed by thorn bushes with several full waterholes and three large caves in which pigeons had their nests. They had with them a guide who had approached their camp as an Arab, and then revealed himself as an Indian soldier who, having been cut off during the last retreat from Benghazi, had been living with the Bedouin ever since. He took them surely down the escarpment, over ground littered with rocks and large stones, and they reached the airfield at 3 a.m., evading the sentries with no trouble. Bombs were placed on fifteen aircraft, petrol dumps and twelve large torpedo bombs were blown up. Too late for the agreed rendezvous they had to walk thirty miles to the next LRDG pick-up point.

For what happened when the four raiding parties eventually reassembled, we turn to the Official SAS Diary. The Diary is a chronological record of the activities of 1 SAS from its birth in August 1941 until midsummer 1945. It is composed of official reports of operations, first-hand accounts, personal memoranda of serving members, nominal rolls of personnel, casualty lists, diagrams, photographs of operations and of locations in Africa and in Europe along with pictures of the original members of 'L' Detachment accompanied by brief biographical notes.

This compendium was assembled by Brigadier Mike Black-man, then Intelligence Officer, in 1945. It is contained in a large leather folder (17 × 12 × 4 in.) stamped CHRONIK der Gemeinde Schneeren, Kreis Neustadt a.rhge. (Records of the Parish of Schneeren, District of Neustadt in the Rhineland) – a folder clearly acquired in 1945. The Diary was appropriated by Blair Mayne when he was demobbed and is now in the possession of his family. It records:

On the evening of the 26th, the party went into action with rum and lime, rum and tea, rum omelette and just plain rum.

Then a fraoli was laid on the sacrificial altar while Captain Mayne went through the weird rites of demonstrating how one should NOT fire and NOT take to pieces at night. MGs, LMGs, tommy-guns, pistols and God knows what other intricate pieces of mechanism.

Casualties: Incredible as it may seem, Nil.

Opposition: Nil.

Blair Mayne paints the picture in a letter to his brother, Douglas: 'At the moment I am about fifteen miles from Benghazi. We did a raid on the local aerodrome three nights ago and we are waiting for one of the party who hasn't returned yet.

'It is very pleasant country here, a great change after the desert. Some of the people who know the South Downs say that it is very like it – low hills and valleys, lots of wild flowers and long grass – it is like a picnic – only annoying thing is the Jerry planes flying about, but we are well camouflaged. Luckily the Italians treat the Senussi (the local tribesmen) very badly so they will do anything to help us. The day and night after the raid we couldn't find our rendezvous. The maps are awful. We had been walking from 1 a.m. to 7 o'clock the next night and couldn't find the damn place – we must have covered about fifty miles, first of all getting to the drome and then coming away, it was getting dark and we were due here at dusk. It was no good walking around in circles in the dark and I had more or less resigned myself to a 250-mile walk to Tobruk, and so we (two corporals and myself) went to the nearest Senussi camp for some water and to see if we could get a blanket. The Senussi were very suspicious at first, but once they were sure that we were "Inglesi", everything changed.

'We were ushered into one of the tents, our equipment brought in and blankets put down for us as beds. There was a fire just outside the door and everyone crowded in. First of all they boiled us some eggs, which were damned good, then platters of dates and bowls of water and a huge gourd of goats' milk was brought in. I think the form with this is that they never wash the gourd and the sourer it gets, the better they like it – they must have liked this stuff very well. This gourd kept going round and round and we soon gathered that the best mannered people take a great suck and the real connoisseurs a hearty belch. The belch wasn't difficult. This went on for a long time. We knew no Arabic and they no English, but everybody knew what everybody else was talking about. Then they started brewing tea, awful stuff, must have been made with dandelions, talk about bitter – this was in little glasses. After the first round, I pretended to be asleep.

'Eventually the party finished, and everyone started for their own tents, the three of us lying on the blanket. I don't think that I have ever been more tired. Nearly every one of the old fellows, before they left, tucked the blanket round, pushing it in under our feet and in at the side – there was a chorus of "Sidas" and the show finished.

'All this time the host's wife had been lying on her bed with two or three smaller Senussi, who looked about three years old.

'The Lord of the Manor then went out, brought in a goat and three kids, tied them to the tent pole and we settled down for the night, and now listen to this, and never disbelieve in luck again or coincidence or whatever you like to call it.

'The men who were waiting for us at our rendezvous – and they would have left next morning – had got a chicken which they had bartered some sugar for, and they wanted it cooked. They had an English-speaking Arab with them and they sent him to get it cooked. In that area there must have been thirty or forty different encampments, spread over the three odd miles we were from each other, and he picked the one that we were lying in to come to! So we don't have to foot-slog it across the desert.'

It was Napoleon who said, 'Give me a lucky general rather than a brave one.' Blair Mayne always seemed to combine both attributes.

Between Stirling and Paddy Mayne there was always good-humoured but intense competition, an almost schoolboyish desire to claim the bigger 'bag' which led them on occasion to tempt their luck. They had been back to the Benghazi area. Stirling had done well with five German planes, thirty new aircraft engines and three hangars full of machinery all destroyed. Paddy had arrived at his airfield – Berka Satellite again – just as RAF bombers unleashed a full-scale raid on it. They lay in the middle of the field with the whole place lit up with flares and the flash of anti-aircraft guns. Once the raid was over there was frenzied activity with nervous and very wide-awake sentries covering every plane.

The enemy was by this time well aware of the SAS, and had re-doubled security against their 'night-raids'. So Paddy, apart from one large petrol dump where they had managed to deposit their bombs, had drawn a blank. When he met David at the LRDG rendezvous, he had to endure some friendly badinage about David's fires lighting up the sky for a change. 'You got all the hangars?' asked Paddy, 'We better have a look. I want to make sure you're not exaggerating!' They borrowed a LRDG truck and set off along the main road to Benghazi again, bent on shooting up what they could find, a typical 'bit of fun'.

It was an eventful night, of which there are several versions, but best described by Paddy himself in a letter to his brother written over six weeks later:

'I have been up in the desert on one of our raids – got back three days ago. It wasn't for my liking. I prefer the long nights, more time to get away though my luck was as good as ever. Still after aircraft. In the last month I got forty odd. I was shot up a couple of times and, bar losing some kit which was burnt, the blighters set my car on fire – I was OK. I had a party last time I was back in the Sergeants Mess. I had just broken the century in planes so it was fairly hectic – a dangerous place to go to – you are never quite certain what is in your glass. I remember in one of your letters you were complaining of not having yet seen a Jerry – that came to my mind forcibly about a week or so later. I had been raiding Berka drome and after I got back to our rendezvous, we decided, the CO and myself, to have a look at Benghazi – so we took a truck. I was driving, the CO beside me and four of our lads in the back [Corporals Seekings, Cooper, Lilley and Warburton], also a free Austrian.* Well, we drove on to the road and started gaily down with headlights on. We got about five–six miles and then we saw a red light being swung. That didn't worry us as always before it was only Italians and we shout out "tedesco" (Italian for German) and drive past. But they were getting wise to us and this time we see a bloody big contraption like a five-barred gate that has got mixed up with a mile or so of barbed wire. So we stopped. The sentry was in the headlights and right enough an Italian. Our Austrian started to do his little piece and shouted out that we are Germans in a hurry and to open up the blankety gate. The Wop wasn't so sure so he hollered for the guard – about ten Germans headed by a Sergeant-Major, tommy-guns, grenades and rifles. I was scared to look further in case I saw tanks and machine-guns. I gathered later that the conversation ran like this: Fritz: "What's the password?" Karl our Austrian: "How the — do we know what the — password is and don't ask for our — identity cards either. They're lost. We've been fighting for the past seventy hours against these — Tommies. Our car was destroyed and we were lucky to capture this British truck and get back at all.

' "Some fool put us on the wrong road. We've been driving for the past two hours and then you so and sos, sitting here on your asses in Benghazi, in a nice safe job, stop us. So hurry up, get that — gate open!" 'But Fritz isn't satisfied, so he walks to about three feet from the car on my side. I'm sitting there with my Colt on my lap and suddenly I remember that it isn't cocked. So I

*This was Karl Kahane, a Jew who had spent twenty years in the German Army before emigrating to Palestine in the 1930s. He knew the German Army ways and the army slang, and had been borrowed by Stirling from a special intelligence unit.

pull it back and the Jerry has one look and then orders the gates to be opened. Which they did and in a chorus of "Guden Nachtens" [sic] we drove on. We thought later that he came to the conclusion, the same one that I had come to, that if anyone was going to be hurt he was going to be a very sick man early on. [This is a prime example of Paddy's quick thinking in a crisis. Stirling, who was seated beside him, is in no doubt that the click of the revolver as the German met Paddy's eye was deliberate. We drove on at any rate and came on a lot of tents and trucks and people (at Lete), got our machine-guns up from the bottom of the truck and started blowing hell out of them, short, snappy and exhilarating. The story is far too long and I am fed up writing, at any rate we cut into the desert, chased by armoured cars.* We climbed the escarpment. We had 40 lb of explosives which blows when set off by our own delayed action fuse. The fuses had got set off by the bumps but it is so fixed that after it cracks there is twenty seconds' safety fuse and we made the most of that twenty seconds. We all got out at any rate. But there is no use writing this stuff, people think you are shooting a line – the most fantastic things happen every time we go out.'

What happened was that Seekings and Lilley smelt the burning fuse just in time and shouted a warning. They all leapt out, Paddy not even applying the brakes. A split second later the truck was blown to smithereens.

The letter to his brother continues: 'On one occasion – I wasn't there, I was on another job – four of our people took a staff car into Benghazi. It broke down while they were there and they had to spend a day in a wrecked house in the main street, [Randolph] Churchill was one of them but he wrenched his back in a car accident and has gone home. He was not a bad lad, plucky enough but very bad manners. He had done a couple of parachute jumps with us but is no athlete.' Paddy's memory is faulty. There were six men in the staff car – Stirling's famous

---

*Survivors recall a nightmare race with Paddy, headlights on, his pedal on the metal of the jolting, bucking, truck reaching the defile into the escarpment just ahead of the Germans; the going too rough for accurate shooting by either side but with SAS firing warning tracer into the headlights of their pursuers.

Blitzwagon – which was a Ford utility painted to look like an Afrika Korps staff car with German recognition signals. The six were Stirling, Fitzroy Maclean, Robin Gurdon of the LRDG, Randolph Churchill (son of Winston), Rose, and Seekings. The raid proved abortive.

6

El Alamein

WHO DARES WINS

IN the larger strategic battle of the Mediterranean, the key was the island of Malta. It lay right in the centre of Rommel's supply lines between Italy and North Africa. During April and May over ninety per cent of freight sent from Italy to Libya arrived safely. Field Marshal Kesselring, Hitler's Commander-in-Chief South, judged that his constant air attacks had neutralised the island, thereby releasing his Luftwaffe squadrons to support Rommel's next Panzer assault. When this was launched on 26 May 1942 from the Gazala position, it proved devastating. Tobruk, which had withstood a siege of eight months in 1941, fell in as many hours. Thirty-three thousand British prisoners were taken, together with five generals and a vast quantity of tanks, guns and supplies. Hitler heard the news in his train between Munich and Berlin with jubilation. By the end of June 8 Army under Auchinleck had its back to the wall at El Alamein, only sixty miles west of Alexandria.

Fortunately Malta had, in the meantime, received strong Spitfire reinforcements which were again causing the Luftwaffe enough problems to divert squadrons from the advance into Egypt. For Rommel's supply lines were now stretched to the limit just as Malta was hitting back. Auchinleck had stemmed the German advance with limited counter-attacks. In all this the role of Stirling and the SAS became more important. The destruction of enemy airfields and aircraft was two-pronged – it helped to protect Malta and it further exposed the enemy communications to the RAF.

'By the end of June,' Stirling had written, '"L" Detachment had raided all the more important German and Italian aerodromes within 300 miles of the forward area at least once or twice, and a few of them even three or four times. Methods of defence were beginning to improve and the time had come to alter our own methods. Therefore we developed the jeep with two sets of twin Vickers "K" guns (machine-guns with a very high rate of fire used on aircraft) and one Browning .50. The astonishing agility of the jeep enabled us to approach a target at night over almost any country. By the end of July the unit was entirely motorised – our transport consisting of 15 jeeps and 20 four-wheeled drive 3-tonners. The LRDG had given us tremendous assistance in training a cadre of navigators and in many other ways we were now self-supporting.'

Jeeps were to play an ever-growing role in the operations of the SAS in the future.

On 4 July the SAS convoy moved off from Cairo for the rendezvous north of the Quattara Depression, about 100 miles behind the enemy lines. The plan was to raid the enemy-held airfields strung along the coast in the Bagush/Fuka area. Three patrols would aim for Fuka, two others would strike further west at Sidi Barrani and El Daba, while the main target, Bagush, was to be attended to by Stirling and Mayne.

David drove his Blitzwagon and Paddy a jeep. A three-tonner carried bombs, grenades and food. They reached the coast road about a kilometre from the aerodrome at 22.00 hrs on 7 July. David decided to set up a road block and destroy any enemy transport that passed. Paddy would take the three others (Captain Storrie and Privates Adamson and Mullen) on to the field with the bombs. There were no lights, not even Arab fires, in the nearby desert. But in the pitch-black void they could smell the sea half a mile away. They stalked the first plane and found that the aircraft were not individually guarded. They placed bombs on six. But there were still a lot of people walking about so they decided to wait before attempting to bomb the planes on the other side of the airfield. Paddy and Mullen went back on their own. After fourteen planes they were challenged and fired on. Two grenades blew the guards apart. Quickly they laid bombs on the remaining planes and withdrew to watch the result. The first bomb went off, then the others in swift succession. The airfield was now alive with the enemy trying to fight the fires. They must have run out of chemicals for some of the fires burned on unchecked. They counted twenty-two explosions. Then, unaccountably, they stopped. 'Damn,' said Paddy. 'We did forty aircraft, some of the bloody primers must have been damp.' A quick examination of one of the remaining primers confirmed his diagnosis. Another twenty planes were tantalisingly near – it was heartbreaking. Then Stirling had another of his inspirations, as always so shiningly simple that anyone, in theory, might have thought of it. They would drive on to the field and shoot up the planes from the staff car and the jeep. With two pairs of RAF Vickers 'K' machine-guns on each vehicle – eight in all – they had a formidable firepower, for the Vickers fired 1200 rounds a minute. Paddy embraced the scheme eagerly. In five minutes flat they swept round the perimeter of the drome, both firing broadside. The roar of the guns was terrifying. The enemy, having scarcely recovered from the first attack, did not know what was hitting him. By the time he had opened up with anti-aircraft guns, they were off and away into the desert night. The raiders reckoned that, with Paddy's initial twenty-two and twelve in the second blitz, they had accounted for thirty-four planes.

A telling comparison is that on 18 September 1940, at the height of the Battle of Britain, five squadrons of the Duxford Wing, led by Douglas Bader – a total of sixty aircraft – achieved what was rightly regarded as a signal success in destroying thirty German planes with six others probably destroyed – the same number now 'written off' by a handful of SAS men. Of course the circumstances and the effects were very different. Bader's success was achieved in the eye of the hurricane. Nor had the SAS eliminated the equally valuable pilots. But the enemy striking power had been dealt a blow that hurt.

Stirling was very conscious of the need to reduce the enemy numbers. Bob Bennett tells how, coming away from a raid, they found about a dozen Italians sleeping by their tents. Stirling's order was 'Open up!' and they shot the lot. Later, on the truck, Bennett voiced reservations about killing them. Stirling pulled him aside. 'The odds are so heavily against us in this war. We have to put the fear of Allah up them. It's the only way we can win. It's against my nature to kill people, but it's got to be done.' Mayne was equally clinical. Major-General David Lloyd Owen clearly remembers greeting Paddy at the rendezvous after a raid on Fuka. He asked 'How were things tonight?' 'A bit trickier tonight,' replied Paddy. 'They had posted a sentry on nearly every bloody plane. I had to knife the sentries before I could place the bombs.' 'And he had, too,' adds Lloyd Owen. 'He must have knifed about seventeen of them.'

War was a deadly business. Malcolm Pleydell, the SAS Medical Officer in the desert, remembers Paddy Mayne saying, just before a raid, 'There should be some good killing tonight.' Paddy's brother Douglas has also said, 'Personally, I think he did enjoy killing. It was very like stalking a deer.' The hunting simile was well chosen. Later, when on a brief leave, Paddy was taken deer-stalking on a Highland mountainside and to the astounded admiration of the ghillies, he killed three stags in one short spell, two of them on the run. Only someone who has tried to approach a stag from downwind in order to get within range will appreciate the marksmanship which that feat entailed. Paddy Mayne had all the skills of the professional hunter, including a cold detachment from the quarry. But none ever thought of him as unfeeling or cold-hearted. He treated his men like children and according to Malcolm Pleydell: 'If you were sitting alone at Christmastime, he would be the first to come over to try to find out why you were getting depressed.'

Paddy once summed up night raids as a glorious binge with the hangover the morning after. The price paid was the long voyage home, exhausting, exposed to constant air attacks. After Fuka, in the first light of the morning, they could see through glasses what looked like an escarpment, the only feature that might offer cover. It was about an hour away, fifteen miles. They made for it with a nervous eye on the brightening sky. Paddy was well ahead in the first jeep, David about half a mile behind and the truck well in the rear. Then the aircraft, two CR42s and a Gibli, appeared diving, spraying machine-gun fire. Paddy, who had done his best to distract enemy attention from David by blazing away at the attacking planes, was the only one to reach some kind of cover beneath an underhanging rock. The truck and David's Blitzwagon, from which the occupants had quickly scattered, were shot to pieces. But no one was hurt. Paddy, with the only vehicle left, asked if anyone wanted a lift. 'After breakfast,' replied David. One of the sergeants reported. 'Nothing left, sir. Petrol, water, food, spares. The whole bloody lot went up with the truck.' 'Not quite,' said Paddy. 'We've got biscuits and some chocolate and here's a bottle of whiskey'. He had confirmed his reputation for coming up smelling of roses.

Stirling was determined that the new technique of charging the enemy by jeep be developed. Since he had become alerted to the prospect of night-raiders on foot, the enemy was strengthening his perimeter guards. Stirling's mind was already running on a mass motorised attack, which would blast through perimeter defences. But in the meantime, the old method was to prove its worth yet again, as employed by Paddy.

On 9 July, accompanied by four others, he descended on El Daba, about fifty miles west of El Alamein. They met little opposition and destroyed fourteen aircraft. Two days later he led another raid on Fuka in which twenty-two aircraft were destroyed. But whatever the merits of this proven system, with its economy of means and manpower, Stirling was pressing on with his set-piece. Perhaps it was the theatricality of the concept, for Stirling was a romantic. But, quite apart from the panache, it would carry a psychological punch which, on top of the physical destruction, could wreak havoc on enemy morale.

So the preparations were set in train. They had to return to Cairo for stores and new transport. Leaving about thirty men in the desert base – which lay fifty miles south of the enemy chain of coastal airfields stretching west of El Alamein – David and Paddy, with trucks and jeeps, embarked on the 400-mile trek back to Kabrit. The only way was through the Quattara Depression, a huge salt bog shaped like a leg of lamb, 150 miles long and seventy miles at its widest. If the thin skin of the bog gave way under a heavy vehicle it would be slowly engulfed. There were two tracks across formed of hard rock salt. Paddy and Sandy Scratchley, a well-known bloodstock breeder and amateur rider whom David had just brought into the SAS, took the southern route.

They were machine-gunned by enemy aircraft before they got down into the Depression – the cliffs surrounding the northern end were 1000 ft high. To avoid the constantly patrolling aircraft they had to cross under the protection of the midday heat haze.

Scratchley paints a vivid picture of that waterless waste of cracked salt. The stifling heat of the solar fireball, mixed with the engine fumes, made even changing a wheel an agonising feat of endurance. Paddy drove one truck – he always preferred to drive – disdaining the Arab headdress which some of the men wore, soaking it in water, which almost at once turned to steam. 'I'd rather roast than boil,' he grunted.

By late afternoon, the salt bog was behind them, and Scratchley gives a glimpse of the Sahara in milder mood: 'The slow grind was forgotten,' he wrote, 'thirty miles an hour or more raised a breeze and the sun was well over the top. Two hundred miles from the western edge of the Depression to where we halted to eat and sleep, in rolling country, spotted with stunted acacia trees. The look-outs relaxed.

'A wonderful desert sunset, when sometimes the whole horizon seemed to be on fire, could be absorbed without another thought. Next morning we continued on our way, the colour of the ground changing with the surface, gravel and sand becoming pebbles and sand until, with the undulations continuing, so that horizon followed horizon, we topped the final ridge and saw in the peculiar technicolour of the evening light, the three triangles of the Mena Pyramids. We were approaching water, civilisation and dirt.'

The desert wore many fascinating faces. Even the most down-to-earth of the SAS men attempted on occasion to capture them in prose. Sergeant Jim Brough, who accompanied Paddy Mayne on many of the raids, wrote this:

'I once heard one of the lads describe the desert as miles and miles of Sweet Fanny Adams. Nothing could be further from the truth. Before you finished the patrol, you would have driven up to 1000 miles without seeing a road, on surfaces like the moon, or the Sand Sea which even aircraft did not like flying over. Expanses of dead flat salt flats on which you could skim along as fast as your engine would allow. Another stretch would be like a ploughed field, composed of hard packed salt. Yet another would be dotted with fossilised tree trunks, just as if they were cast-iron, or covered with lumps of mica. I suppose that the stretches of dirty black-looking sand was oil, you never knew what to expect. So before we took off, we scrounged as many tyres and inner tubes as we could lay our hands on.'

The Stirling/Mayne convoy negotiated that terrain, to Cairo and back, in eight days. They returned to the desert rendezvous with twenty new jeeps with Vickers 'K' on specially welded mountings fore and aft, and spare three-tonners. They brought, too, Eastern gifts of a less martial nature: tobacco, rum, Turkish Delight and jars of eau-de-Cologne.

Reconnaissance had shown that Sidi Haneish, one of the airfields in the Fuka area, was one of Rommel's main assembly areas, and that many Junkers Ju 52 transport planes, of which he was reported to be short, were there. Stirling's plan was to launch a mass jeep attack by full moonlight. The full moon was the last time the Germans would expect an attack. Eighteen jeeps were to take part. They would advance in line abreast, then form into a broad arrow consisting of two columns with seven jeeps on each side delivering their broadsides. The arrowhead would consist of three jeeps firing forward. The navigator's jeep, immediately behind the arrowhead, would be unable to use its weapons. The manoeuvre was rehearsed until the drill was perfect. Absolute precision was vital with so many guns firing at once – the jeeps were only five yards apart.

The cave in which the jeeps were housed was a frenzy of organised bustle, a mix between racing pits and a transport workshop with engines being revved, tyres fitted, spares checked. The weapons, too, had to be stripped and cleaned; plastic, moulded into time-bombs; fuses and primers, inserted; the magazines loaded with rounds in the proper sequence, tracer, ball, incendiary, armour-piercing. During all this activity, Paddy was seen to be asleep beneath a large mosquito net, with his head against one jeep and his feet under another.

It was sundown on 27 July when they set out. They drove for four hours over rough country. Then Mike Sadler, navigating, announced that they were within a mile of the airfield which lay dead ahead. All around was desolation and silence. Was Sadler right? Stirling had no doubts. The order was given to move into line abreast. The die was cast. Clearly visible under a full moon, the eighteen vehicles advanced in a jagged horizontal line that twitched like an ECG trace as they hit obstacles and potholes, accelerating and braking to keep formation. Half a mile to go. Then it happened. The airfield before them was suddenly flooded with light. They had been spotted! Any moment and the enemy would open up.

But no, out of the sky came the roar of a Heinkel coming to land. Stirling did not hesitate. He kept straight on for the runway. Just as the plane touched down a hundred yards away, he opened fire: sixty-eight Vickers, firing 1200 rounds a minute, poured out a torrent of dazzling tracer. The shock and din of that firepower was devastating. The landing lights were switched off. Stirling fired a green Very light, the signal for the arrowhead. They were now moving fast on the smooth surface, pointing between the packed rows of planes. There were Ju 52s all right, but Messerschmitts, Heinkels and Ju Stukas as well. As intended, the deafening initial barrage had left the enemy in temporary disarray. They had no idea of the numbers involved in this thunderous attack. Then a Breda began; followed by the thump of a mortar. The raiders were now moving in a circle, the sky bright with flaming airframes. The heat was so intense – they were blasting the targets from fifty yards – that men felt their hair and eyebrows being singed. The bullets would strike home, then a red glow before the petrol tank exploded and the whole fuselage went up in a funnel of flame.

They could see Germans running about in the distance and the outlines of other planes far out on the field. Stirling's jeep was hit and the columns screeched to a halt. Nobody was hurt but the jeep was kaput, so another moved in to pick up the crew.

There was a quick check-round to see how much ammunition the party had left. Then off again, to complete the circle and make for the Ju 52s they had spied out on the perimeter. These were dealt with, and they were moving off when someone noticed one more which they had somehow missed. The driver of one of the leading jeeps jumped down and ran towards it. They could see him reach up and place something on the wing. Then he ran back to his jeep. It was Paddy Mayne leaving his explosive calling card. On a signal the engines revved and they were off. They had lost one jeep and one gunner killed. The problem now was to reach cover before daylight. They split up to make the rendezvous as independent parties.

Stirling's party got lost. By dawn it seemed as if they would be left totally exposed on the bare desert. Stephen Hastings, later a MP, then a member of Stirling's party, wrote: 'Then the desert became our friend. As the fog cleared we found ourselves on the edge of a small escarpment, dropping about fifteen feet. A large bowl-shaped depression cut by deep wadis covered with thick greenish-brown scrub up to four feet high. Our vehicles bumped uncertainly down into one of the wadis. The men needed no orders; they clambered off and swiftly heaved and manoeuvred the jeeps into the centre of a water course among the tallest bush. In a matter of minutes, enough scrub had been wrenched up and thrown over them. Then only did relief set in. Since the vehicles were hidden it would be easy to run to cover on the noise of an approaching aircraft. We looked round at each other. We were indeed a ragged-looking bunch. Faces, hair and beards were covered in a thick yellow-grey film of dust; eyes were red and strained.

'Our dirty, open-necked battledress and overcoats hung on us like scarecrows. One officer was trying to scrape large and sand-caked bloodstains off his trousers with a piece of stick; the blood of the dead soldier who was lying on his back under a bush with a dirty blanket over his body. Our mouths were dry and ill-tasting and there was a burning behind the eyes, rather like the symptoms of a hangover. But for the moment we were comparatively safe. "Any tea, Seekings?" said David. A large grin from the Corporal, "Yessir!" "All right, then, brew up for everyone" and in a lower voice, "You two – get a spade and bury him." Tea was ready brewed using two charred tins, one full of burning petrol, the other of dirty-looking water. Black tea practically unsugared, tasting of brackish water, but still hot, strong, and unbelievably refreshing. It was 5.30 in the morning. The two men returned with the spade. "We buried him, sir," "Have you got his Pay Book?" They had. There was a moment's silence. What could they do? They had no Prayer Book, they knew no words to say. "I think we'll just go and stand round the grave for a moment," said David. We stood, bareheaded, looking at the grave, a little heap of sand and stones, each man with his own thoughts. It was indeed a curious burial, just a two-minute silence with a handful of tired dirty comrades. Yet for a short fraction of time, lost in the middle of nowhere, there was dignity.'

They reached the rendezvous after another day, three of the jeeps badly damaged and just limping home. Paddy and David were assessing results – they had destroyed at Sidi Haneish at least forty planes. Over the wireless the latest intelligence reports were coming in, when a LRDG patrol arrived, carrying two interesting prisoners.

On the way back from Bagush, where they had been creating a diversion to the main jeep attack, the patrol had heard a plane approach. Taking cover, they watched in amazement as a Fieseler Storch, a small observation aircraft, proceeded to land not more than fifty yards away near a wrecked German truck. From it jumped two German officers laughing and talking, blissfully unaware that they were not alone. The British patrol opened fire on the Storch and emerged from hiding. 'Don't shoot me,' said one of the Germans, pulling a Red Cross armband out of his pocket. 'I'm a doctor. We were just having a look round!' They were duly taken prisoner. One was Rommel's personal pilot. The other, tall and bespectacled, was an eminent Hamburg doctor, Baron von Lutteroti. When they got back, they refused Stirling's offer of parole. So they were put under the charge of the MO, Malcolm Pleydell, and Bob Bennett. The Germans were model prisoners, and the Baron offered to help Pleydell with his medical work. One of the patients was another newly recruited officer to the SAS, Lord Jellicoe. By coincidence, George Jellicoe had lunched with the Baron's wife in Hamburg before the war. The exact circumstances of that social occasion are not established, but clearly Jellicoe and Lutteroti had friends in common.

Word now came from Cairo that the unit had to return to HQ to prepare for some unspecified operation. That directly conflicted with Stirling's plan to remain at the rendezvous and attack German supply lines up to El Alamein. He was furious at what he regarded as interference. Paddy Mayne, more phlegmatic on this occasion, tried to calm things. In the general bustle of leaving the prisoners disappeared. Bob Bennett is convinced that it was 'a put-up job'. He had heard Pleydell explaining to Lutteroti some of the basic facts of navigation, how if he followed the North Star it would take him to the coast – that meant back to the German lines. Again, when their disappearance was noticed, no effort was made to track them down, and finally on the morning after their disappearance a German Stuka dived low over the SAS camp – but dropped nothing. Bennett believes the Stuka's salute was a 'thank you' on behalf of the returned prisoners. It was, Bennett maintains, a small chivalrous gesture on both sides. Paddy Mayne's reported comment was more cynical: 'Cheer up, David, they've only forty miles to walk before they make contact with their own side. By noon tomorrow the Jerries will have a full description of us. It's just as well we're leaving for Cairo.'

By another coincidence, the same Baron doctor was once again to cross the path of Paddy Mayne in the last months of the war in Germany.

Back in Cairo in August, Stirling found his worst fears realised. Instead of, as he had proposed, a series of raids on Rommel's lines of communication behind El Alamein – which 8 Army, under its newly appointed commander, Montgomery, was confident it could continue to hold – the plan from HQ was for a large-scale assault on Benghazi harbour, involving tanks. The SAS force would consist of 220 men, forty supply trucks and forty armed jeeps. 'The whole thing', wrote Stirling, 'sinned against every principle on which the SAS was founded.' To swell his existing force, he would have to take on a hundred newcomers who had not been trained to his exacting standards: he would have to work to a fixed timetable, sacrificing all flexibility; the vital element of surprise would be gone. But the pressures were such and the promise of a continuing role for the SAS so rosy, that against his better judgement he allowed himself to be persuaded.

With the Germans dug in at El Alamein, and protecting their flank as far south as Siwa Oasis, the route to Benghazi, if the SAS were to avoid detection, was daunting. It meant an 800-mile leg south-west down to Kufra Oasis, their staging post deep in the desert, then a further 600 miles north to the mountainous Djebel and the coast. The problems of organisation were huge. The new recruits had to be quickly schooled in SAS desert tactics, even in driving through the treacherous billows of the Sand Sea. But the impossible was achieved. By 7 September they had got the task force as far as Kufra with its palm trees, mud huts and lakes so buoyant with salt one could hardly sink in them. A week later, the whole party assembled in the Djebel, about twenty miles from their target.

Reg Seekings has described their rendezvous in the Djebel as 'rough but good camouflage. There was that sweet smell of danger you got when approaching the coast and away from the desert.'

The news was disquieting. Already in Cairo there were intelligence reports that the enemy was aware of the impending attack. Now Bob Melot, a Belgian working with the British and who lived among the Bedouin, confirmed the rumours. Not only was the enemy alerted, but minefields and machine-gun defences were already in position. When Stirling queried the wisdom of following the agreed plan now that it was 'blown' he was told not to heed 'bazaar gossip'. So on the night of 13 September, the raid went ahead as planned.

On the outskirts of Benghazi the convoy was faced with a road-barrier, unmanned and unlighted. Bill Cumper, the explosives expert and the accepted wag, took a look. The land on each side was undoubtedly mined. He pushed the barrier up with the time-honoured utterance: 'Let battle commence!' The joke went suddenly sour: they were in the middle of a heavy ambush. Fitzroy Maclean has described it: 'Pandemonium, from the other side of the road, a dozen machine-guns opened up at us at point-blank range, then a couple of 20mm Bredas joined in, then some heavy mortars while snipers' bullets pinged viciously through the trees on either side of the road.'

Luckily, the enemy's fire was not so accurate, which gave the SAS gunners a chance to scatter and respond. The Vickers 'K' 'did their stuff', but the situation was hopeless. Jeeps were hit, and men too. The balloon was up, all surprise gone, and the reinforced town garrison was no doubt preparing to receive them. Sergeant Almonds tried to force his way through. His burning jeep now lit up the scene. There was nothing for it but to get back to the Djebel before daylight. Once there, they faced another 800-mile trek.

On the return journey to Kufra, they were strafed and harried unceasingly. In one day they lost twenty-five trucks and nineteen jeeps. In one incident, when Paddy Mayne's jeep was trying to escape from an enemy aircraft which was relentlessly strafing them, one of his men fell off, wounded. They kept on till they got the jeep under cover. Then Paddy went straight back on foot, found the wounded man and carried him back on his shoulders.

The final toll was fifty men and fifty vehicles lost. Stirling's initial misgivings had been justified. The exercise had been a major failure. A simultaneous raid on Tobruk, part of the same grand scheme, proved even more disastrous. Two destroyers and four motor torpedo boats were sunk. The lesson learnt was the one that they already knew by heart: to use the SAS as storm-troops, tightly integrated into a large pre-planned offensive, was a waste of their peculiar and unique talents. They had to be allowed to 'do their own thing', flexible, seizing opportunity as it was offered, working in small elusive packs, and always with the crucial advantage of surprise. Despite the Benghazi fiasco, the future outlook was not discouraging. 'The buggers in Cairo', as Paddy Mayne expressed it, 'were at last beginning to show a titter of wit.'

7
A Proper Establishment

GENERAL ALEXANDER, now overall Commander-in-Chief in the Middle East, did recognise the SAS's proper role and decided to give the regiment a proper establishment. This came about largely through a dinner party in Cairo just before the Benghazi affair, at which Winston Churchill had met David Stirling, now promoted to Lieutenant-Colonel. The Prime Minister had already heard of the exploits of the SAS through his son, Randolph, but he was also impressed by Stirling and described him to Field Marshal Smuts, who was present too, as 'the mildest manner'd man that ever scuttled ship or cut a throat'. The Byron quotation from *Don Juan*, could equally well have been applied to Paddy Mayne – when sober. As a direct result of this encounter, Stirling was informed that his link with HQ would in future be through Colonel Shan Hackett – later of Arnhem – and later still General Sir John Hackett. Shan Hackett and Stirling were kindred souls; but a joint meeting with Montgomery was less productive.

Montgomery – with the self-confidence engendered by the victory of El Alamein still in the future – was prickly and unsympathetic. Stirling, coolly unimpressed and sceptical, did not go down well with his commander. Nor was Montgomery prepared to give Stirling another 150 men, picked men with desert experience. 'What makes you think, Colonel Stirling, that you can handle my men, my most desert-worthy, my most dependable, my best men, to greater advantage than I can handle them myself?' Coming from the commander of 8 Army it was not an easy question to answer, even for someone as self-assured as David Stirling. It was clear that Montgomery's decision was a flat 'no', but what hit hardest was the General's insistence that he was not prepared to reinforce 'failure at Benghazi'. Brigadier Freddy de Guingand, Montgomery's Chief of Staff, proved more amenable. He promised to do his best to help. But Stirling's plan to mount a series of concentrated raids, night after night, against a hundred miles or so of Rommel's communications, would have to be drastically scaled down.

Stirling was always conscious that the fight was not solely against the enemy, but against the so-called top brass, or as he put it, 'the Freemason mediocrities from the First World War who were opposed to the methods of the SAS and objected to its independence'. To defend the SAS, and the enormous potential it held for winning battles, was at times more important than the day-to-day operations. It was advice which was to serve Paddy Mayne well, also, when, later, he too fought for the survival of the regiment.

After the interview with Montgomery, Mayne and Stirling discussed future plans and it was decided that Paddy, with a squadron formed of the old experienced hands, would start off at once for Kufra and establish a base on the edge of the Sand Sea ready to go into action. Meanwhile Stirling would recruit what he could from the fresh troops who had just come out from Britain and whip them through an intensive training course. They should be ready by the end of November.

By 23 October, Major Mayne, with eighty men and thirty-five trucks and jeeps, had arrived at the agreeable oasis of Kufra. They followed the same roundabout route as for the Benghazi raid. Kufra was the rear base also used by the LRDG. 'A' Squadron, as it was known now, moved north and set up a forward base inside the Sand Sea. This was about 200 miles behind the enemy lines at El Alamein and about 150 miles south of the road and railway that followed the coast. It was well placed for raids on both, and largely safe from air attack, for aircraft seldom wasted time and fuel over this desolate ocean of sand. They found a deep hollow in a mass of dunes. One of the new hands, young officers in 'A' Squadron who had just joined the SAS and who were later to distinguish themselves in Italy and France, was Second Lieutenant Johnny Wiseman, newly commissioned in the North Somerset Yeomanry; and it was in Kufra that he had what he termed 'his first terrifying experience' with Paddy Mayne, an example of 'silent ferocity' which he never forgot.

'He was a vast man and when he was speaking to you, as he would normally, he was absolutely delightful,' Wiseman recalled. 'But on this occasion we were all drinking in a tent. We'd had a lot of rum. Someone annoyed Paddy and when he'd had a few drinks – it took a few but we'd been at it for two or three hours – you were very careful indeed. Anyhow, someone had upset him and he said to me "What should we do with this chap?" So I said, rather stupidly, we were only kidding – "Why not shave off half his beard?" We were all growing beards – there wasn't enough water to wash. So he said, "What a good idea!" and he got hold of me, threw me on my back, put his two legs on my arms, said to somebody, "Get me my cut-throat" and took off half my beard without any water, without anything. There was this enormous man sitting on top of me – I've never been so frightened in my life. I was sure he was about to cut my throat. After that nothing in the war ever frightened me! That cured me.'

From the Sand Sea, Paddy immediately got down to action. He concentrated especially on the Matruh railway line, ambushing trucks and blowing up sections of track. Sandy Scratchley recalled the first unforgettable raid: 'All I know is that the night of 23 October was brilliant and clear with a full moon. We figured we were about thirty miles behind the German line at Alamein. As we jogged along under a starlit sky, it seemed strange to be so close to the enemy and hear nothing. It may have been about midnight when the barrage that started the great battle broke the stillness. The effect was colossal. Every inch of the desert between Alamein and the Quattara Depression was lit up with the explosions of bursting 25-pounder shells. From twenty miles it struck me more as a magnificent sight than the horror it actually was.'

A few nights later, Wiseman led three jeeps up to the Matruh railway. The SAS Diary notes: 'Railway blown over a quarter of a mile, and cratered with 20 lb ammonal. On our return, we met Major Mayne at the entrance to the Sand Sea, where he told us that the offensive at El Alamein had begun.' (This was the second phase of Alamein, the final breakthrough, codenamed SUPERCHARGE, which Montgomery had launched on the night of 1 November.)

There are two letters from Paddy Mayne at this time. The first, to his sister, Barbara, or 'Babs', was written on 15 October: 'You ask if my boils are better. Who told you I had any? I haven't. The usual desert sores but bar that I am OK. I write in a native-made grass hut in a P.C. Wren oasis. There is a fort and everything. All we need is a little touch of the cafard, but we haven't run to it yet – we call it sand-happy.

'I was in Cairo for two days last week. Took me ten hours in a slow plane to get there. I had meant to send some Christmas presents, but with the Egyptian holiday, Bairan or something like that it is called, everything was shut. Some time ago you asked me about an MC, I said I had been recommended for. I never heard anything more about it, but after each operation I am told I am getting something but I don't put much faith in it. My CO is very apt to promise things that don't happen. He has promised me leave at home, sort of present for a good boy, but it keeps being postponed. I really don't want it till we clean up the Jerries out here and that won't be very long now.'

The reference to a Military Cross is puzzling, since Mayne had already been awarded the DSO, gazetted on 24 February 1942, for his part in the first Tamet raid of the previous December. His jaundiced view of his CO (Stirling) may have been due to a touch of the cafard – the depression he denied feeling. Or it may be a symptom of his antipathy towards the upper-class Englishman, the same as evoked by Geoffrey Keyes. There was certainly no personal animus on the part of Stirling, who had a great affection for him. Even today, when David Stirling is asked about his feelings towards Paddy Mayne he will say, ingenuously: 'I loved Paddy. I was more fond of Paddy than he was of me.' Equally it is true that Paddy once wrote to David's brother Bill: 'I only wish that D.S. was around.'

The second of these two letters, to his brother, is dated 30 October 1942, the same day as the raid on Matruh railway:

'I am lying here beside a three-tonner, under its tarpaulin in the sand and listening to the wireless. It is pleasant now, cool and fresh, but in the summertime it is no place for any Christian body. We are in the Sand Sea about 200 miles from the nearest oasis (Kufra) and just going out and acting the fool from here. The loot question has looked up very well in the last few days – inside a week first of all we came on a Heinkel, which had force-landed. The crew was tapping for assistance – they got it. Out of it we got automatics, a shotgun and a roller flex [sic] camera. It is a nice one with the reflex view-finder. I bought it off the laddie who found it. Then I was on a job and on the way back I ran into a nice soft convoy. We were like a lot of pirates – 10 days' beard – the poor wee Jerries and Eyeties driving along as happy as you like, 160 miles behind their lines. We whipped in from behind and the first they knew was our bullets, smacking through their three-tonners. Out of it I got another camera, a very nice little one, £15–£20 worth. I'll send you some photographs, not snaps.

'Funniest thing were the prisoners – we can never afford to take many as they eat too much of our rations, so I intended only to take one. I put him on the truck and told the others to beat it, but he started to cry and the others looked so pitiable at being left that I took a couple more – they are useful at washing dishes and keeping my equipment clean.'

Like Wellington in Spain, Clive in India, and many other honourable precedents, Paddy Mayne had the professional soldier's attitude towards the spoils of war. It is interesting, however, to compare Paddy's version of 'acting the fool' with the official report:

'Major Mayne, Lieutenant Marsh, Privates Moore, O'Dowd, Allen, L/C Swan. The party under Major Mayne left Howards Cairn on 19 October and together with remainder of jeeps travelled through the Sand Sea to a point five miles inside the entrance. Here a small advanced dump was made. Travelled north-east for a day, crossing through the boundary wire between Libya and Egypt, a mile south of Fort El Heria, kept on in the same direction for five days, heading for railway at Mersa Matruh. Lay up for a day in a wadi used for a previous job, found guns and ammunition, food, but no water. O'Dowd's jeep developed axle trouble. Major Mayne sent back two jeeps to lying-up area of previous night. Major Mayne, continuing on towards target, was fired on by heavy MG, rifle and 20mm fire. No casualties.

'Decided that they had hit a heavily defended area so turned back and re-joined two jeeps sent back previous night – Lt Tony Marsh and Moore, O'Dowd, Swan. O'Dowd's jeep fixed. Whole party moved off same night to a new lying-up area. Spent three days trying to get news as to when push at Alamein was to start. [It had started four days previously.] Unable to get through on radio. On fourth day whole party moved off in easterly direction, going rough and hilly. Eighth day out, about an hour before dusk, convoy was sighted heading north along the Siwa track: six vehicles. Major Mayne decided to attack. Two jeeps to attack the front of convoy and halt it, other two to race for the rear. We had to chase convoy which speeded up when it spotted us, got straddled out so that only two-thirds of the convoy was caught in pincer movement. All jeeps opened up with K guns. Front truck going very fast got away owing to the fact that we were coming across country diagonally and could not reach maximum speed. Three trucks stopped, searched and then blown up. Twenty Italians taken prisoner. Two prisoners were taken out of bunch, who were crying hard to be taken with us. Here, owing to shortage of petrol and water, party split. Lt Marsh, Moore, Swan and O'Dowd heading due north to blow railway. Major Mayne with two jeeps heading back to the dump at Howards Cairn. During the morning low-flying Ju 52 sighted and party, caught with trousers down, remained still, hoping that the plane would mistake jeeps for wrecks, many of which were lying around the area. It did. Lt Marsh arrived back at Howards Cairn to learn that Major Mayne had had to travel for a day with both front tyres flat, owing to the fact that we had gone off with the only tyre pump in the party . . .' Major Mayne's reaction to that situation is not recorded!

That exercise was carried out many miles behind the German lines, in the middle of the battle of Alamein. It is all there, couched in unexciting matter-of-fact terms – the seemingly endless treks, the lying-up, the false starts, the mechanical frustrations, the Junkers, and the kill. Missing are the blistering heat, the desert sores, the boredom, the flies that 'clustered like a black rosette' on even the smallest wound or 'ulcer', the chlorinated water carried in oil drums that had been burnt out to cleanse them, but which still retained the taste.

It is ironic that, with the speed of 8 Army's advance, the blown railway was likely to be of more hindrance to them than to the enemy. Ten days after the break-out from Alamein the British had taken Tobruk, 300 miles away.

Stirling's plans had to be adjusted to keep abreast of Montgomery's advance. Rommel was now once again dug in at El Agheila. Ninety men under Paddy Mayne were ordered to a wadi called Bir Zalten, about a hundred miles south of Rommel's line. They had thirty jeeps, each self-contained in that it carried all the arms, rations and kit required. The overall scheme was to split up the 400-mile stretch of road linking El Agheila and Tripoli between Paddy's 'A' Squadron and the new 'B' Squadron commanded by Vivian Street. Each squadron was divided into eight patrols of three jeeps each, 'A' being given about forty miles of road which it was to attack systematically.

This constant night-raiding would so disrupt enemy traffic that he would be forced to use the road by day, and thus expose himself to the Royal Air Force. The plan had been approved by Montgomery, who had now come to accept the SAS. Stirling was now his 'mad boy Stirling' and Monty confessed that the plan to focus the SAS assault on road transport 'could have a decisive effect, yes, a really decisive effect, on my forthcoming offensive'.

'A' Squadron got to work at once. Once the offensive began on 13 December enemy vehicles, streaming back towards Bouerat and Tripoli, were counted by a LRDG patrol, on day and night watch, at up to 3500 a day. This was something for Paddy Mayne to get his teeth into. Night after night the rota of his patrols were on The Road. Here is a typical entry in his diary:

'Drove north to attack road, ran into minefield on side of road.

Recced our position next morning and found ourselves west of Sirte. Skirted fort of Ksar Bou Hadi, mined road, blew telegraph poles and cratered road. The first car came along struck our mine. Later the ammonal went up with a loud explosion. Hid for three days, but now were very short of petrol and unable to get all our jeeps back. We ran one jeep on to the road as a roadblock between two trucks in a long convoy. Put mines under the wheels and filled it with our remaining explosive. The convoy stopped and, trying to pass round our jeep, hit one of our mines. Later jeep went up with terrific explosion. Drove south to hit tracks after 100 miles and returned to Bir Zalten. Much frightened by a cheetah, with whom we shared our lying-up wadi.'

With sixteen raids a week, Paddy Mayne and his men made the enemy transport so uncertain by night that, as intended, it was increasingly forced to run the gauntlet of air attack by day.

In the meantime Stirling escorted 'B' Squadron into position south of its allocated coastal stretch west of Paddy's area and east of Tripoli and he then, with his HQ team, carried on to a location 50 miles further west. After a week of raiding operations, Stirling set course for the Gafsa Gap in Tunisia with the intent of making contact with the First Army and with his brother Bill, commanding 2 SAS Regiment based on Philipsville. Thirty miles north of the Gap he was trapped and captured in a boxed-in wadi by a German armoured recce unit. This was to have been Stirling's last operation before going back to the UK to discuss the future of the SAS as a Brigade – with particular reference to planning for the second front.

The Germans had been aware of Stirling's SAS for a long time. Field Marshal Rommel had been so disturbed by their raids that during December he had to divert some of his needed armoured patrols to hunt them down. As early as 8 October 1942 Hitler himself had issued a special order instructing that 'these British saboteurs and their accomplices were to be hunted down and exterminated without mercy'. Fortunately, Rommel ignored that order. But others did not.

The war in the desert was now nearing its end. With the

capture of Tripoli at the end of January 1943, and the US First Army advancing on Tunis from the west, after the landings in North Africa which took place in November 1942, the special kind of SAS operation was no longer needed. Before he was taken prisoner, indeed, Stirling had already decided that Paddy Mayne's squadron should be transferred to the Lebanon for ski-training, training which would enable it to operate in the mountainous northern regions of Turkey and Iran should the Germans move south through the Caucasus. Not only had Stirling been thinking well ahead; but Fitzroy Maclean had been sent to Baghdad to discuss possible plans. The German defeats in North Africa and at Stalingrad, however, effectively removed any threat to Iran.

From his prisoner-of-war camp, David Stirling had nominated his successor. Later he said: 'Paddy was hugely brave. I do not think he could ever have commanded an ordinary regular regiment, but he was exactly the man I wanted to succeed me in command of 1 SAS.'

Paddy Mayne's first battle in his new command now as Lieutenant-Colonel was a battle of survival, an engagement with the higher command, who, having reluctantly come to appreciate the work of the SAS in the desert, were unable to visualise its role in the future. Summoned to Cairo, he had to argue long and hard to convince GHQ that the SAS was still needed.

For a week he argued and defended. He did not have David Stirling's social contacts and acceptance among the top brass, but he had determination and a reputation which, with that of his regiment, pleaded trumpet-tongued to be allowed to continue its work.

Stirling himself says: 'When it came to superior officers, the fact that he was somewhat incoherent in speech never caused him any difficulty. They would wait until he said what he had to say, even if it was rather stumbling, but they wouldn't interrupt him. He was too big a man.'

Captain Derrick Harrison recalled: 'Paddy fought desperately to keep us alive. He managed to do it by changing our role. We became Special Raiding Squadron, SAS.' Undoubtedly Paddy's survival exercise had not been helped by a fracas he was involved in when he was first called to Cairo to talk about the regiment's future. As with so many of Mayne's escapades, accounts tend to be scrappy and varied. According to Reg Seekings, Paddy had applied for permission to fly home on the death of his father, which took place at that same time, January 1943. He had met with a point-blank refusal, which he naturally took very badly. Seekings is quite clear that there was another factor which inflamed Paddy's resentment against the powers that be. This was a growing grudge which the SAS commander felt towards the broadcaster and war correspondent, Richard Dimbleby. Of what this was compounded it is hard to say. Seekings recalls talk of 'this bullshitting so-and-so who reports on the thunder of tanks and big battles from the lounge of a Cairo hotel – never been near the bloody battlefront!'

However it was, Paddy set off on the rampage to seek out Dimbleby. During a wild drinking spree he smashed up several Cairo restaurants. Major-General David Lloyd Owen witnessed the grand finale: 'I was there. I saw Paddy throw the Provost-Marshal and two Military Policemen down the steps of Shepheard's Hotel.' Paddy did not find Dimbleby, but found himself placed once again under close arrest. Someone intervened and, according to Seekings, a signal was sent to Kasmiril barracks: 'Release this man – he is of much more use as an officer than as an other rank.'

It says, in fact, much for official tolerance and common sense that Major Mayne was reinstated, and ordered to prepare the newly named Special Raiding Squadron for the invasion of Sicily.

8

Special Raiding Squadron, SAS

WHO DARES WINS

TRAINING for the Special Raiding Squadron, 1 SAS, began in northern Palestine. Paddy tackled it with such thoroughness that Captain Derrick Harrison, who was there, recalls how 'Paddy was adamant that we started from basics, how to fire and aim a rifle. Right through the whole training routine. He even insisted that we learn to ride horses. There were repeated mock attacks against stone outcrops in a field . . . General Miles Dempsey, the newly appointed Commander of 13 Corps, 8 Army, came to address us. Only then did we learn that our eventual target was to be coastal batteries.' Seekings also has his recollections of General Dempsey's address to the troops. They were gathered in a large assembly hall. 'Dempsey seemed to think that we were all raw recruits. He told us not to be disheartened, that we would see some action soon. We would have our D-Day, he said. I saw Paddy pull him aside and say something to him. Then Dempsey got up again and apologised. He hadn't realised that he was talking to SAS men who had been fighting hard for years. He was very handsome about it.' Dempsey was to be even more handsome when he addressed the SAS again at the end of the Italian campaign.

Harrison's recollections continue: 'We moved south to the Gulf of Aqaba for intensive training in cliff-climbing and assaults in the hilly terrain of Sinai. Back to the Mediterranean coast for endless night exercises in and out of landing craft until we could do it in our sleep. Paddy worked us into the ground.

During these manoeuvres I remember that Paddy usually started out after us, but always managed to get there before us. He was incredibly light on his feet.'

The plan to invade Sicily was the subject of prolonged wrangling between Montgomery, the naval and air chiefs, and Allied HQ under Eisenhower. No less than eight blueprints were produced before Montgomery's views prevailed, and the final plan was for the British and US forces to land side by side on a 75-mile front extending around the south-eastern corner of the island. They were then to drive swiftly north, cutting Sicily in two and preventing the Axis army from escaping to the mainland. In his *Memoirs*, Montgomery observes: 'Although General Alexander [Deputy Commander-in-Chief to Eisenhower] then agreed with this conception of how the campaign should be developed by his two armies and with the role of the naval and air forces, in fact the campaign was not conducted in this way. There was no masterplan. The army commanders developed their own ideas of how to proceed and then "informed" higher authority. The US Seventh Army, once on shore, was allowed to wheel west towards Palermo. It thereby missed the opportunity to direct its main thrust north in order to "cut the island in two".'

But before the invasion, Paddy Mayne and his men were unaware of any dissension at the top. Their task was to capture and destroy the coastal battery at Cape Murro di Porco, the headland like a pig's snout, just south of Syracuse. The mother ships they sailed on were HMS *Dunera* with three LCAs (Landing Craft Assault) and HMS *Ulster Monarch*, with six. *Ulster Monarch* was familiar to Paddy Mayne for, before the war, it had been a regular ferry on the Belfast/Liverpool route. Two incidents occurred on her which throw further light on him.

Pat Riley, an American brought to England at the age of nine, who at this time was a sergeant – he was later commissioned – was involved in the first. *Ulster Monarch*, he remembered, was a 'wet' ship and they were several days en route to Sicily from the eastern Mediterranean. He tells of how he suddenly came across Paddy pushing Tony Marsh – then a junior SAS officer – against the outside wall of a cabin and apparently in the act of throttling him. 'Tony's face was blue,' recalls Riley, 'there was no time to lose. I pulled Paddy round and hit him hard on the jaw. He went down and I straddled over him, waiting and very frightened at the thought of what he would do to me. But he just got up without a word. Then after a minute, he said, "Come on, Pat, let's have a drink".'

If this incident is true, it is the only recorded instance of Paddy Mayne backing off. Perhaps though, through the mist of alcohol, he realised what he had been doing to Marsh. Marsh is now dead – he was one of Paddy's close friends – and there was no other witness. Riley, like Mayne, was a big man and a seasoned heavyweight boxer.

The other light on Paddy's character is thrown by Brigadier Mike Blackman, then a captain, who later became the SAS Intelligence Officer. He relates how, during an air raid when *Ulster Monarch* was off Syracuse, Paddy Mayne strolled calmly around the deck under heavy fire. Blackman maintains that there was no need for such bravado. It was, he believes, either a gesture of showing the flag, or an exercise in self-discipline. It may, too, have been a case of a commander setting an example.

There are many other people, including Johnny Wiseman, who testify to Paddy's complete lack of exhibitionism and almost automatic disregard for danger. 'He had no swagger,' said Wiseman, who recalls other aspects of his CO's character. 'His walk was loose-limbed, almost slouchy, with his feet turned in and he was never tired, no matter how many miles we covered. Nor when he was drinking did he eat – he would fast for a couple of days. No sleep either, and he hated drinking alone. You never dared to leave him to go to bed when he was on a bender. He just would not allow you.'

The convoy reached Cape Murro di Porco on the night of 10/11 July 1943. There was a last-minute check. The SAS had their own favourite weapons. Paddy, except on special occasions, carried only his Colt revolver. Bob Bennett had a 9mm Schmeisser machine-pistol. 'I'd picked it up from a German armoured car in the desert. Tommy-guns were no use on this kind of show because the ammo was so heavy – you couldn't carry enough.' The sea was rough. When the voice of the ship's

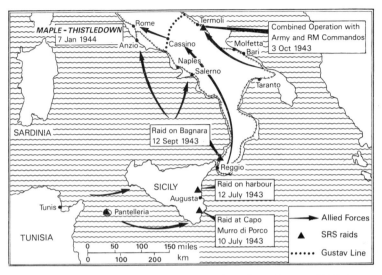

Fig 2 Assault operations by Special Raiding Squadron, 1 SAS, in Sicily and Italy, 1943

captain came over the tannoy with orders to embark, it was very different from the placid Gulf of Aqaba. On the blacked-out ship, with the LCAs bucking and yawing, there were mishaps. Johnny Wiseman's section was the first to embark in the troop commanded by Captain Bill Fraser, a Scot who had been with the SAS from the start. All was quiet except for the drone of the Allied bombers returning to base after hammering the coastal defences. The time was 03.15 hrs.

'Our LCA dropped straight down into the water,' Wiseman says, 'past the oiling doors where we were waiting to embark. Paddy got us across to another oiling door, on a lower level. On the way to shore, we had to pick up Brigadier Hicks, the CO of 4 Airborne Brigade who had come from North Africa. He was clinging to the wing of his glider. We were surprised by the lack of opposition. No burst from machine-guns. No thump of mortars. The beach was not mined. Up the cliff with scaling ladders. We nearly shot the Adjutant of 4 Airborne who was groaning on a cliff-ledge suffering from shock. We cut through the wire and I set off on my bearing for the gun-site. That's when they opened up from all round the site.

'One troop made straight for the battery. The other two were to come in from the flank and rear.

'Harrison's troop had landed in the wrong place. 'For a while we were firing at each other but the Italian guncrew were in the dug-outs under the guns. It was just a matter of winkling them out. They were too shell-shocked or scared to offer resistance. I was in R/T contact with Paddy who was a few hundred yards behind me. The prisoners were coming out when he arrived, "Get your men off the site," he said. "The REs are ready to blow the guns." "Sorry sir," I mumbled, "I've lost my false teeth." "Don't be so bloody silly," roared Paddy. It was true, but by great good luck I found them, God knows how, in the dark.'

Alex Muirhead had been pounding away at the barracks with his 3-in. mortars. 'When we came to the barracks and the Command Post,' says Reg Seekings, 'we went in with the bayonet. That was Paddy's idea – we had trained in the Guards drill, specially for the op. Left, right, fire a volley in step, reload, left, right, fire! It could be bloody terrifying if you were at the wrong end. At one point we shot up a statue – thought it was an Eyetie! We were cleaning out places. There were these big underground bunkers and we could hear voices. We were just going in. The blood was running high and we were in a real killing mood. Then up the steps comes a little girl. It set me back, I can tell you. She looked just like my young sister that I'd left in hospital. "Hold it, lads," I said. I remembered a briefing on cordite. It flares up. If we had tossed a grenade into that ammo store, the whole party would have been burned to death. Some more civvies came up. Then one of my chaps told me that there were British troops down another bunker, 4 Airborne fellows who had been captured. So I shouted down to them not to bugger around, to come quick. No answer so I said, "Right, I'm counting three, and I'm putting a grenade down." They didn't come up so I put a grenade down. They came up after that! A staff-sergeant and two others.' When he was asked why they had not come up at once, Seekings replied with a short, dismissive laugh. 'You ask me! They're not all bloody heroes, you know.'

By 05.00 hrs, the CD Battery had been taken and destroyed:

three 6-in. CD guns, three 20mm light AA guns, along with a range-finder and several heavy machine-guns.

Paddy gave the order to fire the three green rockets – the signal to the ships that, literally, the coast was clear. Prisoners totalled between fifty and sixty. The figures come from the report in the Official SAS Diary. It goes on: 'The main task being successfully achieved, the squadron assembled at farm Damerio and Major R. B. Mayne, DSO, decided to push north-westwards and attack a second Coastal Battery which had opened fire on us.'

It was now 06.00 hrs, daylight, and Paddy was not only effectively but visibly in command. He directed the mopping up of several bunches of enemy snipers and defended farms. Wiseman recalls: 'We set off for Syracuse – about five miles away – taking prisoners as we went. Paddy said: "Don't shoot at them. Send one of the prisoners over to tell them to give themselves up or we will shoot." It usually worked.'

Approaching the second battery site, fighting got harder. The number of prisoners became so unmanageable that Paddy simply ordered them into a field, stripped them of their equipment and told them to wait for the main invasion force. The 3-in. mortars came heavily into play, blowing up an ammunition dump on an AA-gun site. Two troops then went in against strong opposition and took the position adding another five heavy AA-guns to the bag. As they were about to attack the main CD guns, Paddy, who was accompanied by Sergeant-Major Rose, another of the SAS originals, suddenly swung round and fired twice, killing an Italian who was about to drill Rose in the back. Seekings heard him mutter: 'Mr Rose, be more careful!' They destroyed the gun and moved on to the main Syracuse road where they were joined by leading elements of the British 5 Division.

After darkness had fallen and they were clearing a last village, Sergeant Seekings, without provocation, knocked his section Lieutenant, Johnny Wiseman, to the ground. 'It was the first time I hit an officer and got thanked for it!' says Seekings. Wiseman had been standing in a doorway silhouetted against a burning building – an all-too-inviting target.

The next day, with 5 Division taking over, the weary SAS men marched to the harbour in Syracuse; Wiseman managed to pick up an ancient truck but crucially it had no petrol. Once again they went aboard the waiting *Ulster Monarch*, a welcome mother ship. In less than thirty-six hours they had not only destroyed two batteries and much else for the loss of one killed and two wounded, but they had taken nearly 500 prisoners and killed or wounded 200 of the enemy.

Major R. B. Mayne was awarded a bar to his DSO. Major Harry W. Poat and Lieutenant J. M. Wiseman were awarded the MC. Sergeant R. Seekings, DCM, was awarded the MM, as were Lance-Sergeant John Sillito, Lance-Sergeant A. Frame, Corporal C. Dalzell, Lance-Corporal T. Jones, Private J. Noble and Private A. Skinner.

But their well-deserved breather on board ship did not last long. 'We were pretty well knackered after the march into Syracuse and we were all relaxing,' remembers Bob Bennett. 'Then that afternoon, over the blower comes word that we have to do another landing, right away, but not to worry because it was only a mopping-up operation. Only half the usual rations and ammo. We began to think of it as a piece of cake.'

The first assault boats left *Ulster Monarch* about 19.30 hrs on 12 July. They had a rude surprise. Augusta was still heavily occupied by Germans – tough troops from the Hermann Goering Panzer Division. With gun positions sited in the hills, ranging the harbour, they had been ordered to stop the SAS from leap-frogging any further up the coast. The barrage they put up was shattering. Luckily *Ulster Monarch* was close enough inshore. The heavy 6-in. shells from the coastal defence guns whistled over her. But for the LCAs coming in there was concentrated enfilade fire from both sides. Harrison says: 'It was like Dante's Inferno at times.' Wiseman remembers it as a very wet landing. 'No quay, straight into the sea up to our necks in water. With tracer coming at you, you muttered, "I hope that one doesn't quite reach me." A few were killed, but not many.'

Of the landing the Official Diary notes: 'This part of the operation was carried out very successfully against the Navy's advice [the Navy had opposed a frontal assault] in broad daylight under heavy MG fire from the northern peninsula, and CD fire from the west, splendidly counteracted by MG fire from the LCAs and by guns of *Ulster Monarch* and supporting ships.' Once in the town, the fight for the shell-torn buildings and through rubble-strewn streets was a grim house-to-house operation. 'Down both sides of a street with each group covering the buildings on the other side,' Bob Bennett describes it. 'With a "Back Charlie" of each section walking backwards to cover the rear. If a building was occupied we used grenades. You threw a couple in, then smashed through the door spraying the room with fire as you went. We killed quite a few that way and there weren't many prisoners.' Harrison came up with Paddy in the main central square as usual giving orders, buildings burning behind him. 'He told me to take my section up to the citadel at the crossroads.' Wiseman was told to take his section up to where the very narrow road which led up the peninsula joined the main road and to hold the peninsula there. 'Paddy had very precise ideas of how he would defend the place now that we'd taken it.'

As the Diary puts it, 'Major Mayne then pushed forward patrols to test the enemy strongpoint 081509, and other possible defences round the railway on the left, in order to decide further movement.' By early morning the Germans had pulled out as 5 Division arrived at the outskirts.

There was some strenuous celebration in Augusta once the place was safe. In the main street, a SAS corporal, in a top hat, played a piano. Over 280 SRS men felt that, after three hard days, they deserved a break. The wine flowed freely, one of the 'happy hours' when no one paid. There is some debate among survivors of that raid, as to whether or not Paddy gave permission to loot for twenty-four hours. Bennett recalls that he did. Others are not sure. The feeling is that Paddy, who did not agonise over the spoils of war, had condoned the general expropriation of what his men wanted or required. Certainly the piano was taken aboard *Ulster Monarch*. Johnny Wiseman had promised the Purser a typewriter and managed to make good his word. He was stopped by Military Police who were indulgent. So, clearly, there was some pretence of control. Paddy himself took his explosives expert, Sergeant W. A. Deakins (later commissioned) and, with the aid of grenades, blew a safe on the first floor of a bank. Deakins recalls that the entire haul consisted of some Italian receipts, six silver spoons, a cameo brooch and an ornate gold ring. These Paddy handed to Deakins for his trouble. Clearly Paddy had entertained hopes of something better. But he took it philosophically – the luck of the game.

Johnny Wiseman makes the practical point that loot had anyway to be limited: there was nowhere to keep it and no way of carrying it. Each man had up to 55 lb of gear to carry with a tommy-gun or rifle, signal flares, pistol, knife; also ammunition, which was too heavy to waste.

'Paddy *never* allowed a bren to be fired automatic – ever – it had to be single aimed shots,' says Wiseman. 'If you hadn't something to aim at, you did not fire.' Paddy Mayne possessed the canniness of his Ulster Scots background. He subscribed to the saying, 'If you see a stick cut it!' meaning 'Grasp your opportunity, seize the good Lord's bounty when you can!' He would have agreed with Wiseman, for example, that the Anzio landing would have been a big success had the brigadier in charge pressed straight on to Rome, living off the land for a week, instead of waiting for supplies.

On the other hand Paddy always weighed up the odds. Alex Muirhead remembers his calling off, at the last moment, a Brigade plan to raid the coast north of Taormina, when he heard that the Hermann Goering Panzer Division had arrived. He decided the opposition would be far too strong. In a letter to his sister, Barbara, Paddy gave his own thoughts on the Sicilian invasion:

Lovely weather here, and we are all getting browner, if that is possible. I would like to bring this unit home and swagger about Great Britain with them. They would make the home troops look pretty pallid. They look damned smart. We wear blue shirts with our parachute wings on the left breast if they have done three successful operations behind the line, and on the right arm if they haven't. We have a very snappy beret, beige, and our own badge – I'll send you one sometime. Altogether we look pretty nifty.

Before we came on this op, we were inspected and spoken to by all the Generals and, I believe, impressed them with our looks and turnout. I was pleased about that, but I was more pleased by the way we impressed the Jerries and Eyeties, and we did that to no mean tune.

We went at them like terriers after rats. We had only one man killed in our first operation and he, poor chap, had been with me since Commando days in Galashiels. I was very fond of him.

Incidentally, we made our second landing on the 12th [12 July is the Orangemen's holiday in Ulster, celebrated with parades]. All we needed was some drums and banners and we would have felt right at home. That was an attack on Augusta. I wonder if you heard anything about it on the wireless or in the papers. Probably didn't – we never have had much publicity.

Absolutely beautiful day, blue Mediterranean, a pleasant cool wind blowing and nearly lunchtime. We eat pretty well, good rations and we supplement with tomatoes, almonds and grapes – thousands of them about. I hope Dougie got the watch I sent him. Be Good. B.

The watch for Douglas was probably 'won' in Augusta. The letter is enlightening in other ways. His resigned disappointment that the people at home never hear of what his boys are doing is a recurring theme in his letters. Perhaps in that lay the germ of his grievance against Richard Dimbleby. And the youthful pride in their smart appearance reminds us that, when he wrote that letter, Major Mayne was only twenty-eight years old.

About the bar to the DSO he was awarded: the official citation reported as follows:

On July 10th 1943, Major Mayne carried out two successful operations, the first the capture of CD battery the outcome of which was vital to the safe landing of 13 Corps. By nightfall SRS had captured three additional batteries, 450 prisoners, as well as killing 200 to 300 Italians.

The second operation was the capture and hold of the town Augusta. The landing was carried out in daylight – a most hazardous combined operation. By the audacity displayed, the Italians were forced from their positions and masses of valuable stores and equipment were saved from enemy demolition. In both these operations it was Major Mayne's courage, determination and superb leadership which proved the key to success. He personally led his men from landing craft in the face of heavy machine-gun fire. By this action, he succeeded in forcing his way to ground where it was possible to form up and sum up the enemy's defences.

The taking of Augusta was the last action of the Special Raiding Squadron in Sicily. A Greek destroyer took them out to *Ulster Monarch* again but they were on board only for a day or two when the ship was dispatched back to the Middle East and the SRS sent ashore to form a camp and enjoy a leave near Augusta.

9

Italy: Bagnara and Termoli

WHO DARES WINS

DESPITE the Allies' strategic mistakes, and the tenacious resistance of the Germans, Sicily had fallen by 10 August. Attention now switched to invasion of the Italian mainland. On 3 September 1943, 8 Army crossed the Straits of Messina and made a direct assault near the town of Reggio. Simultaneously the US Fifth Army and the British 10 Corps would land at Salerno, south of Naples. In a handwritten note from General Alexander to the newly knighted General Montgomery, the Deputy Commander-in-Chief made the point: 'The greater the extent to which you can engage enemy forces in the southern tip of Italy, the more assistance you will be giving to AVALANCHE [the Salerno landing].'

As 8 Army pressed home its attack on the Reggio beachhead, the Germans began to withdraw, fighting skilfully all the way.

Dempsey ordered the SRS to capture the port of Bagnara, some miles to the north of Reggio. Their task was to disrupt the German lines of communication and expedite their retreat up the toe of Italy. The SAS Squadron, consisting of 245 men, all ranks, left Catania on the east coast of Sicily on 1 September. They were in an American Landing Craft Infantry (LCI), a much bigger vessel than *Ulster Monarch*, accompanied originally by six LCAs. After a series of mishaps with the LCI going aground and LCAs breaking down, they had to put in at Riposto, further up the coast. At last they got under way and reached the Bagnara beaches on 4 September.

It was essentially another coastal assault operation accompanied by other units, including Commandos. They landed at 04.45 hrs and occupied the beach and road without opposition. At first they were greeted by cheering Italian civilians who hailed them as 'Liberators'. As Johnny Wiseman recalls: 'Then the Germans started firing at us from a ridge – long-range machine-guns and mortars. The troop beside us, who were moving south from the beach into the town, lost two killed and several wounded.' Lieutenant Pat Riley takes up the story: 'We had Intelligence reports about the huge women in Bagnara – real Amazon types – and that many Germans had come to an untimely end through interfering with these women. Paddy said to me – we were in the dark – 'Don't go up the hill, Pat, go down the bottom of the hill and hold the bridge down there. Get it quickly!' I went into this tunnel. Biggest fright I ever had in me life. I met my first woman and, by God! they were big! Anyway we got into this tunnel where the Germans had been taking cover from our mortars. We got three or four of them and by the time we were out at the far end the rest were away. We got out and went up the village. Suddenly my batman came to me. He said, "Look!" We were in a garden. I looked and, beautiful, the Germans were facing the other way – away from where we were. I left my bren-guns up on the hill and I told them to open up when I waved my hand to them as I got closer – just a couple of short bursts. Then we went in. We had a bit of a scuffle, but we took them – twenty-one prisoners we took – then I discovered I'd lost my batman – he was a very good bloke and I was furious. Then we got shelled. The Germans are peculiar. One of our blokes got hit, and this German prisoner jumped up. I thought he was making a run for it under the shell-fire and I nearly let go at him. But not a bit of it. He went straight for our fellow and rendered first-aid to him. Paddy was at the top of the hill – Bagnara is built on a hill. At the bottom was a key bridge which Paddy got our troop – Wiseman's section – to hold until reinforcements came up.'

Despite repeated German attacks, they held it. Paddy Mayne was directing things from the centre of town. During the advance up the deep ravine north of the town, when a section was held up, he was seen to grab a Schmeisser and eliminate three Germans manning a MG post.

The SRS accounted for forty-seven Germans killed and wounded, and took thirty-five prisoners. Their own losses were five killed and six wounded. The Diary records: 'Prisoners questioned stated that they were completely taken by surprise and were unaware of a landing until we engaged them. It can therefore be presumed that had our landing taken place at 02.00 hrs as intended, the whole position would have been cleared with far fewer casualties.'

By holding the bridge, Mayne and his men enabled 8 Army to continue their advance up the toe of the Italian mainland. A footnote in the Diary records that on 5 September, Corporal Corps, Paddy's batman, carried out a demolition scheme on the Post Office, but failed to open the safe!

After two days' hard fighting, the SRS squadron was withdrawn to Sicily for a rest and to prepare for their next assignment. This was to take Termoli, on the Adriatic coast, due east of Rome, then occupied by the Germans. By the beginning of October, the Americans had captured Naples, but just north of it the Germans were well dug-in, and in heavily defended positions.

The Termoli operation was timed for 02.45 hrs on 3 October 1943. The SRS squadron, along with 3 Commando and 40 Commando, had left Manfredonia on the Adriatic, south of Termoli, in a US LCI fifteen hours previously. Their objectives were two bridges. They advanced to the top of the beach ridge and over the railway, then through the 3 Commando bridgehead and up over the road from Termoli to Vasto, a coastal town about ten miles further north.

'That night is very vivid to me,' Wiseman remembers. 'It was pitch-black. I told my section to follow in single file. We were just getting to the main road and I didn't want us to lose each other. That wasn't Paddy's way. "What the bloody hell are you doing?" he yelled. "Spread out or we'll be here all night!" Anyway, we ran straight on to a German tracked tricycle towing a 10.5mm gun. We shot them up. Germans in a farmhouse around the bend were giving battle. Some of them surrendered

– we were firing heavily at them – a group came out with their hands up. One said, "Will you shoot my brother?" I speak some German. His brother was lying there, terribly wounded, and clearly beyond hope. I said to Chalky White, "I suppose I'd better do it." But Chalky said, "Leave it to me," and he put the man out of his torment. It was very decent of Chalky. Then I had a R/T message from Paddy: "Come back into the town. You've done your job – we've now got the town and we're holding it. Bring them back to the schoolhouse building." By then we had the town and were manning defensive positions all round it.'

Meanwhile, Captain Alex Muirhead had been ordered by Paddy to site his 3-in. mortars on the railway cutting on the edge of the town. He was heavily shelled and moved back to a less vulnerable position, to a ditch behind the building. He describes what happened next:

'Paddy came up. "Are you scared?" he says. "Why did you move?" I defended myself angrily. I said that I was not going to expose my men to unnecessary risk. He accepted that. Several officers had been "Returned to Unit" by him because, in Augusta, they had abandoned their position on the peninsula between the town and the mainland. But he always listened to reason.'

Next morning, the Germans rallied swiftly and counter-attacked with everything they had. They used seasoned troops of 1 Parachute Division who had come across from Anzio. Wiseman got the message from Paddy's batman. 'He wants you back in line. We've run into a lot of trouble.'

Reg Seekings takes up the story: 'We were lying in a monastery, a big garden. We had a truck parked in this side-street. I was in a café when word came – the Germans had broken through. I rushed to find Paddy – he was at HQ some distance away.'

When the shelling started Paddy, according to Pat Riley, was playing snooker with the MO, Phil Gunn, Major Bill Fraser, and Riley. Though the shells were falling near enough to shake the building, Paddy insisted on finishing the game. 'Like Drake and bowls,' said Riley.

Paddy then gave orders for everyone available to get up to the cemetery where the immediate German thrust including armour was taking place. 'Get the cooks, bottle-washers, everybody up there at once!' Wiseman and Seekings with their section were loading up the truck they had commandeered. 'The Germans had been ranging mortars on this street,' said Seekings. 'We were just kicking the tail-gate down, the section was getting aboard, when this bloody shell landed right in the middle of the truck. It blew us to hell. We were carrying detonators for the "78" 2-lb grenades in our packs – you never loaded the grenades till you needed. Mine was the only pack not to explode.

'A family who lived opposite the truck – three or four girls who did the washing for us – the women were just blown open. The eldest son was running around screaming, with his guts hanging out like a huge balloon. I caught him and shot him – it was the only thing to do. Wounded all over the place. I was covered in blood and bits of flesh – I stank for days after it. Lance-Corporal Grant picked up his own arm, his own arm, and set it to one side. "I've had it this time," he said. He died of wounds that day.'

From the different and confused versions of what happened, several first-hand accounts emerge. When Paddy came up and saw the carnage, what was his reaction? Riley says: 'He was silent, very silent. He just told us to get the rest up to the cemetery right away.'

Wiseman also escaped miraculously: 'We all got in the truck. I was sitting beside the driver. At that moment I see the messenger again. I said, yes, what do you want? That was when the shell dropped. There wasn't a living soul beside me. The fellow I was talking to disappeared. The driver was sitting unwounded but dead. Part of the top of the truck had gone right through my sergeant, right through him. I just got out of the truck, just like that. Untouched. I don't think there was a single person alive. I went round the corner. Phil Gunn was bandaging up a fellow who'd got some shrapnel. I said, "Phil, for God's sake, come and see some real tragedy." He came round but there was nothing he could do at all.

'I obviously went to report to Paddy. When I found him he

said: "I hear from the CSM [Rose] that you've had one or two casualties." "I haven't got a section any more." "Right. You join up with my unit, at HQ." We got up to the cemetery. Things were really hotting up. A lot of flak was coming down.

'Some 4.5 mortars – heavy stuff – had arrived and had just got across the river. These chaps had just come out from England with one of the infantry brigades, and they were cowering, uncertain what to do. Stuff was really coming down. Now this is Paddy at his best. He went up to them – I had to follow him. I wasn't as brave as Paddy, but I had to follow him. Paddy says, "Listen chaps, how do you fire these mortars? I've never seen them. I want to take some photographs of them." 'Absolutely true! There's Paddy snapping away. There are these fellows firing their 4.5 mortars, and there's all hell coming down. They had forgotten about that – they were so pleased to show the Colonel how they could fire their mortars. Paddy at his very best. I doubt very much if he had a film in the camera, but there he was, flicking away at them, while they were firing for all their worth at whatever was coming up, tanks or self-propelled guns – and my God! – those heavy mortars – they were doing a lot of damage. Paddy had a thing about cameras. If anyone had a camera he wanted to see it. We used to say that Paddy went into action with a camera! I'm told he later brought back a dark-room from Norway, dismantled it and took it with him.'

There is a story in the regiment that, after the shelling of the truck with the death of twenty-nine men, Paddy went off to exact some terrible vengeance. We can find no evidence for this. But it is recorded how, as they were entering Termoli, Squadron HQ, with Paddy in charge, they engaged a party of Germans over forty strong with mortars at a bend in road 820755 going up the wadi or ravine. Somehow he managed to appear suddenly on the enemy's flank above them. With a grenade he killed a mortar crew and, standing there, using a bren-gun like a carbine, with repeated bursts he decimated the rest. Subsequently twelve bodies were counted. With the help of 40 Commando, the remainder were captured.

During the final battles, Riley remembers General Dempsey arriving and having a word with them. 'I never saw anything like it. There he was with the red band round his hat. A General, right up in the front line!'

When the worst was over, there was the usual post-mortem. The traumatic loss of a whole section at once began to sink in. 'We stayed awake all that night getting drunk,' says Seekings. Some had the theory that a German look-out in the clock-tower had directed the fatal shell. Wiseman says, 'I went up to the tower. Someone had undoubtedly been there, but I don't think that was the reason. It was just a lucky shell. One of those things.'

Brigadier Mike Blackman recalls how 'During one of the counter-attacks at Termoli Paddy was in a basement playing his wound-up gramophone, "Lili Marlene" and "The Garden Where the Praties Grow" (a song by Percy French who wrote "The Mountains of Mourne"). The latter was usually a storm signal.' Paddy had a penchant for the Irish songs of Percy French. Bob Bennett had a fine tenor voice and used to sing them for him, right from desert days. 'Paddy couldn't sing a note,' says Bennett, 'but he loved a sing-song when we were drinking and he used to mouth the words.'

Paddy's own thoughts on Termoli were expressed in a letter two weeks later to his sister Babs:

I'm glad you wrote. I wouldn't have liked to have gone through all that mail from HQ and found none for myself. I was looking at an old letter from Frances [his other sister] tonight. I keep letters for some time and often reread them. It was written on 26 August and starts off "Blair dear, it is ages since I have written to you. Time simply flies and I have been terribly busy."

'My unit got cut up a bit in our last operation. It was at Termoli and we had to withstand some heavy counter-attacks. We had 29 killed with a series of shells, for it was the only way they could touch us. A very nice wee lad called Canning was wounded there – he comes from Belfast, and had done four raids with me. I haven't his address here but I'll write it on the back. If you could call round and say he is not too bad – only a flesh-wound and that he did awfully well, I would be very grateful. You might get Mother to send me her recipe for soda farls. We have a cook from Lisburn [Co Antrim] who thinks he could make them but he's worried about having no buttermilk. He thinks he can manage with cream of tartar. You'll probably know better than me what he means. Have you heard they have given me a bar to my DSO? – still managing to bluff them. Hope you are fit as I am. Give my love to Mother. Yours B.

Appended was the address: Mrs Canning (Mother), 73 Jamaica Street, Belfast. There is much of Paddy Mayne in that simple letter.

The Diary sums up the operation in Termoli:

Almost all the German troops were from the 1st Fallsch Army Regiment or the Fallsch Jaeger Regiments ['Fallschirm' means 'parachute' – these were élite paratroops]. It is a good sign that, although the fighting of 5 October was an all-out attempt to regain Termoli through the cemetery and down the railway, and the enemy forces had ample forces and heavy support to smash our light forces which were there, he was unable to do so. It seems as if their troops were without the morale to advance far – again through fear of being cut off to which they have been subjected since Sicily – and the attack was abandoned when the threat to the town was greatest.

Termoli was the last operation carried out by the SRS, 1 SAS, in Italy, but, according to Reg Seekings, another project was being considered immediately after it. This was to be an attack across the heavily held Sangro River about fifty miles from Termoli. The Guards Division had twice attempted to cross it and been repulsed with heavy casualties. Paddy called Seekings in to tell him that he was planning to use another troop for the job. Seekings argued hard to be allowed to go with his own. 'You're sure your chaps would be quite happy?' asked Paddy. 'They could do with a rest you know.' 'I'm sure,' said Seekings. 'Right,' said Paddy, 'I'm coming with you. Are you a good swimmer?' 'I told him I was good enough,' says Seekings. 'We reckoned that we were lucky enough to be able to get a line across. Once we had a line across the rest could follow.' 'By the way,' said Paddy, as Seekings was leaving, 'I've been told there are two VCs for this. I've put my name on one. You put yours on the other.' In the event the scheme was turned down by Corps HQ. Paddy and his men were deemed to be too valuable for such a chancy exercise.

Instead the SRS was sent south to Molfetta, on the east coast just north of Bari. There they kicked their heels and got down to some serious drinking. Inevitably, there were several incidents there. Paddy systematically broke up the mess. He tore down the iron railings from a balcony. He picked up the unit MO, Phil Gunn, who was over six feet tall and of whom he was very fond, and threw him against the wall, damaging his shoulder badly.

'In action he was superb,' commented Johnny Wiseman. 'Out of action we were terrified of him. He was compeletely unpredictable. Particularly when we were hanging around. It wasn't a blind fury. He wasn't particularly cross. He just became destructive. Especially after several days' solid drinking without a single bit of food. In Molfetta he once said, 'I'm going to Naples.' Off he set, alone in a jeep. He got about five miles and overturned the jeep. I found him lying underneath it. He was unharmed.'

Mike Sadler, who was with Paddy from the desert to, eventually, Germany, confirms this. As do many others. 'When the pressure was off,' Sadler remarked, 'it was the violent element which attracted him. He wasn't happy unless he was involved in something which resulted in violence.'

Derrick Harrison recalls one night in Molfetta when the officers wanted to have a few local girls in for a party in the mess. 'Paddy agreed reluctantly,' he said, 'and when they arrived, he took a bottle of whiskey into his room, shut the door and let us get on with it. Sometime during the proceedings he'd obviously had enough. Out he came. He wasn't angry. He was towering. "Out!" All the women fled. Then he started to get hold of the officers, picked them up and physically aimed them at the door. Some went through and some landed against the wall.'

This aversion to women other than sisters or mothers is well documented in the life of Paddy Mayne; but there was one other manifestation of it, even less attractive that occurred in Molfetta. This is recounted by Sergeant Dave Kershaw, another of the old desert hands: 'There was no part of Paddy Mayne I disliked,' Kershaw says. 'One night he dragged an Italian bint into the bar in the Sergeants' mess. He had a rope around her neck like a dog on a leash. He didn't mean any harm. He was just having fun. As if to say, "This is my bitch".' For a man who was known to shun sexual relationships of any kind, it was somewhat puzzling and distasteful behaviour.

Before the SRS left Italy to return to Britain for the D-Day invasion which was to come, generous tribute was paid to their work by both Generals Montgomery and Dempsey. In his farewell speech to them Dempsey praised their work in Sicily: 'Brilliantly planned and brilliantly carried out,' he said, and went on: 'Then came Bagnara and finally Termoli. The landing at Termoli completely upset the Germans' schedule and the balance of their forces by introducing a threat to the north of Rome. They were obliged to bring to the east coast 16 Panzer Division which was in reserve in the Naples area. They had orders, which have since come into our hands, to recapture Termoli at all costs and drive the British into the sea. These orders, thanks to you, they were unable to carry out. It had another effect though. It eased pressure on the US Fifth Army and, as you have probably heard, they are now advancing. In my military career and in my time I have commanded many units. I have never met a unit in which I had such confidence as I have in yours, and I mean that.'

Those words gave to no one present more satisfaction than to Lieutenant-Colonel R. B. Mayne, DSO and Bar.

10

Retraining for France

BY the beginning of 1944 it was apparent to the Allied High
Command that the Special Air Service had distinguished
itself in the Western Desert, and in Sicily and Italy. It was also
becoming clear that Germany was losing the war. Even Hitler
seemed to acknowledge the possibility of defeat in November
1943 in his War Directive No 51, in which he said, with regard
to Western Europe: 'Should the enemy succeed in breaching
our defences on a wide front here, the immediate consequence
would be unpredictable. Everything indicates that the enemy
will launch an offensive against the Western Front of Europe, at
the latest in the Spring, perhaps even earlier. I can therefore no
longer tolerate the weakening of the West in favour of other
theatres of war.'

In Eastern Europe, the areas captured so easily by the
Wehrmacht were now falling just as quickly to the advancing
Red Army, and the Germans, like Napoleon in the previous
century, were facing a terrible reality. Goebbels was asking the
inevitable question: 'Where will it ever end?' Meanwhile the
Allies were agreeing on the date and the preparations to carry
the war into Western Europe. Stalin, Churchill and Roosevelt
decided that May 1944 should see the start of Operation
OVERLORD, which would take the Allied armies into Normandy,
while the Red Army would launch an offensive in the East.

So how could the SAS contribute to the Second Front? This
was not an easy question to answer. After all, as Paddy Mayne

was to point out in 1944, the SAS did not always receive the credit for its exploits and some of those in High Command still did not fully appreciate the kind of role for which it was trained; and it was because of such lack of understanding of the nature of the contribution the SAS could make, in relation to the role for which its members were trained, that Bill Stirling of 2 SAS, David's brother, resigned his command. In the midst of debate about what role was appropriate for the SAS, he wrote a memorandum to the High Command:

> Everyone needs a bonus now and then. We should be used as a stiffener to SOE [Special Operations Executive] and the Maquis. We did that kind of work well in Italy. I don't think the question before you is whether SAS troops are worthwhile or not, but under whose command they should come.

As it turned out, when the SAS returned to the UK in 1944, the decision was taken almost to double the numbers and reform the command structure with strategic planning under 21 Army Group, led by Montgomery, and the Supreme Allied Headquarters of General Eisenhower. This would result in operations from Abbeville as far as Paris and the River Loire, under the direction of 21 Army Group, with those in the rest of France and Belgium under Supreme Headquarters. The plan was for bases to be established in relation to the main battle zones and the SAS to be parachuted into these areas with the object of disrupting the enemy's lines of communication, providing a tactical diversion, and fighting alongside the French Résistance.

Early in 1944 1 SAS and 2 SAS were sent to Darvel in Ayrshire where they were joined by a squadron of Belgian SAS and two battalions of the French SAS. They were to be trained for a new role although they were not told exactly what that would entail. To some of the men that seemed strange, since the SAS had, after all, experienced numerous battles and developed outstanding fighting skills. The combined number of the SAS was now 2500 under the command of Brigadier R. W. (Roddy) McLeod. 1 SAS was reconstituted from its previous units under the command of Paddy Mayne. What had previously been a troop in the Special Raiding Squadron would now be a squadron, and each section a troop. In terms of the command structure, Harry Poat was now promoted Major and second-in-command to Mayne. At Darvel 1 SAS found itself with the other elements of the Special Air Service. The bringing of all these men together effectively produced a textbook for new recruits and created a more cohesive fighting unit. The SAS was not by nature a parachute unit but the role intended for it in France would demand that parachuting be an essential part of operations. The area chosen to prepare for this was the bleak and often hostile climate of the Scottish moorlands. As one veteran of the North African campaign later remarked: 'We thought it was tough dealing with extremes of heat. It was a treat compared to those bloody windswept moors, the biting winds and fog.'

They spent months on those moors, with men carrying heavy rucksacks and equipment and navigating their way in difficult and uncharted terrain. Frequently the rucksacks were filled with sand and the men were given a compass to find their way to dummy targets. Captain Derrick Harrison, who later proved to be one of the best fighting men in France, remembers wading through cold rivers. Like many others, he made parachute jumps on to lonely Scottish hillsides in darkness, and reckons it was the sort of training which proved invaluable when subsequently he had to find his way to places in France which were only 'a pinpoint on a map'.

Many of the parachute jumps were designed to acquaint the men with the 'leg bags' they would have to carry with them when dropping. The bags were about the size of a rucksack and secured to the right leg with two straps and a quick-release cord which allowed the bag to swing twenty feet or so below the descending parachutist. This 'leg bag' was intended to allow for a quick escape on the ground. The previous method was to drop supply containers which were unloaded on the ground thus delaying an escape in the event that the enemy was close to a dropping zone. Additionally, the bag touched the ground before the parachutist, giving him the knowledge that the ground was close, thus assisting his fall.

At Darvel there were, of course, the stories which have always followed the SAS. High jinks were inevitable when the regiment was so close to the civilian population. One particular episode concerns a SAS team sent to elude the sentries in a dockyard. Not only did they avoid the sentries, but they spent the night sleeping on a submarine.

The Army authorities were so angry that Paddy Mayne was obliged to make a report to the Brigade Commander in May 1944. This followed a request from Brigade HQ to investigate breaches of the offences against the Army Act by some of his men. His reply was: 'My men are well behaved and no flagrant cases of ill-discipline have been noticed.'

His report suggests that: 'Some sensible publicity would help the unit. It must be the only unit which has never had any. In the Middle East, our work was credited to the Long Range Desert Group and everyone therefore heard of them. In Sicily and Italy, the credit went to the Commandos.' He adds: 'I understand that in the 8 Army history we are referred to as the Sussex and Surrey Yeomanry. The Germans and the Italians know more about the unit than the ordinary soldier or civilian here.'

Five days after this communication, Mayne was again obliged to report in writing to his Brigade Commander:

Herewith my opinion and action taken on various incidents reported:

Navy at Campbeltown

The entering of his house and the holding up of the Naval Officer in charge is considered to be well within the bounds of our scheme [the scheme being to test security].

(a) The Navy were asked to co-operate and said they would.

(b) The house was guarded by a sentry and barbed wire.

(c) It would appear to be an obvious place to attempt to neutralise.

No action has been taken in this matter.

The taking of the RAF Truck

This truck was found unattended and immobilised. The party through over-enthusiasm and considering themselves, possibly too thoroughly, to be enemy parachutists, took it.

The officer concerned has been reprimanded for not returning it sooner.

Interfering with Civil Police

The civil policeman was seen collaborating with the enemy, i.e. the Home Guard. He was put into a truck and removed some distance and then released. This is the method which would probably be adopted in action. The party have been reprimanded for the crude method they adopted, and apologies have been made to the Chief Constable of Ayr.

One would think that in the course of the war games, which Mayne and his men were playing enlisting the assistance of the Home Guard and the Civil Police, that that list would have been sufficient, but Mayne was obliged to brazen it out. There was more:

The taking of the Polish Truck

The Officer has been reprimanded for retaining the truck and has been instructed to apologise to the Polish Officer for the inconvenience caused. Allegations made in the letter from 4 Liaison Group are not considered correct.

(1) They were warned of the exercise.
(2) The Officer concerned, Lt Cooper, states that at no time did he wear the overcoat. He was not in the Inn at Eskbank. He did not promise on his word of honour to return the coat or truck. I have no reason to disbelieve him.

In my opinion the incidents were caused by over-enthusiasm and were done in a playful rather than malicious spirit. I do not consider it is a question of bad discipline. There does not appear to have been any wilful damage done to the truck or the owner's belongings. The trucks were taken in a fair manner and were returned to official authorities. Had they been dumped by the road and their removal denied, I would have taken a very severe disciplinary action, had it been possible to prove who had taken them. We have benefited greatly by these schemes.

It was his manner of dealing with his men which gained him loyalty. There was certainly no one better prepared to recognise or indulge in 'over-enthusiasm' than Paddy Mayne himself.

The Rev. Fraser McCluskey, who became Chaplain to the SAS, has described his first meeting with Paddy Mayne, at Darvel: 'I arrived in the Officers' Mess in the early hours of morning. I advanced into the Hall where a strange and some-what confused sight met my eyes. Officers were passing through the Hall into the dining-room to the strains of a small and somewhat wheezy gramophone playing "Mush, Mush, sing Tooral-aye-ady". Round the fireplace and the ashes of a dead fire, and oblivious of the breakfast procession and the orchestral accompaniment, sat several officers, in varying attitudes of repose. From this somnolent party a large man – a very large man – detached himself on my entry and heaved himself in my direction. If he didn't actually ask me who the devil I was, or what the devil I was doing there, I gathered at least that that was at the back of his mind.'

Paddy Mayne reminded the Padre that since he was in the mess, he should remove his hat and have breakfast. With that, Mayne returned to the 'lifeless' bodies at the fireplace.

The war games played in Scotland with the assistance of the Home Guard were to prove invaluable. There were courses also in sabotage techniques and even a trip to Kilmarnock power station to examine the workings of the plant and the best way of causing maximum damage to it. Kilmarnock railway station was used as a blueprint to study the means by which trains could be derailed or destroyed, and how trains could be driven. There were lectures by intelligence officers who had worked in Germany about the symbols used by the various sections of the German military and the titles used at all levels of the German Army. There were crash courses in French and German. Despite all the training, the instruction in the demolition of communications in enemy territory and the learning of simple phrases in French and German, the men at Darvel were not told what their next job would entail.

As it turned out, the plan was to drop SAS teams into France hours before the D-Day invasion. It was decided, however, that such teams would require more than a few hours in which to locate and destroy the network of German communications linking the beachheads. There was also the danger that if SAS teams were to fall into the hands of the Germans, this could put in jeopardy the whole Allied invasion. So the plans were changed.

II

TITANIC and its Lessons

TOWARDS the end of May 1944, small groups of men were moved from Darvel to the SAS HQ base at Chelmsford in Essex. From there they were taken to the airfield at Fairford in Gloucestershire, known as the 'cage'; this was because SAS personnel were held in secret there, and their movements limited, until they were to leave for France.

Just prior to D-Day a scheme was hatched to fool the Germans. Shortly after midnight on 5/6 June, six men of 1 SAS were dropped into France, south of Carentan. Dummy parachutists were also dropped with them to create the impression of a full-scale airborne landing. The party consisted of the following personnel: Lt Poole, 'A' Sqn; Lt Fowles, 'B' Sqn; Tpr Dawson and Tpr Saunders, 'A' Sqn; Tpr Hurst and Tpr Merryweather, 'B' Sqn.

The decision to undertake this operation, which was code-named TITANIC, was indicated in Brigade Operation Instruction No 11 on 19 May 1944 and signed by Brigadier R. W. McLeod, Commander of the SAS Troops. Several aircraft were assigned to different dropping zones to carry both members of 1 SAS and 2 SAS into France. In respect of 1 SAS, under the command of Paddy Mayne, the dropping zone was to be in the area of Marigny, beyond the Normandy beach-heads, with the codename TITANIC IV. Instruction No 11 states:

SAS personnel will be dropped before the dummy parachutists and on landing will remove ballast from the containers
which normally carry supplies to indicate to the enemy that
weapons as well as troops are being dropped; they will then do
anything in their power to make their presence felt, e.g. setting
Hawkins mines on roads, holding up solitary staff cars. On
completion of these tasks they will hide up. It is hoped to make
special arrangements for evacuation by sea. All parties will be
equipped with MCR I receivers.

The same instruction No 11 adds:

All defences from Le Havre to Dieppe are held by static
low-category infantry divisions. However, even though such
static troops do not generally extend more than three miles
inland, this is not the case in the Le Havre/Boldec area.
Information about the exact whereabouts of German troops is
imprecise but it is almost certain that on D-Day the towns in
the area will be full of troops and many of them will be
earmarked for a counter-attack. A vigorous reaction to
TITANIC is almost likely.

Brigadier McLeod's assessment of TITANIC also included the
surmise that, on D-Day, the towns under German control would
be under strict curfew, so that the SAS teams could not expect
much help from the civilian population.

Six aircraft were allocated to the various TITANIC operations
(TITANIC I and TITANIC IV). Each aircraft was to carry thirty-nine
dummies, six pintail bombs, fourteen rifle simulators Mk II, and
seven machine-gun simulators. The dummy parachutists were
cleverly made from sandbags and equated to approximately
one-third the size of a man and the parachutes carrying them
scaled down accordingly. The pintail bomb was a small bomb
containing a Very-light cartridge which was released at the same
time as the dummies. The pintail reached the ground first since it
travelled at a speed greater than the dummies, and it activated the
Very light. The purpose was to attract the attention of the enemy
to the dropping zone and indicate that there was a reception party
on the ground waiting to receive the parachutists. British

ingenuity did not end there. Mechanisms were attached to the back of each dummy with a time-delay to indicate the time the dummy left the aircraft. After the dummy struck the ground the simulator exploded to represent either rifle or machine-gun fire and this lasted for five minutes.

The six men from 'A' and 'B' Squadrons of 1 SAS were briefed by Paddy Mayne before they left Fairford airfield at 00.40 hrs on 6 June. Fortune, sadly, was not with them. They baled out of their aircraft but found they were two miles north-west of the intended dropping zone. On hitting the ground and gathering their equipment it was discovered that Lieutenant Poole and Lieutenant Fowles were missing. The four remaining members of the party buried their parachutes without too much difficulty. It was a mild night and visibility was good, so they began a search for the containers that carried the additional gear, but not one could be found. Not to be outdone, the four men began to lay Lewes bombs, twenty in all, over a 500 square yard area and ignited them. By 03.00 hrs the Lewes bombs were exploding. Light was beginning to crease the horizon, so they decided to find refuge. After a short time, they came upon thick hedging about half a mile north of the area where they dropped. They remained there the following day and the only activity in the area was a cyclist travelling up the main Carentan road. That evening, to their delight, they were contacted by a Monsieur Le Duc Edouard of the Résistance. He promised he would find a way of getting them out of their predicament. He returned unexpectedly an hour and a half later and encouraged them to follow him. Sure enough he escorted them to a ruined abbey. It was wet and miserable but at least they were safe. Just after midnight, the Frenchman returned to the abbey bringing with him an ample supply of food and cider. Trooper Hurst later reported that 'they were well hidden and everyone was happy'.

To the amazement of the SAS team, their French guide saw them again at 10.00 hrs that morning, accompanied by Lieutenants Poole and Fowles. Poole had knocked himself out on leaving the aircraft and was unconscious on the ground for almost one hour. When he recovered, his injuries included a cut lip and a grazed chin. His immediate reaction was to send a message indicating that he had lost contact with the remainder of the party. The device for this purpose was a pigeon. The pigeon was a marvellous means of sending messages home, and many SAS personnel dropped with a pigeon in a small box strapped to their equipment. It was not unknown for pigeons to suffer the unfortunate fate of being eaten by their handlers, but in this instance Lieutenant Poole's pigeon was dispatched and returned safely to base.

Lieutenant Fowles had dropped only a field away from the party of four, but he searched in vain for them and the containers. The others noticed that Fowles was without his MCR I receiver and his bombs. He said he spent much of his time lying up in a farm three miles from the dropping zone. He shot at some Germans, but did not hit them. He said he also cut telephone wires which led to a German HQ.

The men remained in the vicinity of the abbey for three weeks, rarely gaining sight of any Germans. However, on 28 June, a German parachute regiment took over the nearby village of Romilly-sur-Lozon. The Frenchman became very agitated and told the SAS team he believed that the enemy knew of their presence and that it was vital they move camp. Fowles and Poole agreed with this assessment and set off immediately with the others to find a safe haven. Ironically, they ended up three miles south of the dropping zone where they had originally intended to land. A small wooded area became their base. Poole and Fowles, however, felt uneasy and the following day moved camp once more to an old brush cabin several miles away. They remained there for three days and nights. It was now 2 July, and their food was running low. A decision had to be made to sit it out or make for the Allied lines which they reckoned were six miles to the north of their position. That night, under cover of darkness, they all set out but by now enemy patrols were everywhere and over the next six days their progress was slow. The German patrols consisted of six or seven men with either light machine-guns or Schmeisser submachine-guns.

On 25 July the Frenchman arrived with three American parachutists, one of them a medical officer, Captain Berry. The three were from the American 508 Parachute Regiment and one of them was wounded. They had been taken prisoner on 7 June at Edensville and on the same day were being taken by the Germans in a convoy along the Route Nationale when the convoy was strafed by American planes. The enemy trucks were fully loaded and many Germans were killed or wounded. The three Americans took advantage of the chaos and escaped.

With the three Americans Poole and Fowles now decided to press on and on the night of 9 July they found themselves close to a German position which was being mortared by the Allies. The party, now consisting of nine, narrowly escaped injury when mortar bombs landed close to their hiding place. The following morning, they were on the outskirts of a village and unanimously decided to make a break for it when darkness fell.

Luck was not with them. At midday, two German parachutists were seen advancing towards them. The Germans responded quickly and tossed grenades before running off. Hurst was seriously injured by shrapnel in his lower legs and Trooper Merryweather was hit in the back. Lieutenant Fowles also received back wounds and two of the Americans were injured. Those who escaped injury quickly carried the wounded to a farmhouse 150 yards away.

Fowles was distraught at the damage inflicted on his small party and, although wounded himself, set off in search of the two Germans to exact revenge, and more importantly, to stop them reaching their HQ. Within half an hour, however, the farm was surrounded by forty German parachutists all dressed in camouflage jackets. The Germans were heavily armed with light machine-guns, Schmeissers and rifles. They were all young, with 'white faces and appeared jumpy'. To resist would have been hopeless, and so the SAS men walked or were carried from the farmhouse and lightly searched for weapons. They were then taken to the German HQ and interrogated by a captain who merely asked for their ranks and serial numbers.

Escape kits, still in SAS possession, remained undetected because they were sewn into the lining of their battledress. Each man was given ten German cigarettes, sweets and candy, and the wounded were taken to a German hospital for treatment. At the dressing station Fowles was carried in by a German. His back wounds were by now in a serious condition. Hurst and Merryweather spent three months in a German hospital, which was eventually liberated by the Allies. Trooper Dawson was held in a Stalag and later released when it was overrun. The Frenchman who assisted the party, Monsieur Le Duc Edouard, was executed by the Germans. He was only twenty-eight years old and in peacetime was a pilot. This was the first SAS raid into France and it taught the regiment many valuable lessons. Should the operation really have been undertaken, and what did it achieve? The Brigadier commanding the SAS sent this memorandum to HQ, SAS Troops:

(a) Owing to the loss of containers the party were without their bren-guns and heavier equipment.
(b) There is no evidence of the effect of the dropping of dummies and sonic warfare. It does not appear that the simulated drop of an Airborne Division did in fact cause any abnormal German activity in the area, since no abnormal drives or searches seem to have taken place. I consider that this tends to show that TITANIC was not worth doing.

However, this was not the true picture. From 6 June onwards, 1 SAS under command of Paddy Mayne began parachuting into different areas of France in operations with different codenames such as BULBASKET, GAIN, HAFT, HAGGARD, HOUNDSWORTH and KIPLING. These operations were to undertake a much more comprehensive role than the one led by Fowles and Poole. They were not only to engage in sabotage and harass the enemy but provide intelligence for the bombing of enemy targets, arm the Maquis, and teach them the art of guerrilla warfare.

Important lessons were devised about dropping zones. The advice was to choose a site from which in daylight there was a view of three kilometres. This meant that when fires were being lit to bring in an aircraft, there was sufficient room to light the fires in shallow pits. It was recommended that a nearby farm was essential so that a bullock cart could be used to handle containers quickly since as many as twelve were often dropped. The drill for a dropping zone was as follows:

Immediately containers and panniers have been dropped, douse the lights and then roll up the chutes. After that, dispose of the containers and, at daylight, check that there is nothing about. If jeeps are dropped it is essential to have a wood nearby to ensure that you can get rid of the cradles in which the jeeps are dropped, because they are too big and heavy to bury. It takes about three-quarters of an hour to remove the jeep from the cradle. Parachutes are easily disposed of and the local people will willingly hide them for the cloth.

The SAS teams were advised to find themselves camps. It was soon apparent that, for a permanent camp, guards were needed – at a minimum of five kilometres round it. It was recommended that SAS men should try to live off the land by purchasing food from farms. The Maquis was split into two groups: the FTPS (Franc-Tireurs Partisans Français) or Communist Maquis, and the FFI (Forces Français de l'Intérieur).

From all accounts, Paddy Mayne never fully trusted either of the Maquis groupings, and there are examples of SAS personnel being lost because they were given away by members of the Maquis who talked loosely or broke under interrogation. As a rule, however, they were keen fighters and provided valuable support for the scattered units of the SAS.

It is difficult now to imagine that, after 6 June when SAS teams were dropped with jeeps, they travelled about the French countryside in daylight in uniform. It was always a rule not to use the jeeps near a main SAS camp but to resort to the use of civilian vehicles. The Gestapo were always a source of concern because they observed every suspicious movement in a neighbourhood. They also used the tactic of infiltrating agents, often local people, into the Maquis. Major John Tonkin reported that at his base camp in July 1944 the Maquis discovered five German agents, who included women, and executed them.

Mayne stressed to all of his men to remain in a constant state of alertness, because they might have to go for several days without seeing action and become complacent. The friendliness of the French villagers encouraged men to believe that they were not really behind the enemy lines. As Tonkin told Paddy Mayne: 'There is a general tendency to relax. They need constant reminding of this point and the highest discipline has to be maintained to discourage them from wandering from the camp. The British soldier's aptitude for scrounging will make him see "no harm" in going to the nearest farm for eggs, whereas such a thing could be highly dangerous.'

Within weeks of the landing of 1 SAS, many observations were being conveyed to Mayne about kit, the Maquis or simply the standard of rations. Some men complained about the distinct track left by the rubber soles of boots. Others humorously noted that 'the local wine and cider is stronger than one thinks and kirsch or schnapps is nearly pure wood alcohol'.

At each camp the SAS met up with the local Maquis, equipped them and often carried out operations with them. The Maquis had a password which was general to them in a camp and which was changed every twenty-four hours. The SAS continued to use pigeons for carrying messages, but not always successfully. Major Tonkin wrote a message whilst sitting on the edge of a cornfield after landing with Operation BULBASKET. After attaching the message to his pigeon, he decided it was time the pigeon did his duty. 'I launched the pigeon with perhaps more force than skill, for it circled us twice and made straight for the nearest big tree fifty yards away. I believe it may still be there,' he wrote.

Each team was issued with MCR I receivers and Jedburg transmitters. Also in use was a device called the 'S' phone which was used to guide aircraft to dropping zones. Another piece of equipment was the Eureka which could be worked off a small generator and was reliable for bringing planes to a reception committee. Its advantage was that the hum given out by the set could not be heard beyond twenty-five yards on a still night.

Each man was issued with 24-hour ration packs. The biscuits and meat were not always popular with the men, though the sweets and chocolates in each pack proved irresistible to the French. One group reported that the men were sent too many biscuits and used only six tins in three months. The fruit cocktail and sultana pudding proved the most popular. Sardines, though not very high in the popularity stakes, proved to have a high barter value with the French. One tin of sardines was worth a chicken or several dozen eggs. Stewed steak and Irish stew were described as 'unbearable after several days'. The recommendation was that bully beef or spam was preferable. Other items in the food kit which came in for criticism were chocolate, cigarettes, jam, tea and margarine, which were just 'adequate', but more sugar was required for the 'dehydrated' tea. When it came to weapons, these did not escape the critical eye of the men of 1 SAS. They told HQ that some form of webbing pouch was required to hold spare magazines; four magazines should be carried in each pouch with one on each weapon thus giving each soldier a total of seventy-five rounds.

After some time the Maquis requested that they be sent no more sten-guns, because they had proven unreliable. Many men used German weapons or opted for the light American carbine which was considered excellent for personal protection. There were reports that brens were often damaged when being dropped; the break occurred at the magazine catch of the body-locking nut. Overall, however, each SAS unit was well equipped.

When it came to fitness there was never a better group of men. In France SAS parties had only four to six hours of sleep per night. The operators and coders were most at risk from fatigue. Sleeping in the open in some respects helped the men to avoid lice and fleas, and the proximity of most camps to running water enabled them to keep clean. Boots were greased regularly, otherwise they cracked after about six weeks. The sleeping bags were excellent, but lighter waterproof covers should have been made available.

A report from one camp even mentioned snakes and the fact that 'though none was encountered, the locals assured us that there are local snakes with bites poisonous in the extreme'.

At first, Paddy was unaware of many of the operating difficulties emerging in France, but his suspicions about the risks of sharing sensitive information with the Maquis were about to be realised. A member of the Maquis at Chelmsford was involved in the planning of the first drop in Operation GAIN. The Frenchman returned to France with the signal needed to bring the plane to the DZ. Meanwhile, at Chelmsford hopes were high for the next unit to parachute behind enemy lines. The question was, would the details of this forthcoming drop remain a secret?

12

The Garstin 'Stick'

A T FAIRFORD a team of twelve men waited for the order to go. This party was commanded by Captain Garstin and Lieutenant Weihe. It included a young man from Randalstown in County Antrim who had served with the Royal Ulster Rifles. Another man from the same regiment was also scheduled for this mission but his name was withdrawn at the last moment. He was Lance-Corporal Billy Hull from Belfast. Hull begged Paddy to let him join the Garstin 'stick' (slang for parachute drop) but Paddy refused because he was assigning Hull to another role; but the fate of the Garstin 'stick' was nonetheless to have a profound impact on Hull, and on the whole SAS.

At 23.34 hrs on 4 July, the twelve-man party boarded a Stirling aircraft not at Fairford but, as a last-minute change, at Keevil airfield in Wiltshire. There they were briefed and wished good luck by Paddy.

On arrival in France their aircraft descended to 800 ft. The recognition letter was 'B' for Bertie and, when it was received, the men baled out. Five of the party landed in a wood bordering the DZ and the others in the zone itself.

Those in the open were fired on as they landed. The Germans' automatic weapons sent a swathe of bullets across the landing area. It was a bright moonlit night and the SAS men were silhouetted like 'sitting ducks'.

Among the last five men to bale out was Trooper Norman who landed in the trees of a wood. His first contact was with

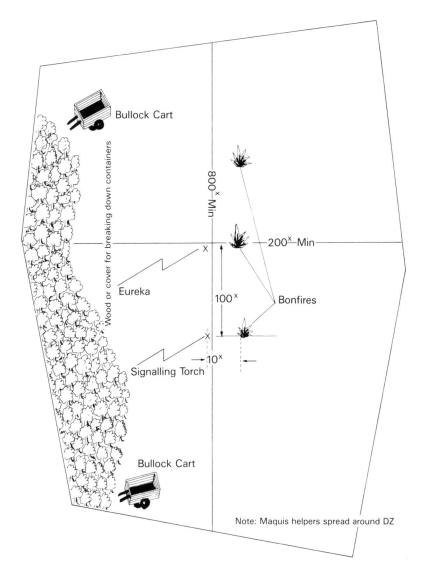

Fig 3 Diagram of a typical SAS dropping zone (DZ) in France, 1944

Trooper Morrison who had left the plane just before him. They decided to make their way out of the wood back towards the dropping zone. As they arrived at the edge of the wood they heard Lieutenant Weihe call out: 'Who's there?'

Both men answered with their names and were told by Weihe to remain in the safety of the wood. In hushed tones Weihe explained: 'I've caught a packet and I can't crawl, never mind walk. Stay where you are.' Norman thought otherwise. 'I'll come and fetch you,' he told Weihe. 'You'll stay where you are and that's an order,' Weihe responded sternly; he knew that anyone seen in the open was likely to be shot, because the moonlight enhanced the accuracy of enemy fire. Weihe advised Norman and Morrison to make a run for it and so they headed through the wood in a north-westerly direction. Just as they reached the outskirts of the wood, two bursts of automatic fire passed over their heads, forcing them to dive for cover. There was nothing for it but to crawl. Two hundred yards on they reached a cornfield. Firing had ceased and they hurried across the field and within an hour were in the vicinity of the town of La Ferté Alais, fifty kilometres from Paris. Having assured themselves that there were no sentries around they crossed the Paris railway line and found, to their amazement, that they were in the town's main street.

They finally left the town and reached a river where they discovered a boat; it was padlocked and there were people nearby. Norman entertained the idea of cutting the padlock with the aid of the file in his escape kit. Morrison felt it was not worth the effort owing to the size of the chain and the likely noise. The river was too deep to wade, so they both went in search of a crossing. They found a bridge and, an hour later, a hiding place on a nearby hillside. The next morning their first problem was their food supply. They decided to cut their daily ration to a minimum. In the afternoon, hunger got the better of them and Norman decided he would go on a recce. He soon found a farmhouse where he scrounged supplies.

For the next few days, Norman and Morrison kept on the move, scrounging food and evading German patrols. They kept to a compass bearing which they hoped would lead them to the Allied lines.

On the evening of 12 July they had a narrow escape when crossing a secondary road. Norman turned to the left and found himself speechless. Morrison noticed the expression on his face and looked in the same direction. Ahead of them was a German sentry at a barricade. Fortunately he was looking in the opposite direction.

In the days that followed, both men hid in farms and eventually reached the Allied lines. Norman returned to join his unit at Fairford in August after being fully debriefed. The others who dropped with Garstin and Weihe were not so lucky. When Garstin landed he was faced by a group of men in civilian clothes at the edge of the dropping zone. They greeted him with the words: 'Vive la France.' Suddenly there was a burst of gunfire and Garstin and the others went to ground. In the initial onslaught Garstin, Weihe, Trooper Barker and Lance-Corporal Lutton were wounded. Within an hour nine men were in the hands of the enemy. However, like Norman and Morrison, one of the party, Trooper Castellow dropped into the wood. He was eventually caught by the Gestapo and forcibly interrogated but managed to escape and reach the Allied lines.

The nine held prisoner were taken to a converted hotel behind the Champs de Mars in Paris and from there to a Gestapo HQ for interrogation. Lieutenant Weihe and Lance-Corporal Lutton were transferred to hospital where Lutton died of his wounds. Weihe was later operated on for a shattered spine. Garstin and Barker were taken to the hospital to have their wounds bandaged but no more. The five others were held at Gestapo Headquarters for three days and were tortured by the Germans. On the fourth day, they were taken back to the hotel where they were joined by Captain Garstin and Trooper Barker. Garstin was in a very weak state, but the Germans did not seem to care. On 8 August they were given civilian clothes and told that they were going to be exchanged for German agents being held by the British in London. When the Germans were asked about the issuing of civilian clothes they told the SAS party that this would enable them to pass safely through civilian territory. At 1 a.m. on 9 August the men were awakened by German guards and loaded on to a lorry which proceeded out of Paris in a northerly direction. Even at this stage none in the party was certain of his fate. The lorry stopped at a wood near Beauvais, to the east of Noailles. By now it was dawn. The Germans ordered their captives to walk along a narrow path which led to a clearing. Corporal Vaculik tentatively asked the Germans if he and his comrades were going to be shot and was told, yes.

The SAS men were lined up from left to right: Jones, Garstin, Vaculik, Barker, Walker, Varey and Young. Facing them were two officers of the Gestapo with sten-guns at the ready. Close by were two other Gestapo officers, one acting as an interpreter and another who was preparing to read a statement. These two were in civilian clothes. As the SAS unit waited, Garstin was held erect by Jones and Vaculik. Their death sentence was read to them:

> For having wished to work in collaboration with the French terrorists and thus to endanger the security of the German Army, you are condemned to the penalty of death and will be shot.

On hearing the word 'shot' those who could run made a dash for safety. Vaculik managed to get clear even though the Gestapo kept firing after him. Corporal Jones tripped and fell and the Gestapo ran past him, thinking he was dead. When he finally got to his feet there were five bodies in the clearing. Jones and Vaculik managed to evade being recaptured and eventually returned to their units. The bodies of the dead remained in the open for three days, until a party of Germans billeted in a nearby château, dug a grave and buried them. The grave chosen was in the cemetery of Marrissel at Beauvais.

The Gestapo went to great pains to disguise their crime. It was thought at first that the SAS dead were buried in graves numbered 326–329 in the Marrissel cemetery. Eventually Captain Mike Sadler and Major Harry Poat interviewed a woman collaborator who worked for three weeks at the château from where the burial party was formed. The woman thought the burial group belonged to a Luftwaffe Signal Section since their shoulder straps bore yellow edging. When the grave was found, so were two other graves containing the bodies of members of the Résistance.

The members of the Gestapo responsible for the killings were never traced despite extensive inquiries.

Lieutenant Weihe survived torture but was not operated on until twenty days after his capture.

The failure of this mission can be attributed to a member of the Maquis who was captured, interrogated and shot.

The treatment of prisoners by 1 SAS was different. Over the years some of the mythology surrounding Paddy Mayne has included allegations that he often shot enemy prisoners, but we have found no evidence to substantiate such claims. In fact, before the French operations he put some of his thoughts on this subject on paper in a Top Secret Document requested by the Psychological Warfare Branch of the Allied Forces:

Ultimate leadership will be assumed by the person on the spot with the greatest determination and ability. One thing I believe must be stressed is that SAS parties must not be put under the command of any person outside the SAS and the Resistance Groups must be told that SAS parties are their own masters and that their weapons etc. must not be touched or borrowed. Otherwise, I can visualise parties being sent out to murder some local Vichyite. Suggestion as to possible collaboration with Resistance Groups may be given or sent to SAS troops, but the ultimate decision as to what is done must be left to the local SAS Commander. I would also suggest that Resistance Groups be told that instructions given by any SAS Commander as to the treatment of German prisoners must be implicitly obeyed.

It has generally been found that ill-treatment of captured prisoners is very rare amongst front-line troops. Before surrendering, they may be bayonetted or shot unnecessarily, but in the heat of the battle that is only to be expected. With rear troops, headquarters staff, guards, civilians etc., the position is different. It is usually from them that such remarks as 'Shoot the swine' and 'Why do you bother to take prisoners?' emanate. It is believed that a great deal of this bloodthirstiness will go as they lose the feeling of comparative security. It can be taken as accepted that they will lose this feeling of security after the units commence to operate.

As to using propaganda to teach the Germans to 'play the game', it is thought here that a stronger weapon than a wireless set is needed. The great objection to propaganda on the suggested lines is that it implies, or could be twisted to imply, that we are frightened of bad treatment and are frightened of being captured. To a logical German mind it would suggest that to make us frightened they would use bad treatment or threaten bad treatment. Propaganda which might be useful would be to tell the Germans that there are armed British soldiers behind their lines and if they (the Germans) surrender to them, they will be taken to a safe place and will be unharmed.

In characteristic Paddy Mayne fashion, he adds: 'We will probably not be able to cope with many owing to feeding problems, but a few are always useful for fatigue duties. The reasons for driving this into the Germans' heads are obvious.' The document continues:

The greatest difficulty will be controlling the local Resistance in their attitude towards prisoners. They must be given definite orders and must obey the rules of warfare in dealing with prisoners. Before they surrender, the Germans must be subject to every known trick, stratagem and explosive which will kill, threaten, frighten and unsettle them; but they must know that they will be safe and unharmed if they surrender.

1 Paddy (*in centre, white shorts*) in his first rugby union international for Ireland *v* Wales at Ravenhill, Belfast, 1937, seen here warning off Haydn Tanner, the Welsh scrum-half. Ireland won 5-3

2 British Lions' Tour of South Africa, 1938. Paddy in Johannesburg with a fellow Lion, Duncan Macrae, and the Springboks' Manager, Frank Mellish

3 The springbok killed by Paddy with some new-found Afrikaner friends on the night of the Pietermaritzburg ball

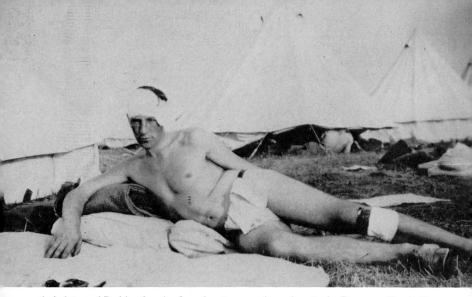

4 A dejected Paddy after the first abortive parachute drop in the Desert at Tamimi in Nov. 1941 in which a number of his comrades were taken prisoner and his best friend at that time, Eoin McGonigal, died

5 Paddy, the Desert Raider, with a .50 Browning, near Kabrit 1942

6 Paddy (*r*) and Raymond Shorter sampling dates near Kufra; note bandages covering Desert sores on their hands

7 Maj Lea (*2nd from r*) with members of 'B' Squadron, 1 SAS, at the entrance to an abandoned underground fort at Bir Zalten on the old French Mareth line, Nov. 1942

8 Col David Stirling, DSO, OBE, 'in the beginning' in the Western Desert. Stirling, who was later captured and sent to Colditz was the great strategist and, before his capture, moulded his men into the fighting force which was to produce some of the finest fighting men of the Second World War

9 RSM Bob Bennett, BEM, MM, was a superb fighting soldier and one of the members of 'L' Detachment, David Stirling's original group of 66. A close friend of Paddy, he served after the war in Malaya as part of the 'new' SAS

10 Brig J. M. (Mike) Calvert, DSO and Bar commanded SAS Brigade from Dec. 1944 in NW Europe until its disbandm in Nov. 1945. He had earlier served wi distinction with Wingate's Chindits in Burma. He later raised the Malayan Scouts (SAS) during the Malay campa

Malcolm Pleydell, Desert MO, seen here in 1942 examining the growth of his beard with the aid of his hip flask

12 Capt Mike Sadler, MC, a brilliant Desert navigator who later guided Paddy through the enemy lines in France

Smiling in the Sand Sea: Capt (later Maj) Bill Fraser, MC

14 Capt Alex Muirhead, MC, prior to parachuting into France, May 1944

15 Two veterans of 1 SAS who saw action from the Western Desert to the end of the war under Paddy's command: Sgt Reg Seekings, DCM, MM (*r*) and Sgt Johnny Cooper, DCM, seen here on leave in Cairo, 1941. Seekings miraculously escaped death in Termoli in 1943 when a German shell hit a truck as he was kicking its tail-gate closed (*see Pl 21*)

16 Nahariya, Palestine, May 1943: Paddy was never without a camera throughout the war and very often took cameras from captured Germans. (He even dismantled a complete darkroom in Norway and took it home.) In this photo he is the tireless cameraman (*l-r*) E. L. W. Francis, Bill Cumper, Dr R. M. Gunn, and, out of picture, R. V. Lea

17 Men of 3 Section, 3 Troop, Special Raiding Squadron, 1 SAS, looking jubilant after taking one of the three gun batteries on Cape Murro di Porco, Sicily, 10 July 1943

18 A lull in the fighting on Cape Murro di Porco, Sicily, July 1943. Paddy, seen standing in the doorway, was regrouping his forces after having taken the main coastal battery; they were to take two more batteries. In the centre of the photo is Maj John Tonkin, MC, with men of 3 Troop, SRS, 1 SAS

19 When the fighting was over after Bagnara three of Paddy's officers decided the best way to relax was to swim in the Tyrrhenian Sea (*l-r*) Harry Poat, Tony Marsh, Phil Gunn

20 Paddy on an American Landing Craft Infantry (LCI) prior to setting out for the Termoli landing, 1943

21 The scene of carnage in the Adriatic port of Termoli, 4 Oct. 1943, when a German mortar shell hit a truck killing 29 of Paddy's men. The SAS section had just got into the vehicle, many of them carrying detonators for the 2-lb grenades in their packs

22 Officers of 'C' Squadron in the 'cage', Fairford, Glos: (*back row, l-r*) Tony Marsh, Roy Close, Stewart Richardson, Charles 'Titus' Oates, Tom Bryce, Derrick Harrison, Tom Reynolds, Mike Mycock; (*front row, l-r*) Peter Davis, Tim Iredale, Colin Rosborough

23 Maj Mike Blackman, MC (later Brig) was Paddy's linkman with the Canadian HQ in Germany; he was also the co-author of the citation resulting from the famous episode on the road to Oldenburg

24 Cpl William Hull, who was Paddy's driver for part of the time in Germany, was a fellow Ulsterman. 'Billy' Hull was involved with Paddy in some of his daring exploits towards the end of the war

25 Lt John Scott, MM (r) with Sgt J. Edwards in the Netherlands shortly before Paddy earned his fourth DSO

26 A German tracked tricycle, towing a 10.5 mm gun, and its crew, ambushed by Paddy with Lt John Wiseman, MC, and his section during the break-out from the Termoli bridgehead, 1943

27 While on leave in 1944 Paddy went to Scotland to shoot and to fish. Flyfishing for salmon was one of his favourite pastimes

28 A KIPLING patrol makes contact with Gen Patton's forward elements at Courtenay, near Lyons, after an 80-mile dash through German-held territory, Aug. 1944 (*l-r*) Cpl 'Kit' Kennedy, two Maquis guides, L/Cpl Jimmy 'Curly' Hall, L/Cpl Paynter, Capt Derrick Harrison, MC

29 The KIPLING patrol returns to base. One hour later, 'Curly' Hall (*second left*) was killed and Derrick Harrison (*left*) wounded in a fire-fight with German SS troops at Les Ormes. The Germans lost some 60 dead and wounded

30 Mrs Hanbury with a stirrup cup for departing SAS troops at Hylands, Chelmsford, Essex, May 1944. It was in this house, a temporary SAS HQ, that Paddy attempted to drive a jeep up the staircase

31 Tanks of the Canadian 4 Armoured Division in their drive towards Oldenburg, Germany. Paddy and his jeep patrols were officially operating as left flank-guard to the Division, but had got ahead of the armour

32 Maj Harry Poat's jeep patrols in the forest beyond Lorup after the battle with the Germans on the way to Nienburg, April 1945. The patrols were under continuous enemy fire, so Paddy allowed the German prisoners to withdraw to safe ground, on parole

33 Members of Maj John Tonkin's 'D' Squadron, 1 SAS, before entering Kiel in early May 1945. Their target was the U-boat base. In front is an American staff car commandeered for comfort rather than warfare

34 Paddy (*centre*) seen here with Maj Roy Farran, DSO, MC, (*r*), who commanded 'H'
Squadron, 2 SAS, on their arrival at Stavanger airport, Norway, in May/June 1945.
The role of 1 and 2 SAS was to 'pacify' the 300,000 or so captured German troops
in the country

35 Paddy (*r*), Tony Marsh, naval rating (*under hat*) and John Tonkin (*out of view*) having
fun with a captured – and defused – German speedboat in the harbour at Bergen,
Norway, June 1945

36 Paddy with his niece, Margaret, at Mount Pleasant, Newtownards, shortly before the war. He adored children and it was said by his brother Dougie that if only Paddy had been able to have a family of his own his life might not have been so fraught and ended so tragically

37 Paddy's funeral procession to Movilla Churchyard, Newtownards, December 1955; he died at the age of forty

13
Operation GAIN

WHO DARES WINS

THROUGHOUT the French campaign, Paddy Mayne alone decided when it was best for him to drop into enemy territory. This was another example of his single-mindedness. He saw himself as a fighting soldier and, while others would have preferred him to remain at base co-ordinating operations, he often decided otherwise much to the consternation of his superiors. Mayne preferred to be in the thick of it and considered it vital to check on his men personally and observe their operations.

Initially, much of his attention was focused on Operation GAIN which was designed to harass enemy communications in the Orleans Gap not far from Paris. The SAS complement was divided into several teams with bases in the forests of Orleans and Fontainebleau. It was to prove hazardous because of the proximity of the bases to large enemy concentrations, traffic routes and dumps.

The first party Paddy sent into France to begin Operation GAIN was on 13 June. They were joined by another party commanded by Major Ian Fenwick and established a base camp in the Forêt d'Orleans. Within days they were blowing up railway lines and sixteen railway wagons containing sugar. A sortie was made to the town of Dourdan after reports that there were no Germans in that vicinity.

Lieutenant J. M. Watson of 'D' Squadron approached Dourdan in his jeep accompanied by his driver, a gunner manning the twin Vickers, and a Frenchman who knew the locality. When Watson's jeep passed through the marketplace of the town, to his astonishment he spotted a German convoy guarded by only five troopers. The Germans did not take much notice of Watson's jeep and so he ordered his driver to pass on through the town. On the outskirts he told the driver to stop, and contemplated his next move. 'A German convoy guarded', he thought, 'by five men' was too great an opportunity to miss. Watson decided to return and shoot it up. The Vickers in the front and rear of the jeep were checked and the driver was given the instruction to take the jeep on a 'speedy tour' of the marketplace. As Watson's vehicle entered the market square, both his Vickers were swiftly brought into action. Bullets tore through the German trucks causing considerable damage and wounding soldiers sitting inside them, but the Germans were prepared. From some of the trucks, machine-guns were firing at Watson's jeep as it was being driven wildly round the square. The Frenchman in the rear was hit and spilled out of the jeep on to the roadway. He managed to crawl to safety as Watson shouted to his driver: 'Get us to hell out of here!'

In this way the SAS ensured that the enemy from Dourdan to Orleans were not safe from attack even in the centre of towns and villages. The German security methods were generally very poor. There was often no check on identity cards, and road blocks were left unmanned.

'German sentries are not inquisitive and, if in pairs, normally stand in twos,' Watson reported. 'None has been seen using a torch. Near the lines many villages are used for billeting but woods are never used much except on the edges for transport. All German vehicles carry green foliage and so do we. Our jeeps are usually mistaken for German ones. If resistance is suspected in a wood they will burn it or, failing that, mortar it. They seem to have formed a flying column for this purpose. Estimation of German fighting quality is difficult but I would say that it is good. I have never seen a German surrender though the French Résistance say it is common. In retreat the Germans carry their weapons to the last.'

SAS operations took their toll also on French civilians

because Gestapo policy was to seek retribution each time a German soldier was shot or a convoy attacked. To compound matters the French police, 'Milice', who were under German control, were brutal towards their own people. After two German sentries were killed at Estouches, the Gestapo opened fire on six Parisian refugees, killing a seventy-year-old woman and wounding several others. In another incident, the Germans discovered a store of petrol in a house owned by a member of the Maquis. They shot him in the leg and then burned him alive. The Maquis retaliated. A German sergeant who was captured by them was killed by seven shots from a Colt .45, a burst from a sten-gun, and a grenade. The Maquis did not believe in taking prisoners.

The Maquis in the Forêt d'Orleans was badly organised, for there were too many leaders vying for power. Watson told Paddy Mayne that the Maquis contained 'too many shady characters' and 'they operated too close to their own camps thus giving away their positions to the Germans'.

The SAS camp at Fontainebleau was discovered by the enemy after a tip-off from a member of the Maquis and was surrounded by over two hundred heavily armed troops. The section had a miraculous escape and fought their way to safety, wounding some of the enemy in the process.

Just before Mayne dropped into France, the command of the squadron in charge of Operation GAIN changed owing to circumstances which resulted in the death of Major Fenwick.

A message was received that Paddy was dropping on a Sunday night if a dropping zone could be prepared. That night, Ted Griffiths was in the vicinity of Chelmsford and was summoned by Paddy for a drink; but first there was a meeting with Captain Brownrigg at Northolt, the HQ of Airborne Troops where Mayne was to be briefed for the drop. The briefing over, they drove to the 'cage' at Fairford where Griffiths was taken on a conducted tour. The evening was spent drinking with Corporal Tommy Corps, Paddy's driver, who, according to Mike Sadler, was a disreputable fellow but in the best SAS tradition. Corps, in fact, though heavy-drinking and often loud-mouthed, was a brave and loyal soldier. He had a dog-like devotion to his CO partly because Paddy excused many of his excesses. Most of their stores that evening were packed in a jeep which was to be dropped with them. Griffiths recalls a .50 Browning mounted on the vehicle, but their personal belongings were stored away in leg bags. There was the matter of whether they would take two grenades or more. There was a little wound-up gramophone like something out of Woolworth's and records, among them two of Paddy's favourites by Percy French, 'The Garden Where the Praties Grow' and 'Come Back, Paddy Riley'.

Corps was insisting in including a bottle of John Jamieson Irish whiskey. Apparently Paddy, untypically, was not keen, but eventually conceded that it might come in useful.

While Paddy was preparing for his journey, the base camp in France was attacked by over six hundred enemy. The battle lasted several hours. Each man was told to look out for himself and given the order to rendezvous later at a pre-arranged point with Lieutenant Watson. When darkness descended, this was the opportunity for the three SAS parties at the base to escape the ring of enemy troopers.

Unfortunately, the next day, 8 August, news of the attack was conveyed to Major Fenwick when he arrived at Nancray-sur-Rimarde. The Résistance people, who were recounting details of the battle, gave the impression that all of Fenwick's men were wiped out and all the jeeps lost. Fenwick decided to proceed without delay to another camp under the command of Captain C. L. Riding. He was joined in a jeep by Sergeant Duffy, Corporal Dunkley and two members of the Résistance. Fenwick was seething with rage at the news that his men were dead. As he was driving along a German spotter plane passed on information about the whereabouts of his jeep. Fenwick was now on his way towards Chambon. On the outskirts of the village an elderly woman stopped his jeep and informed him that there was an ambush waiting for him up ahead. Fenwick turned to the woman and told her: 'Madam, I intend to attack them.' Ahead the SS, with plenty of warning of the approach of Fenwick's jeep, were setting up an ambush on both sides of the roadway. Fenwick's rage may well have got the better of his judgement. There were other lives he was about to put at risk, though there is no question of his bravery, or of the hatred he felt at that moment for the Germans. Fenwick met the German ambush with 'all guns blazing'. His jeep was almost through the ambush when he himself, who was driving, was shot through the forehead.

The jeep careered wildly along the road with the SS firing at it indiscriminately. It crashed into woods at the side of the road. Fenwick was dead as was the Résistance member of the team, Lance-Corporal Menginou. As the vehicle crashed Corporal Duffy, who was in the rear, lost consciousness. When he came to, he was surrounded by SS. Nearby, he saw the other member of the group, Corporal Dunkley, being led away, wounded and handcuffed. Duffy lost consciousness again and woke in a hospital, north of Fontainebleau. Duffy had an altercation with other patients, probably because they were Germans. They were hostile towards him and Duffy was not slow in pointing out to them that he would sort them out if they continued to hurl abuse at him. The hospital authorities decided that Duffy's presence would lead to trouble and they moved him to another ward. His new ward consisted of eight Germans and one Russian. His thoughts turned to freedom and fortune was with him. A young French girl came to clean his ward and he made a point of talking to her, acquainting her with his plight and the details of the ambush which led to his capture. The girl returned to see him several days later to tell him that the Americans were at Chartres and that, if he was going to escape, it had to be done quickly. The Germans were planning to evacuate the hospital before it was overrun.

The only way he could get out of the hospital, the girl suggested, was to dress up as a medical officer. She would steal a uniform for him that day. Duffy told her he was prepared to go as soon as possible. The girl left the ward and returned carrying a bucket, accompanied by several female orderlies. The orderlies crowded around the beds of the other patients to shield Duffy. The girl with the bucket approached Duffy's bed and, to his delight, retrieved a uniform from inside it. He reckoned the best time for his escape was in the afternoon, when the other patients in his ward habitually enjoyed a siesta. When the time came, Duffy examined the uniform only to discover that one important element was missing – shoes. He was not to be deterred, however. He put on the uniform, and crept stealthily out of bed, amid the snores of the other patients. He quietly opened the door of the ward and peered down the nearest corridor. Fortunately, one of the girls who was in the ward earlier passed by. Duffy pointed out that he had no shoes. She told him to return to his bed and wait. Duffy lay in bed anxiously hoping that matters would be resolved. Much to his consternation, the other patients were beginning to waken. Within half an hour the girl returned to the ward carrying a bucket and, as previously, accompanied by her friends who congregated round the beds of the others while she removed a pair of shoes from the bucket and passed them to Duffy. He was now obliged to wait until his fellow patients resumed their siesta.

'I now spent a tedious time waiting for those bloody Huns to fall asleep,' he recalls. 'When they did, I did one of the fastest, if not the fastest, quick-change acts in history. When I had finished dressing, I walked rather painfully, for the shoes were two sizes too small, out of the ward, down the corridor and across a courtyard which was crowded with wounded. Vehicles were ready for evacuation. As I got to the main gate, I saw a sentry standing there. I walked by him and as I did so he saluted me and I returned the salute, out of courtesy.'

Duffy made his way along the main Milly/Fontainebleau road. The shoes made walking unbearable and at the first opportunity he took to woods to get rid of them. Luckily, he came across a deserted log cabin and spent the night. The next morning, he was awakened by firing and decided it was best to head in the direction of the gunfire. He reached a road south of Milly and, to his delight, saw an elderly man leading a horse-drawn cart. Duffy's feet were swollen and bleeding. There was nothing for it but to approach the Frenchman and ask for assistance. He was well received. He clambered on to the back of the horse and the farmer continued on his way. Half a mile along the road they were met by two Germans. Duffy must have appeared a strange sight sitting on the back of a cart-horse with swollen feet. The Germans were more intent asking directions to a nearby village. It was to Duffy, in his German Medical Officer's uniform, that the questions were directed. Though he did not fully understand the detail he pointed in the opposite direction to which he was heading and the Germans left. As they walked away, they thanked Duffy for his assistance.

'A bit further down the road we came upon a Hun tank which had been knocked out. A group of men were round it and they turned out to be the Résistance. They took me to a house and entertained me. A doctor bandaged me – I had twenty-one blisters on my left foot and twenty-eight on my right. I later went to Milly and contacted the Yanks.'

While Duffy was in Milly, he was awarded the American Purple Heart. Corporal Dunkley, who also survived the ambush, was later released when the Americans took a German hospital in which he was held. The courage of Sergeant Duffy and Major Fenwick illustrates the calibre of the men who were under the command of Paddy Mayne.

Mayne took a considerable risk in operating behind enemy lines. With the death of Ian Fenwick, Mayne decided it was vital he was with his men. He dropped into France with his wind-up gramophone strapped to his leg. Two days later, Paddy Mayne and Mike Sadler, his navigator, joined Captain Riding at the Forêt d'Orleans, where Riding was now in command of the late Major Fenwick's operations.

Jim Almonds remembers Paddy arriving that day and the mood he was in. His CO arrived in the midst of his men as though 'he was on an afternoon stroll'. During the forty-eight hours which followed, Mayne decided the squadron should lie low. He spent his time assessing and re-assessing the role of his men and what benefits were accruing from Operation GAIN. He also assigned small groups to recce the nearby roads of Orleans/ Pithiviers and Orleans/Montarges. Information gleaned about German troop movements was radioed to England. Mayne stressed it was vital that recce parties remove the lamp masks from jeeps and cover them with foliage. He knew the Germans were excellent at using this kind of camouflage and it was a tactic which he and Mike Sadler were to make use of frequently while travelling to meet his men in different areas of France.

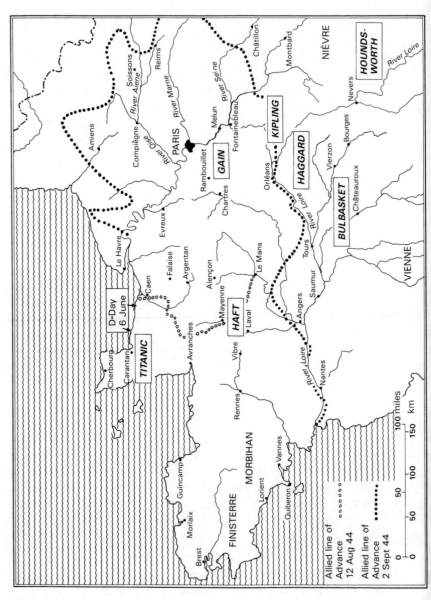

Fig 4 SAS operational bases in France, 1944

One of the recce parties chosen by Paddy Mayne consisted of two young troopers, Ion and Packman. They were instructed by their Colonel to check on the Orleans/Pithiviers road. As they left the camp in good spirits with a farewell nod from Paddy Mayne, he could not have known the fate that was about to befall them. The Germans were well aware at this time of the presence of the SAS in the forest. Ion and Packman were captured and taken to Château Chamerolles near Chilleur-au-Bois which was the Gestapo headquarters, and also the billet for two battalions of motorised infantry. Little is known about the two days they spent in the hands of the Gestapo except that they were constantly referred to as 'saboteurs'. Four days later the caretaker found two bodies in a decomposing state near the château. The German who ordered the killing of Troopers Ion and Packman was an Oberleutnant, who was later described as having a pronounced scar from the left corner of his mouth. The shootings ordered by this man were carried out at Château Chamerolles by a staff sergeant in a field grey uniform. Both men had SD on the left cuff of their uniforms (Sicherheits-dienst). Further investigation revealed their names and that they belonged to the 1010 Motorised Regiment commanded by Rittmeister Marschler and Hauptmann Kubale, who were judged to be ultimately responsible for the murder of the troopers. The caretaker buried the bodies in the local cemetery and kept mementoes from the corpses which later provided identification. When a member of the SAS visited the spot where the bodies were discovered, he found a tuft of blond hair which corresponded with the hair of Trooper Ion. The disappearance of the two illustrated how difficult things were becoming for the squadron.

In another part of the forest at Lorris there was a Maquis camp of several hundred men under the command of a Captain Albert, who was preparing for an attack on Orleans. Mayne sent Lieutenant Leslie Bateman to join them to provide liaison but Bateman was no sooner with them than the camp was attacked by a large force of Germans on foot and in patrol cars. Bateman and his small band of SAS were asked if they could knock out the patrol cars with bazookas but Bateman reckoned the range was too great. There was also the danger of accidentally hitting Maquis personnel.

The Maquis commander decided it was better to move camp quickly. His decision was accelerated by the fact that the Germans were using flame-throwers to set trees and undergrowth alight. Bateman assembled his men and a United States Air Force officer and got them into civilian cars. The Maquisards climbed aboard trucks. The Germans opened up with heavy machine-guns as the Maquis and the SAS made their separate escapes to the main road, north of the river Loire. Behind them, the woods were alight. The SAS party found itself on its own. Corporal R. Wilson, who was in one of the civilian cars, later described what happened next:

'Lance-Corporal Essex was in the back of our car with a member of the Maquis. He happened to look around and saw a German patrol car coming up the road. He informed me, but before I could do anything the patrol car was overtaking and the next thing I knew was a bullet coming through the windscreen. It hit me just above the right eye and a fragment of the windscreen struck me in the jaw. It knocked me out, and when I came to, the car was empty except for myself and the American airman who was lying outside the vehicle. I watched as the American tried to crawl under the car, but he was spotted and fired on twice and killed. Four Germans came towards the car. I'm sure that they were unaware of my presence. I took out my .45 pistol and waited until they were about fifteen yards from me and I opened up on them. Three of them fell and one ran away. Machine-gun fire was being directed at our men who were escaping into the woods. The next thing I knew, the windscreen of my car was blown in completely and I was hit again!

'When I came to, I found myself tied to a tree with my hands tied behind my back. All my personal belongings were removed from me. A German staff car arrived and six Gestapo men got out. One of them approached me and asked how many of our men were with the Maquis. When I ignored him, he hit me in the mouth. I was then taken to Orleans and on the way the Germans picked up some Maquis who were captured while escaping from the wood. We were driven to Orleans and I was taken before a Company Commander who asked me about ourselves and the Maquis. When I refused to answer he told me that he regarded me as a terrorist in the same way as he would classify the Maquis, and as such I would be treated in the way that they were treated. I was taken into another large building where I was again interrogated. I could hear the Frenchmen being taken out and shot. I was in the presence of two Gestapo officers. I passed out and later awoke to find myself in hospital in Orleans. Two days later the Americans arrived and I was rescued.'

Lieutenant Bateman, who was in the same car as Wilson, later recalled how he ran from the car despite an injury and joined two other injured men in the woods. He looked back to see Wilson lying in the car and thought he was dead. Bateman estimated the German attack to consist of eighteen patrol cars. Bateman and his companions hid in a wood pile until they were contacted by the Résistance. Apart from Corporal Wilson, the other members of the SAS team returned to the forest to contact Mayne. Leslie Bateman remembers Paddy arriving from Poitiers wearing his uniform and driving a French civilian car. 'Paddy never deigned to wear civilian dress. And I got the impression that he had been driving round France for some time. We met in the thickly wooded area near a safe house I was using, the Château d'Ouchamps owned by the Duhamel family. Paddy didn't stay long. He never did. Gave us our instructions and moved on.' Batemen was ordered to remain with Maquis de Lorris. Mayne then took the men to Le Mans to meet 'C' Squadron and then to Ouzouer-sur-Loire. As for Operation GAIN, it achieved demolition tasks despite extreme difficulty because of the close proximity of large numbers of Germans. It kept the Germans on their toes and disrupted life for them.

14

Operation KIPLING

BY early August 1944, Le Mans was becoming a vital area as General Patton's US Third Army pushed eastwards from Le Mans towards Fontainebleau and Orleans. In front of them was Paddy Mayne's 'C' Squadron, designated with the task of Operation KIPLING. Like so many other operations of this kind, KIPLING also began in the barbed-wire 'cage' at Fairford airfield where a party of six men awaited orders to head for France. This group was led by a man well known to Paddy, Captain Derrick Harrison. Mayne knew he could rely on Harrison to accept responsibility for much of the planning of KIPLING and for decisions on the ground.

On 14 August Harrison and his men parachuted into France near Auxerre, 150 miles behind the German lines. Before long, other drops brought Harrison's command to twenty-seven men and five heavily armed jeeps. Harrison waited for the word to go into action. To this day he will admit that in those early days the advice and theories of Paddy Mayne were always in his head. At Chelmsford, Mayne tapped his forehead, looked at Harrison and said, 'I have a mental blueprint of the ideal SAS man. No one fits it exactly, but when I look at a man and listen to him, he must come close to it.' Harrison knew the blueprint to contain the following qualities: stamina – mental as well as physical; intelligence; the ability to work as part of a team; versatility; and confidence without rashness. Those qualities, which may best describe Mayne himself, were exactly the criteria which Harrison sought to apply to his own men, and it was these same qualities which Harrison brought to bear in action and earned him the Military Cross.

The action took place on the afternoon of 23 August. Harrison was in the KIPLING base when he overheard one of his men saying that he intended travelling in his jeep to the Maquis base at Aillant, to have a gun mounting welded into position. Derrick Harrison reckoned it was not safe to have one jeep travelling alone, so he called for his own jeep to be brought forward. The driver was a man he knew well – Lance-Corporal Jimmy 'Curly' Hall. The man driving the jeep with the damaged gun mounting was Stewart Richardson. He was accompanied by a member of the French SAS, Fauchois, and the driver was named Brearton. The two jeeps set off towards Aillant-sur-Tholon.

Along the road Harrison's attention was directed towards a huge wall of smoke which seemed to be coming from the village of Les Ormes. Unknown to Harrison, the SS were burning buildings in the village and preparing for the execution of twenty villagers in retaliation for actions carried out by Harrison's men. There was nothing for it but to proceed further along the road. At this stage Harrison was unaware of the extent of the German presence, but he felt he needed to investigate. As they reached a hill outside the village Harrison saw a woman cycling towards them. As she reached the two jeeps Harrison noticed that she was crying. Firing was coming from the village and the smell of dense smoke was reaching the crossroads, where the jeeps were parked. The distressed woman screamed at Harrison and his men to save themselves because there were two hundred Boches in her village. Harrison was faced with a frightening dilemma. If he waited for the Maquis, there was no knowing what devastation the Germans would cause or the number of villagers they would kill. He had two jeeps and four men against what could be vastly overwhelming odds. Harrison asked his men if they were 'willing to have a go'.

The first man to accept the challenge was Fauchois. Unlike the others he carried a Canadian passport, so that his capture would not lead to his identity being discovered and bring harm on his family. 'Curly' Hall agreed that it might take too long for the Maquis to arrive and Brearton's view was that it was worth having 'a crack at them'. Richardson decided to make it unanimous. It was time for the kind of quick thinking which Paddy Mayne always encouraged in his men.

Harrison, knowing the odds, decided that the only thing which might favour his small party was the element of surprise. If they approached the village from the rear, they could tear through it with the Vickers blazing. Harrison's jeep was the first into the village with 'Curly' Hall's foot hard on the accelerator. Close behind was the other vehicle. As Harrison's jeep entered Les Ormes, the first sight which met him as he stood in the jeep, manning the powerful twin 'K' Vickers was the village square and a SS Officer with a pistol in his hand. The German had one second to stare at Harrison, before he was shot in the roadway. Instant reaction allowed Harrison to record the scene around him. At one end of the square stood the church and in front of it a group of SS men with two staff cars and a truck. Harrison concentrated his fire on these, sending the cars and the truck into flame. As the SS men ran for cover Harrison raked the square, leaving it bloody with dead and screaming wounded. Hall reversed the jeep until it was a reasonable distance from the church. Harrison was coming under fire as the jeep came to a halt. He wondered why Hall was not driving out of the German line of fire. He looked down to see blood oozing out of his comrade. 'Curly' was dead.

German bullets tore through the engine block, leaving Harrison stranded. Behind him the other jeep was busy raking the square and surrounding buildings. Worst of all the twin Vickers which Harrison had fired so furiously were now jammed. He jumped into the rear of the jeep – the only thing left to him was to get the other Vickers into action. But after one burst it too jammed. Leaning over the body of 'Curly' Hall, he seized the bren and fired several bursts from it. 'Christ, it jammed as well,' remembers Harrison.

He grabbed his carbine and got out of the jeep firing it from a standing position on the roadway. The Germans had recovered from the initial SAS assault, and were concentrating accurate fire on the two jeeps. Blood was flowing down Derrick Harrison's right arm. As he loaded and reloaded the carbine, he felt considerable pain. Added to that, firing was difficult because of a broken finger he had received in a previous action. In the other jeep, Richardson saw that Harrison was about to be killed as twenty Germans moved towards the square from a nearby orchard. He screamed a warning. Harrison opened up on the Germans, wounding some and sending the others scattering. Fauchois got out of Richardson's jeep and retrieved Hall's body. Richardson suddenly spotted a German sniper lining up his sights on Harrison. He promptly drew his .45 pistol and with one shot killed the sniper. Brearton recognised the situation they were in and turned the jeep to allow the twin Vickers to operate freely. Richardson drove his jeep, until it passed Harrison, who ran after it still firing as he leapt aboard. As they made their escape from Les Ormes they were still unaware that, on their arrival, two villagers were being shot and eighteen others were lined up for execution. In the subsequent confusion those destined for execution escaped. Harrison and his men left some sixty dead and wounded SS. Today in that village there is a monument which commemorates the bravery of Lance-Corporal Jimmy 'Curly' Hall.

There were good memories for Harrison too. He had lunch with Paddy Mayne as guests of the Maquis Camille. Harrison remembers that the chat was good, better than ever. 'When I first met him he was Zeus. He was a god. At that time he was just one of the gods or Zeus on earth. I found it easier to converse with him,' says Harrison. Paddy normally wore the same battledress as the other men in France with no badges that would indicate rank, though on one occasion Derrick Harrison remembers him arriving in service dress with his Sam Browne belt and crown and pips. Paddy Mayne had sent to Chelmsford for his service dress because Bill Fraser was reported to be wearing his kilt.

Mayne was pleased with Harrison's progress in KIPLING and the way in which he dealt with the pressures in the full knowledge of Hitler's shoot-to-kill policy. Harrison says: 'We took the view that we would not be taken prisoner.'

Paddy Mayne did not know, however, the full extent to which the pressures of operating behind the lines affected some of his men, and Harrison in particular. To this day, Derrick Harrison finds it painful to talk about the measures he took to keep himself alive and to maintain the fighting level and alertness required. How, in fact, did men like Harrison cope with the strain of operating for long periods behind enemy lines? Harrison himself provides the answer:

'We didn't realise just how much tension we were under. It manifested itself in a scent for danger – quick reactions. When laying an ambush you waited there knowing that, after it, you had to get away quickly. We carried Benzedrine tablets which kept us going. I found that state of alertness stayed with me. In Civvy Street everything spelled danger, even though it wasn't there. The Army sent me to a place to be debriefed where I had to recall my experiences over and over again under the influence of drugs. You were held between consciousness and anaesthesia. I found that in Civvy Street I reacted quickly and physically to everything, to the point of hitting people. I was finding that it was still happening. The debriefing took three months with a half-hour session every night. One or two others were in the same position – re-living it all again. Initially I was sent to an Army psychiatrist at Chelmsford and then to an Army establishment in north London.'

It was Derrick Harrison's honesty and his willingness to face up to these problems which saw him through to the point where he was able to develop a career as a journalist which he still pursues.

Paddy Mayne himself was also under pressure in France, constantly on the move to avoid capture, travelling from base to base. Most of the time his driver was the navigator from the Western Desert campaign, Mike Sadler. There are those who still believe that Paddy Mayne was never frightened, but Mike Sadler has a different view. 'In conversations with me, he admitted that he was frightened. Unlike some of us, he was not so scared that he would fail to act. He kept it all very much under control.'

The high jinks, always an integral part of his behaviour, were in evidence in France and it resulted in him being brought before the commander of the US Third Army, General Patton.

When the Americans took Le Mans, Paddy Mayne drove through the town with his twin Vickers firing into the air. For American soldiers and civilians who must have thought the war was over in that area, the sound of those heavy guns came as quite a shock. Mike Sadler remembers the episode vividly:

'We drove through Le Mans and into the countryside where we were apprehended by the Yanks. Orders had been sent out to arrest us. At first we began speaking to each other in French, in the hope of fooling the Yanks. We almost managed to convince this young soldier, when a sergeant came over and said to him: 'These guys speak English better than you do.' We were then taken back to Le Mans and led in front of the General. Paddy knew we were in trouble, but he carried it off beautifully. He said to Patton, "I hope we didn't frighten your men." There was nothing even Patton could do but to reply that of course we hadn't done that. However, once he got that over, he told Paddy that firing his guns in the town was not the way to behave. We left and Paddy just laughed about it.'

15

Brave and Brilliant Exploits

THROUGHOUT the French campaign, there were men whom Paddy Mayne never forgot and whom, even after the war, when in the company of those who had fought close to him, he would mention with reverence. In addition to Derrick Harrison, there was Sergeant Frederick White, known to his friends and fellow soldiers as 'Chalky'. When we met him in 1986, the scars of battle were still evident. He was part of Operation HOUNDSWORTH. The following account of Chalky White's bravery was written by Captain Ian Wellsted, who was parachuted into the Morvan area on 6 June, and on 7 August took over 3 Troop:

> While at the Chalaux camp, on 20 July, I learned that 3 Troop was moving into the Forêt des Dames area. The advance party of Ooly Ball with Sergeant Jeff Duvivier had set off on bicycles on the evening of 17 July. Captain Roy Bradford [not the co-author of this book] with Sergeant Chalky White as rear front gunner, Sergeant 'Maggie' McGinn as rear gunner and Trooper Devine as driver, set off in a jeep on the evening of 19 July to join them. Bradford took, as his interpreter on the trip, Jacques Morvillier from the Maquis Jean. Chalky, who was a very fine soldier, having won the DCM and MM on previous operations with the SAS, had been a peculiar jinx to his officers. His platoon commander had been killed on every operation and up to this point, six officers had lost their

lives on patrols or skirmishes with Chalky. This time it was intended to outwit the jinx by giving Chalky command of his own section.

The next I heard of the movement of the troop was on 21 July. It was almost dusk when a message came from the Maquis, via the station guardroom telephone, to say that a British soldier had been brought in and wished to see us. A jeep was sent down to fetch him and when he was brought to us he looked a sorry sight. His shirt was torn, his face was white and drawn, and as he spoke he quivered with nervous tension and the strain of what he had been through. It was 'Maggie' McGinn and the tale that he had to tell was a sad one.

He said that, after setting out from Chalaux in the late evening, the jeep moved all night travelling in a north-easterly direction by side roads and taking all the usual precautions. By eight in the morning, they found themselves in the little village of Lucy-sur-Yonne. There they came face to face with a German officer and his sergeant. At first the officer did not realise the car was British, and waved them down as though it was one of his own vehicles. Chalky answered him with a burst from his twin Vickers and the Boche dived for cover. Almost immediately the jeep came upon a German lorry parked at the roadside and behind it they could see another. Jerry troops on both sides of the road were lazing in the fields and, in a matter of moments, the jeep crew knew they had found a German troop convoy preparing breakfast. It was too late to turn back. Already the Germans were sprinting for their guns. There was only one thing for the SAS lads to do and they did it. On Roy Bradford's orders Sergeant 'Maggie' McGinn put the accelerator to the boards and, as the jeeps passed the trucks, Chalky White riddled them with his twin Vickers. There were seven lorries each containing at least twenty men. In the jeep, apart from the rattle of the Vickers, there were explosives which could blow at any minute. However, a burst of machine-gun fire from a Spandau hit the jeep from behind. Devine slumped over the rear guns and Bradford was hit in the arm. Chalky kept firing. Three times he stopped to change magazines as he fired something like 800 rounds into the Germans at point-blank range. Jacques and Roy Bradford passed the magazines to Chalky. But the final straw for Chalky White and his team was that the rear gunner was unable to give them protection. As the jeep passed the last truck, a long burst from a Spandau almost cut Bradford in two and severely damaged the elbow of the Frenchman. Chalky White himself was badly wounded. He had fired the Vickers and changed magazines even though his left hand was shattered. He also had bullet wounds to the leg and his shoulder was torn. The engine of the jeep was in a bad state and it was only just possible for it to coast out of sight, before it finally came to a standstill. 'Maggie' McGinn leapt out and after ensuring that Devine and Bradford were dead, he quickly helped White and the Frenchman from the jeep. He dragged them both across the roadway and pushed them through a hedge. Behind he could hear Germans running down the road in hot pursuit.

From the cover of a nearby wood they watched the Germans search the jeep and the bodies of the dead men. When night fell, McGinn insisted that the wounded should move in case the Germans began to search the area at dawn. When the wounded were eventually too weak to travel, he built them a shelter from corn sheaves. At daylight, the three moved on. At one point McGinn swam the river Yonne and brought back a lock-keeper's boat. He ferried Chalky and the Maquisard across the river and the party remained in an orchard throughout the day. McGinn persuaded the injured Jacques to contact civilians which he did and the Maquis came for them that evening.

Chalky White gave the authors his account of the action and it did not differ markedly from the account above, though there were interesting details which only someone such as Chalky White could provide. Chalky never did like officers. He reckoned that they were often family men and in his opinion they were always concerned about surviving the war to be with their families. This may seem a curious statement, but it adequately sums up a man who loved action, who lived for war. He was not very pleased to have Captain Roy Bradford with him, and his justification for that turned out to be as follows:

'I made a mistake which I should never have made about Roy Bradford. He was always taking photographs and before we went on that operation, I should have searched him and removed any incriminating material. As it turned out, when the Germans searched his body they found photos. A photo of me was made into a poster and plastered on walls with a reward. It was a mistake I shouldn't have made.'

Even to this day that 'mistake', as he describes it, still lives with him. He was so exacting about his professional role as a soldier. When describing the battle in the village, there is a glint in his eye as he relives it:

'When that officer appeared I tripped the Vickers. I could feel the jeep running over the bodies of the Germans in the street. I had a field-day. But the problem was the tail-end-Charlie. When the Germans laagered up, they always left a tail-end man with a Spandau and he was the one that got to us.'

When you mention Paddy Mayne, Chalky White's face lights up and then he addresses you with a look of anger: 'They should have given him the VC and the SAS should do something. After all, they renamed Hereford Barracks, Stirling Lines – what's wrong with naming one of our places after Blair?' Chalky White first met Paddy Mayne in Palestine. His first memory is of Mayne and McGonigal riding horses. He remembers also at that time that some of the men were making complaints about their mail not being sent home on time. 'Mayne and McGonigal sorted out the mail officer. They were lucky not to have been put on a charge.'

When Chalky is asked for his assessment of his hero, he reflects quietly and then makes the comparison that David Stirling was a thinker and a gentleman whereas 'Paddy was an action man':

'Paddy was the best professional killer I have ever seen,' says Chalky White. He adds: 'The best thing that happened to the regiment was when David Stirling was captured. He was too much of a gentleman – in our job you needed a killer. You knew not to mess with Paddy. It was not that he was menacing, but people knew there was a line never to cross. After Stirling was captured, Paddy began to take life more seriously. He knew his settling in period was over. Our job really was about killing, resting – killing and resting and of course some lads drank a lot. The war did something to you. You lose all sense of feeling. You became almost a sadist. Paddy was to me a man without faults. He wasn't under stress when the war was on. At the end of his life he let drink get the better of him.'

Chalky White stands out as one of those men from the Desert campaign who in many ways were moulded in a fashion which has echoes of Mayne's own character. In the battle at Lucy-sur-Yonne he sustained wounds to his left hand which resulted in the amputation of three fingers, but this did not prevent him from fighting on. His name sits easily alongside names such as Seekings, Harrison, Riley, Brough, Kershaw, Bennett and so many others. There was a ruggedness, determination, bravery and the quality of the loner about them all and they enjoyed and lived for action.

There are so many brave and brilliant exploits during the French campaign which demand to be recalled. There were yet others of a bizarre nature which, thankfully, illustrate the humour which even men in battle can bring to a situation.

Lieutenant Anderson of 'D' Squadron was travelling along a road dressed in civilian clothes and riding a bicycle when he passed three German soldiers on foot. Suddenly the pump fell from his bike, engaging itself in the chain, sending him head over heels.

'As I hit the deck, the bike rolled over and hit me. I let go one mouthful: "Fuck me you bastard." Suddenly I remembered the Jerries. They were walking towards me. I just began cursing in French but all the time thinking I'd had it. However, they just laughed, helped me on my bike and off I went – pedalling like hell.'

Ian Wellsted, promoted Captain on 7 August, of 'A' Squadron was pleased when one of his men was able to demonstrate that German technique was not always what it should have been. 'On the day of a big ambush by our lads and the Maquis,' his report read, 'a German Staff Captain came down from Nevers to instruct the local "grey Russians" in the art of laying ambushes. Having given the Russians a short talk on the theory of laying ambushes, he took them out for a practical demonstration. This was, however, most ably provided by ourselves and the first burst from Sergeant Noble's bren killed off the Staff Captain.'

Perhaps one of the most interesting and humorous reports concerns a Corporal Thompson of HQ Squadron. It seems that in action he suffered occasional blackouts which lasted thirty-six hours. He was reported sick and sent to hospital. After being there a short time he was transferred to another hospital and interviewed by the medical officer who asked him about his past. He was told his nerves were shattered and he would have to remain there for some time.

Eventually Corporal Thompson was made Provost Corporal. While inspecting the buildings closely, he noticed that padded cells and barred windows were conspicuous throughout the establishment. There were numerous nationalities in the hospital including Czechs and Poles. There was a wireless in Corporal Thompson's ward and it was customary for the British troops to listen to the BBC six o'clock news bulletins. One evening a Czech came along and re-tuned the radio on to another programme. Thompson told the Czech that he could listen to any programme once the BBC news bulletin had ended. He persuaded the Czech to listen to the BBC by depriving him of two teeth. Unfortunately, this method of persuasion was witnessed by the Ward Sister who reported the matter to higher authority. During her absence the Czech recovered from unconsciousness and retaliated by trying to cut Thompson's throat with an open razor. Thompson defended himself by throwing his locker at the Czech's head and scoring a direct hit. Thompson was put in a padded cell and given time to ruminate. He quickly reached the conclusion that he was in a lunatic asylum and his conduct would label him a raving madman. This realisation caused him great concern and he reported sick with an old injury and put his case before the medical officer. His plea was successful, for the medical officer carried out an inquiry which revealed that Thompson's papers had been mixed up with those of a man of the same name who was suffering from severe shell-shock and mental fatigue. The matter was cleared up and Corporal Thompson was given a certificate stating that he was sane. Thereafter he claimed to be the only man in 1 SAS to be in a position to prove his sanity.

Captain Wiseman, of 'A' Squadron, must have wondered on at least one occasion about the sanity of his Maquis colleagues when they were directing a drop near Is-sur-Lille. The Germans were five miles from the village, loading troops on to a train for Dijon. The Maquis were otherwise busy, flashing torches at RAF planes to indicate a dropping zone, but as it turned out, the lights of the railway station at Is-sur-Lille were much brighter than the torches at the dropping zone. As a result the RAF dropped sixteen heavy containers on the heads of the assembled Germans.

There are so many varied reports on the Maquis in SAS files that it is difficult to assess them properly. One thing on which, it seems, most SAS men were agreed, was that it was never safe to carry out combined operations with them. The Maquis consisted of two ideologically separate groupings between whom there was much rivalry (see p. 104). Many of their operations were aborted or failed because of informers. Some SAS men were appalled at the brutality of the Maquis but it has to be remembered that many of them were witnessing the destruction of their own homeland by the Germans and atrocities against their own people, often their own families. But, as one SAS report put it, 'The Milice or Militia are the real bastards. They have been hypnotised by the Boche, drilled, disciplined and injected with Boche frightfulness. They are traitors to their own country and will stop at nothing.' The Maquis shot any Milice they could capture.

Equally, the shooting of prisoners was not simply confined to the Maquis. There were men in France who remembered the murder of the men in the Captain Garstin 'stick'. Lieutenant Richardson and his patrol captured four Germans towards the end of the campaign in France. The Germans were in uniform and armed. There were two sergeants, a sergeant-major and an officer. As soon as they were captured, one of the SAS patrol brought it to Richardson's attention that these men were from the Kriegsmarine or Marines. Richardson decided to bring them back to his camp. The patrol and the captives arrived at the camp in the early hours of 27 September and the Germans were interrogated to establish where they were stationed at the time when Garstin and his men were executed. A brief report describes what happened next:

> They were very arrogant, and as they were attempting to return to Germany it was thought that they might have had something to do with the murder of Captain Garstin and his party. They were taken out and shot.

Summary justice for men against whom there was no proof. Prior to this Richardson and his party were in receipt of information that small parties of armed Germans might be moving in their vicinity in darkness, in an attempt to get back to Germany. There was no order issued to execute such enemy if taken prisoner, but merely to establish their identities.

In fact the men responsible for the decision to shoot the Garstin team were from Gestapo HQ in Paris and those at the château from where they were led to the execution site were believed to be members of a Luftwaffe Signal Section. This information was known to the SAS. Indeed, there was a constant attempt throughout the campaign in France to establish the identities of German officers who ordered or took part in the killing of SAS troopers. A secret document on atrocities against 1 SAS during this period reads as follows:

> The Allied Expeditionary Force of Inquiry found that Lt Stephens was murdered by the Germans near Verrières on 3 July 1944; that 31 men were murdered near ROM on or about 7 July. The Germans actually responsible for the murders are not known but there is a prima-facie case against Major Herold, the senior German authority near Poitiers at the time.

This report was compiled from information being gathered in France during the campaign, but it was only possible to begin to act on it in the summer of 1945.

The killings of Garstin and his men had marked the beginning of the murders of many of the Allied Forces and reports of these back home caused great distress to families. In this context, Paddy Mayne fulfilled a role which was appreciated by the men and, more importantly, by families waiting at home. He wrote numerous letters from France and on trips back to Chelmsford. An example is to the mother of Captain Alex Muirhead, who was involved in Operation HOUNDSWORTH:

Dear Mrs Muirhead,
Alex is in very fine form. Although he has no way of writing to you, we hear from him regularly. He has now been in France some time and is doing terrific work.
We can send your letter to him and I hope it won't be very long before you hear from him personally.
Very best wishes and try not to worry.
Yours sincerely, R.B. Mayne

Leslie Bateman has a similar letter written to his father.

September 1944 saw the end of the French campaign. Paddy Mayne, Major Melot and Major Marsh left for the HOUNDS-WORTH base on 27 August 1944. Tony Marsh, who was in charge there, told his Colonel that he desperately needed a number of jeeps and Mayne agreed to send down 'C' Squadron to HOUNDSWORTH situated at Chalaux. The following day a second party of twenty jeeps and forty men arrived at Orleans and were met by Derrick Harrison. Marsh took the whole of the squadron, less thirty-four men and twelve jeeps, and set up a base close to the existing HOUNDSWORTH camp. Mayne was happy with the decision. Within three days, one of Marsh's patrol destroyed three vehicles and killed or wounded twenty Germans. On 1 September, Paddy Mayne decided that someone should go and collect a trailer that was dropped when Harrison and his men were leaving KIPLING base. The man who volunteered for the job was Lieutenant 'Monty' Goddard.

Paddy Mayne looked at Goddard and then at Tony Marsh. 'I'll go along for the ride,' he said. Marsh smiled since it was never certain exactly what Paddy meant by 'going for a ride'. Paddy climbed into the front of the jeep alongside Goddard and they set off with Paddy checking the twin Vickers in front of him. The two men travelled along the road which led towards KIPLING. The road was devoid of traffic except for the occasional farmer with a horse-drawn cart. Paddy Mayne, who was always one to sense danger, heard the rumbling of heavy vehicles in the distance. He gestured to Goddard to pull the jeep into cover at the side of the road. To their astonishment the two men found themselves in the company of a Maquis patrol. The Maquis said they were about to lay an ambush for a German patrol, but Mayne saw that the Frenchmen were not adequately equipped to deal with a large force. Paddy told him to get the jeep out of sight and to bring him the bren, the single Vickers, and an ample supply of ammunition. He also told Goddard to leave the jeep in a position that would make for a quick getaway.

Goddard parked the jeep under cover of nearby trees and returned with the weapons. He then proudly took the single Vickers and handed Mayne the bren which, in Paddy's hands, looked like a rifle. As the German convoy came into sight, it was led by a 36mm mobile quick-firer and behind it several trucks loaded with soldiers. In the rear was a staff car. Mayne motioned to the anxious Goddard to wait until the range was right. He appeared unconcerned about the Maquis who, in turn, looked as if they were beginning to doubt whether they should get involved in the action. They were a motley group, armed merely with an assortment of carbines and revolvers, who did not evince authority or confidence. Mayne, therefore, ignored them, and simply ensured that Goddard and himself were prepared. Twice he looked towards the jeep to reassure himself that it was properly sited to allow for a clear escape into the nearby woods.

As the Germans approached the Maquis men stood in a group. Their staccato conversation suggested that there were several conflicting views on what they should do next. One of them carried several grenades attached to his belt. This did not escape Mayne. Without so much as a please, he strode into the midst of the Maquis, took hold of the man with the grenades and roughly removed the bombs from his belt. Mayne then returned to his position which afforded him a clear view of the approaching Germans. As the convoy came within fifty yards range, Mayne waved to Goddard who was holding the Vickers at the ready. In seconds Mayne was on his feet firing the bren from his shoulder, and Goddard was crouching, aiming the single Vickers from his hip. As the first salvo hit the Germans, the convoy came to a halt. Mayne and Goddard just reloaded and kept up a lethal hail of bullets on their target. As the quick-firer at the head of the convoy came into action, enemy soldiers leapt from the truck and spilled across the roadway into a hail of bullets from the bren and the Vickers. Mayne looked round for support but the Maquis had gone. If there was any question of escape, Goddard put paid to it. He headed for the 36mm quick-firer, the Vickers bucking against his hip as he poured burst after burst into the enemy vehicle. It was a suicidal tactic.

Mayne watched as enemy soldiers piled into the ditches either side of the road. In an attempt to deal with them he crept with the bren in search of a vantage point which would afford him the upper hand. Fifty yards away he spotted raised ground which would give him a clear view of the ditches and the trucks. There was no time to worry about Goddard, the heavy sound of whose Vickers was beating out its own rhythm nearby.

Mayne reached his objective. Below him Goddard was running zigzag along the roadway firing the Vickers. A final sustained burst finished off the quick-firer and its crew. Fifteen feet from it, Goddard was cut down as a cannon opened up from one of the trucks. Mayne reacted in anger, and fired a full bren magazine into that truck. It was a carefully directed burst, which killed those inside it. As the truck exploded, he could still hear the cries of German wounded. Sadly the bloody body of Lt Goddard stained the road. Alongside him lay the single Vickers.

A voice was screaming at Mayne from the cover of the woods. He looked behind and saw one of the Maquis. Mayne's own position was now coming under heavy fire from a Spandau set up close to one of the German trucks. As one last desperate act Mayne reached for the grenades and transferred the bren to his left hand. Quickly he rose, firing the bren wildly and tossed a grenade down the embankment into the ditch where the Germans were sheltering. He went to ground again and loaded another magazine into the bren and repeated the exercise. The

Maquisard was now alongside Mayne on the ground, tugging at his sleeve. Below them was mayhem, but the Germans were re-grouping. As a parting gesture, Mayne fired one more burst from the bren and took off into the woods. The Germans did not follow. Mayne's jeep was gone, but he made his way on foot with the assistance of his guide – and, after commandeering a civilian car, arrived back at the camp. Tony Marsh looked at his Colonel and knew it was better not to discuss the matter. It was left to the Maquis to describe the heroism of both Goddard and Mayne.

Mayne ensured that his part in the action was not referred to again. In Tony Marsh's company much later, he referred to the episode as 'just a scrap'.

A day later, Mayne was having dinner at the Hotel Morvandelle on Lac des Settons with Major Melot. Some of the wine may well have come from a consignment liberated by Lieutenant George. He was sent on a 'recce' in Meursault where twenty-five bottles of a good vintage were presented to his troop. While he was in the cellar of a château collecting the wine, Germans were setting up an AA-position in the garden. The wine trip turned out to be fraught with difficulty. On the way from the château, George's vehicle broke down and was abandoned, though the wine was rescued. They transferred to a Citroën but had difficulty at a river crossing. Fortunately, they arrived in time at the Morvandelle hotel with the consignment intact. George and his companions enjoyed their meal with Paddy Mayne and Bob Melot and headed back to camp at Chalaux at midnight. Once again, the Citroën gave them trouble and they were obliged to freewheel most of the way. When they arrived in the camp, they were surprised to hear that the Maquis had reported that they had all been ambushed and killed by the Germans. It was explained that they had provided Meursault for a dinner with Colonel Mayne, which they had managed to survive!

When it comes to examining the calibre of the men who fought under Paddy Mayne, it is impossible to mention the exploits and the heroism of them all. 1 SAS and 2 SAS achieved exceptional feats in France. One of the most apt tributes came from General 'Boy' Browning in September 1944 when he said the SAS achieved more in hastening the demise of the German 5 Army and 7 Army than any other single effort by the British Army.

The commander-in-chief, Eisenhower, wrote to Brigadier McLeod: 'The ruthlessness with which the enemy has attacked the SAS Troops is an indication of the injury you were able to cause to the German Armed Forces, both by your own efforts and by the information which you gave of German dispositions and movements.'

Paddy Mayne was awarded a second Bar to his DSO for his contribution to the campaign in France. The official citation stated:

Lt-Col. R. B. Mayne DSO has commanded 1 SAS Regiment throughout the period of operations in France.

On 8 August 1944, he was dropped to HOUNDSWORTH base, located west of Dijon, in order to co-ordinate and take charge of the available detachments of his Regiment and co-ordinate their activities with a major Airborne landing which was then envisaged near Paris.

He then proceeded in a jeep in daylight to motor to the GAIN base making the complete journey in one day. On the approach of Allied Forces, he passed through the lines in his jeep to contact the American Forces and to lead back through the lines his detachment of twenty jeeps landed for Operation WALLACE. During the next few weeks, he successfully penetrated the German and American lines on four occasions in order to lead parties of reinforcements. It was entirely due to Lt-Col. Mayne's fine leadership and example, and his utter disregard of danger, that the unit was able to achieve such striking successes.

Mayne, with his peculiar sense of humour, provided a fitting finale to the French campaign. When Paris was liberated, he arrived to spend a few days relaxing. He had just been awarded the Croix de Guerre. With him was his faithful navigator, Mike Sadler. Sadler recalls that one day they decided to have lunch in a small café off the Champs Elysées with some members of the

French SAS and civilian members of the French Résistance. The food was good and was washed down with ample quantities of wine. As the meal ended, Paddy Mayne took a grenade from his pocket, pulled the pin and placed the grenade in the middle of the table.

Mike Sadler still remembers the scene: 'Some of the party dived under the table, while others of us just sat there thinking the end had come. After all the thought crossed my mind that he was so unpredictable that he might just have decided that he was going to end it all at that moment. He then lifted the grenade, placed it in his pocket and said, "What are you all worried about?"

'It was a cruel joke because there was that element of doubt. He wasn't laughing. When the grenade was first placed on the table, I remember smoke emitting from it. He must have tampered with the detonator. It was planned.'

16

A Different Role in Germany

BETWEEN the ending of the French campaign and until the final assault began in Germany early in 1945, Paddy Mayne commuted backwards and forwards between SAS HQ in Chelmsford and Allied HQ in Brussels. His Christmas plans, in particular, were interrupted by a summons to Brussels. He wrote to his mother on 24 December: 'I am crossing over to Holland today. I had several arrangements made here including shooting partridges which should have been great fun and we had several parties arranged over Christmas, and on Boxing Day I was to have played rugby at Cambridge, but I'm afraid we have to earn our living some time. Mrs Hanbury is a very pleasant old woman, her husband is dead and her only son was killed with the RAF. She lives in three rooms of her house. She is a wonderful talker, quite interesting, but unending. I called in to see her last night and she opened a bottle of Champagne, then insisted I stay for dinner, when I had a remarkable venison cutlet, some excellent red wine, good port and a very fine cigar. She has asked for your address. I think she wants to write to you.'

Hylands, the house of the wealthy brewing family, the Hanburys of Truman, Hanbury & Buxton, played a continuing role in Paddy's life as the SAS HQ. Mrs Hanbury had the highest regard and affection for Paddy and there is in the Mayne family file a letter from her to Paddy's mother about her pleasure at having 'your most gallant son' under her roof. To her, he had always behaved in the most deferential and courteous manner. David Danger, who served under Paddy from Sicily to the end in Norway, rising through the ranks and ultimately to Lieutenant-Colonel, recalls one occasion, late at night, after Mrs Hanbury had retired to bed, when Paddy attempted, for a bet, to drive a jeep up the main marble staircase of the mansion. Roused by the resulting uproar, the lady of the house appeared in her dressing-gown on the landing and remonstrated with him in motherly fashion: 'Now, Paddy, that is quite enough of that, I think. You're keeping me awake. It's time you all got to bed.' According to eyewitnesses, Paddy could not have been more apologetic, dismissed the cheering crowd and, suitably chastened, gallantly escorted her to her bedroom door and bade her good night.

For someone who, despite the constraints of army life during wartime, had often spent leaves in both London and Cairo and who had, after all, been around with an international rugby side, at home and on tour, Paddy Mayne showed at times a surprising innocence of the ways of the world.

Ted Griffiths, who had given tuition to Paddy Mayne in Latin before becoming a life-long friend, tells of how they spent that same Christmas leave together when Paddy arrived from Chelmsford. It was in the middle of the last great German offensive through the Ardennes and the atmosphere in Brussels must have been rather less relaxed than on the famous night before Waterloo. Mayne had managed to acquire a case of Queen Anne whisky. The party broke up at a late hour and the two friends returned to the hotel where Mayne had a room. This, he insisted, was where Griffiths would sleep. They had a few more drinks and eventually Mayne departed downstairs. He was confident the night porter would find him a bed somewhere. Mayne's French was of the most basic, but francs changed hands and the porter got, as he believed, the message. He led Mayne to an annexe around the corner where the Belgian Madame in charge effusively welcomed this magnificent looking British officer, so impressively covered with decorations, including the Croix de Guerre. A room was found and Mayne – as he later related to Griffiths – had just got his uniform off and thrown himself on the bed when the first of his night visitors appeared. It was a plump young female, wearing little and anxious to give of her best in the Allied cause. Her reception was rudely brusque and unmistakable. She hastily withdrew. Madame, jealous of the reputation of her house, and aware now that she was dealing with a client not easily pleased, dispatched another of her most voluptuous *filles*. This one met a similar rebuff. Two more young ladies in alluring déshabille attempted in vain to penetrate the Mayne defences. The last fled the room in alarm at the demeanour of this impossible officer. It was at that stage that Mayne, now thoroughly annoyed and surely at last aware of the nature of the establishment, barricaded the door with a wardrobe. Madame, greatly agitated at this turn of events, summoned the night porter who in turn brought Griffiths to deal with the developing crisis. Griffiths remembers Mayne shouting, 'What the hell's going on? There's no peace in this bloody place.' Eventually the virgin soldier was persuaded to emerge. It was now after 5 a.m. Peace was restored and he spent the remainder of the night in Griffiths' bedroom. The following night accommodation was provided in Griffiths' RAF mess at Melsbroek.

During the frequent visits to Brussels, active forward planning was going on for the advance into Germany itself. The future role of the SAS was a matter for constant discussion. One of Paddy's officers, Major Tony Marsh, now OC 'C' Squadron, wrote to his chief on 14 January 1945 describing the then role of the Belgian SAS who were attached to the 61 Reconnaissance Regiment:

They are doing recce patrols in jeeps and on foot, and are thinking of trying out patrols, penetrating the lines on foot to a depth of four to six miles, probing for information and the odd bit of mucking about that they can manage. The only trouble is that, in the case of information patrols, the difficulty is getting information back quickly. The Recce people tell me that if they were offered some 1 SAS patrols at a future date, they would certainly take them. The choices seem to be two:

(a) Jeep patrols working with the forward Recce people, jeeping so far and foot patrols after;

(b) foot patrols penetrating the lines for information and the odd spot of strafing.

The great thing seems to me to be that parties cannot be expected to live out for more than 48 hours either on foot or in jeeps on account of the weather.

At this time the winter weather was especially severe, with temperatures well below zero. Marsh goes on:

21 Army Group have asked 2 Army for our release. GI Ops 2 Army thinks it's because they may have something for us.

That 'something' turned out to be the rather bizarre and confused role in Germany, combining recce, intelligence gathering and that of forward assault troops that was eventually assigned to 1 SAS in the advance towards Oldenburg. It was a role which was later to be questioned by the officers concerned.

In the final months of the war, the SAS was an integral part of the Allied drive into northern Europe. The role dictated that they should operate independently or with armoured divisions. Paddy Mayne's men were given the job of punching a hole in the German defences for Canadian 4 Armoured Division. Known as Operation ARCHWAY, this task would take 1 SAS to the Baltic port of Kiel and it would also see some of the worst losses for the regiment.

When the Allies crossed the Rhine towards the end of March 1945, Lieutenant John Randall, who was with Phantom Signals Group which worked alongside the SAS, remembers meeting Mayne:

'At Wesel the Germans fought hard. There was a lot of hand-to-hand fighting in the streets and the scene was one of carnage. I saw Paddy arriving in his jeep. He sat openly in the vehicle, while some of his lads scoured the area to ensure there were no Jerries around. Mind you, we all thought it unlikely there was a German left in the area. The Yanks had gone in there with everything, including flame-throwers. Dead Jerries lay in rows with their throats slit. There had obviously been no time to take prisoners. I tell you, there were bodies everywhere and the place was like a wasteland.'

Two men in Randall's patrol found a German soldier hiding in a dugout and brought him to Mayne. 'He must have been the only German left alive,' remarked Randall. 'The guy was terrified. The lads walked him up to Paddy's jeep and asked the Colonel what they should do with him. Paddy got out his revolver. Then, slowly, he returned it to his holster as if he was having second thoughts. He looked at the lads and then told them to make the German bury his own dead.'

Reg Seekings has his memory of the carnage. Before crossing the Rhine, he was leading a jeep patrol along a road when he spotted objects hanging from trees at the side of a farmhouse. He took some of his men, crossed fields and, on reaching the farm buildings, was shocked to discover that the objects on the trees were bodies.

'There were eight or nine elderly men and women,' he says, 'and they had been strung up and left there. The American paratroopers had been there the day before us. Possibly these people were caught in hiding. Luckily I went into the barn and, with my training, I detected the smell of explosives. The place had been booby-trapped with a wire attached to some farm implements. My lads could have been blown to bits. The Yanks should have cleared it. I had to clear it.'

The beginning of April saw 1 SAS making the final push against the enemy. The regiment was divided into four squadrons. While 'A' and 'D' Squadrons operated further east in Germany under Major Poat, 'B' and 'C' Squadrons were under Paddy Mayne in the area Meppen/Pappenburg/Oldenburg, with the objective of advancing north-east towards Oldenburg and Wilhelmshaven. The jeeps were believed to be sufficiently reliable and rugged, and with the firepower to enable the squadrons to punch a hole in the German defences so that Canadian armour could be used more effectively. There is no doubt that the topography did not lend itself to jeep warfare and the forested road often concealed

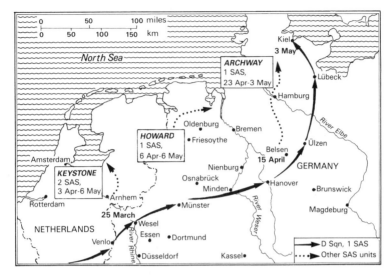

Fig 5 SAS operations in NW Germany, 1945

snipers which made travelling jeeps vulnerable to sudden attacks.

Sergeant Bob Bennett remembers the jeeps and their design: 'The whole front of each jeep was covered in armour plate, with semicircles of bullet-proof glass to protect the driver and front gunner. Some vehicles were also fitted with a wire-cutting device above the front bumper. Armament consisted of twin Vickers for the front gunner, another pair for the rear gunner and every third or fourth jeep carried a .50 Browning heavy machine-gun. The driver had a bren-gun.'

Armed in this way 'B' and 'C' Squadrons under Mayne's command left Tilbury on landing craft in the early morning of 6 April. The force was self-contained in transport, equipment and rations. The sea journey took twenty-four hours before the force disembarked at Rotterdam. After concentrating in the town Mayne, with his Intelligence Officer Major Mike Blackman, motored forward to the main Canadian Army HQ situated in the area of Nijmegen.

After driving all day, Mayne arrived at the HQ and was greeted by Brigadier Mike Calvert. Calvert briefed him and outlined the plans for the way Mayne's squadrons should operate. He pointed out how vital it was that the SAS force should get to its operational area as soon as possible because the Germans were regrouping in the Oldenburg region. Mayne saw there was no time to waste and decided to push on the same night to reach Canadian 2 Corps HQ early the next day. This was done after one night spent just over the Dutch/German border. On reaching Corps HQ, Mayne met the brigadier of the General Staff and was asked if he would place his force under the control of Canadian 4 Armoured Division. This was agreed and, while he was still in discussion, Lieutenant Schlee arrived to inform him that the two squadrons would arrive with him in the late afternoon.

The following day Mayne went to Divisional HQ to discuss the operational capabilities and objectives of his men. Much of the time was spent examining the topography of the ground where the SAS would operate. The area outlined for Mayne was almost entirely criss-crossed with dykes and canals, making it extremely difficult for jeeps to operate with any degree of freedom. It would be virtually impossible for his vehicles to drive off the roads and there were few places where vehicles could reverse and turn. There were innumerable culverts and bridges which the enemy were likely to have prepared for demolition. The majority of fields were boggy, even in dry weather, and with April rainfall they would be worse.

HQ did not know it, but the enemy facing Mayne's troops were the remnants of a parachute division which was known to fight well and at times even fanatically. Mayne decided to leave the liaison with HQ to his Intelligence Officer, Major Blackman, who remembers seeing little of Mayne in the days and weeks ahead. Contact was kept by radio, although for much of the time Mayne was operating in his jeep across a reasonably wide front to keep in touch with his men. The Canadians wondered why a senior officer, such as Mayne, was always out in the field and not in contact. Fortunately in Mike Blackman Paddy Mayne had a very able linkman who constantly kept him informed of developments at Headquarters.

The Germans were also aware of Mayne's presence on their native soil. A captured document from a General Staff Officer refers to Mayne, though his name is spelt as 'Kaine'. From their experience of the SAS in France and Italy the Germans knew they were highly trained in sabotage. The presence of SAS units was always reported therefore without delay to the German Divisional Command. Indeed, the seriousness with which the SAS was regarded can be gauged in the following correspondence:

Generalkommando A. K.

Armee oberkommando I
Ic/AO Nr. 23/44 g.Kdos

From captured enemy orders and papers it has been learned that the enemy intelligence service has tried to infiltrate single agents and teams and to build up resistance groups in the rear of the present German front (that is to say in Alsace-Lorraine, and also in the Saar and the Rhineland), in the same way as it did in France and Belgium during the years of occupation. In this work, the SAS troops will share the principal role with special espionage agents. By SAS troops are meant specially trained parachute troops. The enemy will probably set up SAS troops partly composed of German-speaking elements which can be less easily detected in a German-speaking area and, while carrying out sabotage, can also carry out active seditious propaganda.

These troops will also attempt to establish connections with the prisoners of war in the neighbourhood and with foreign workers in order to form them into resistance groups.

When the troops jump, they are equipped with everything they need for the penetration. Besides the equipment and weapons which the paratrooper carries with him in his jump-bag, on every mission containers are dropped holding the usual supplies of food, extra weapons, ammunition, explosives and other material. The penetration is usually carried out by groups ranging from three to forty men.

The combat methods of SAS Troops may be summarised as follows:

1 External marks of identification; coloured neckerchiefs – in darkness phosphorescent ones; in the case of American parachute and airborne troops, orange-coloured bits of cloth in enemy areas.

2 On landing, speedy assembly of the units by means of whistles and metal rattles. So far as possible, in large airborne operations, communications at greater distances by Eureka UKW sets.

3 Jumping with all weapons (see the remark on the jump-bag), thereby obviating search for weapon-holders.

4 Dropping of containers with only ammunition, supplies, explosives and equipment.

5 Dropping of life-size parachute dummies, filled with explosives.

6 Single combat, characterised by ambush, deception, utilisation of all the weapons of hand-to-hand fighting (brass knuckles, 'flammendolch').

On the landing of the SAS troops in France, it was learned that every member of the SAS had a pass in French and English. This stated that the bearer of the pass was a regular member of the Allied Forces under the command of General Eisenhower and that he was to be given every kind of support, information, means of transportation, care and lodging. It was signed by the leader of the Resistance groups in the area of France. The pass is a means of recognition for the introduction of SAS units in connection with the local resistance groups, partisans, escaped POWs, etc.

Units in this command will immediately report all observations pointing to the presence of SAS troops in the Army area.

Captured SAS members are to be turned over to the AOKI.

For the Army High Command

Chief of the General Staff

On Monday 9 April Mayne and his two squadrons left the Meppen area to penetrate the enemy lines. Major Blackman wrote: 'The plan basically is good, but practically not a workable one. The reasons being, first the difficulty of the terrain, and second the apparent slowness of the Canadian advances. However, this is not a criticism, but purely a statement of facts.'

Mayne was undeterred, however. His attitude, as always, was 'if the enemy are there, we'll destroy them'. At this time he was accompanied in his jeep by two of his men, Lance-Corporal Billy Hull and Trooper Williams. Both were from Ireland. For the remainder of the campaign in Germany, Hull played an important part in Mayne's life and it is through Hull that much of the information about Blair Mayne's exploits in Germany has emerged.

Hull is one of those characters in the SAS who came out of the war with an acute perception of Blair Mayne. This may have been due in part to the fact that Billy Hull was an Ulsterman from the Shankill Road in Belfast. He was twenty-two, seven years younger than Blair Mayne, when he first came into contact with him at the SAS depot in Chelmsford in 1944. Hull had lied about his age when he joined the Royal Ulster Rifles, and though he heard stories about Paddy Mayne's exploits in the Western Desert, it was not until the campaign in France that Hull was chosen by Mayne to join the SAS. Hull and eleven other members of the Royal Ulster Rifles became part of the regiment. Two were returned to their units, and, of the others, Hull was one of only two of the chosen group to survive the war.

Unlike Mayne, Hull was short and stocky, but he was good with his fists, and Mayne liked that. Prior to his becoming closely involved with Mayne, there were incidents which have a direct bearing on why Mayne chose Hull to accompany him in Germany. It illustrates the kind of men that Mayne preferred to have around him.

While at Chelmsford, Hull and other members of the Royal Ulster Rifles were being prepared for an operation behind enemy lines in France. Twenty-four hours before the drop, Hull was issued with new orders. He was to proceed to France on a separate operation with a Captain Anderson. They were to undertake a reconnaissance mission with orders to destroy a German train which the Allies believed would be carrying a large number of German soldiers and supplies. Hull went to see Mayne and pleaded with him to be allowed to accompany the men from his parent regiment, but Mayne dismissed the request with the explanation that Hull was required for a mission which was just as important. Those men whom Hull regarded as his closest buddies were part of the Captain Garstin 'stick' and were either killed in the drop or executed later. This left a bitter impression on Hull's mind, and a craving for revenge. When he dropped into France with Captain Anderson, Hull was unaware of their fate.

On 12 July 1944, Hull and Anderson made their jump in the dangerous hours before dawn when daylight was slowly beginning to streak the sky. Hull remembers his parachute catching in the upper branches of a tree. More significantly, his trained ear told him that, nearby, a German convoy with half-tracks was making its way down a road. The sound of that convoy may very well have saved Hull's and Anderson's lives by covering the sound of the aircraft which dropped them off. Hull quickly released his harness and, to his astonishment and fright, his body ploughed through the roof of what turned out to be a pig-sty. Sitting in the middle of the mess, Hull tried desperately to control his thoughts. 'Had the convoy been alerted? Where was Anderson? Were the Germans billeted in the farmhouse? If there weren't Germans on the farm, how long would it be before the farmer discovered him and alerted the enemy?' and, as he recalled later: 'What am I doing sittin' in this mess, anyway?' These questions raced through his mind.

His thinking was soon interrupted by the sound of footsteps and voices outside the pig-sty. His instinct told him that if Germans came through the door, it was better to go out of life fighting rather than face capture and certain torture and death at the hands of the Gestapo. Quickly he got to his feet, folded back the metal butt on his MP38 Schmeisser, cocked it and waited. The door opened gently and framed in the doorway was an elderly French farmer carrying a torch. The farmer was more shocked than Hull, and without more ado Billy pushed past him and headed for cover and safety. Before long he came across a small stream. As he made his way along it, the cold water reached to his waist, but there was no time to worry about discomfort. He needed to find a secure vantage point close to where he believed his officer dropped.

There was also little time to search for Captain Anderson. Hull decided that if he could find a spot where he could survey the landscape at dawn it would be easier to find his colleague. However, it was essential that he should first ensure his own safety, so that whatever happened he would have a chance to proceed with the mission. Eventually he found a clump of bushes which was the only shelter in what seemed to be fairly open countryside. Nearby the convoy was still winding its way along the road, fumes from the engines of the large trucks wafted over the fields and mingled with the rising dampness and mist. Hull settled into a clump of bushes as though he was working his way into the folds of his favourite armchair. Meanwhile, Captain Anderson was facing a more dangerous predicament.

As he left the plane, the wind played havoc with his attempt to control his descent. Within minutes he found himself suspended, as if in a hammock, between two trees. His body up to his shoulders was wedged in the upper branches of one tree and his chute was held tight in the branches of another. He, too, could detect the sound of the convoy. In the next hour, with the threat of dawn and capture impending, he worked quietly and meticulously to free himself. Eventually, he lowered himself to the ground. It did not matter that the roughness of the branches tore into his hands and wrists and opened wounds in his face. If he failed to release himself, there was certain death in store and for members of the SAS, it could be preceded by interrogation and torture. There was no time now to worry about removing the parachute. Anderson headed in the direction in which he believed Billy Hully might have landed and found shelter. The convoy took over two hours to pass and was out of sight when Hull and Anderson had their first real view of their surroundings. They found each other by using a similar technique; moving slowly along hedgerows and calling each other's name quietly.

Their reunion was soon interrupted by the sound of vehicles

and raised voices. The noise seemed to be coming from the farmhouse where Billy landed. They decided it was best to separate and meet at a prepared rendezvous.

Hull considered it wise to remain in the vicinity on the basis that, if the Germans knew of his presence, they would throw a cordon round the area and make escape impossible. That is exactly the tactic the enemy used. They deployed a cordon over a three-mile radius. Hull retired to his hedgerow armchair. The next few hours proved crucial to his survival. German soldiers came within yards of his hiding place constantly firing into the hedges lining the field. Anderson had a similar experience, although the enemy did not get as close to him. For the next three days, in their separate hiding places, they lived by eating berries though Billy Hull resorted to a method of providing food for himself which kept Blair Mayne amused when he later recounted the episode to other officers in the SAS.

Billy's pigeon survived the parachute drop and even the trip into the pig-sty, though Billy reckoned 'it was its stay in the sty which seemed to silence it!' After two days of eating berries, his stomach demanded something more substantial. He decided the pigeon could serve a useful purpose. To this day, Billy, stocky as he is, looks for all the world like a man with a good appetite. The pigeon, he says, 'met its end gracefully'. At nightfall on the third day, when Billy was convinced the enemy cordon had been removed, it was roasted on a small fire.

When the story was later told to Paddy Mayne, his retort was 'So Hull's the man who eats pigeons.' Later, while Mayne and Hull travelled together in Germany, Paddy was often heard to say to Billy: "Eaten any pigeons lately, Hull?" Billy would reply: 'Only when the Army provides them, sir.'

On the fourth day, Anderson and Hull met up and proceeded towards their objective – to blow a rail link and an enemy train. In all well-laid plans, there is always an element of the unexpected. Hull and Anderson were told they were to blow a train as it went through a tunnel on the outskirts of Paris. They were not told that the tunnel would be guarded. When they came within 500 yards of the tunnel, they took out binoculars and surveyed its siting. The first thing they noticed was an

armed guard at each end of it. Before they discussed the best
way to place charges, Anderson turned to Hull and smiled. It
was a knowing smile and one that mirrored itself exactly in
Billy's thoughts. One of the guards would have to be dispatched
quietly with a knife. The reason was simply that he was standing
outside the tunnel while the other was inside. If one was
dispatched quietly, it would be easier to shoot the man in the
tunnel and, at any rate, the guard on the outside was easier to
get at. Anderson decided they should toss a coin to decide which
job would fall to each man. The smile did not leave his face.
Billy won the toss and turned to his colleague and said: 'You're
doing the knifing'. Anderson replied: 'You don't understand,
Billy. The toss was simply to allow the winner to have the best
job. You're using the knife.' Like a good soldier who knows not
to argue with his senior officer, Billy made his way towards the
outlying sentry.

Meanwhile Anderson trained his American carbine on the
man Billy Hull was stalking. The sentry at the other end of the
tunnel was now almost visible so Anderson decided it was wiser
to go down and use a .45 revolver at close range on the second
soldier. He would wait until Billy had neutralised his target.
Hull got close and without 'ceremonies' pulled the Jerry out of
sight of the far end of the tunnel and plunged the knife up
through his ribs, holding his left hand across the German's
mouth to prevent him screaming. Twice he plunged the knife,
the second time striking bone, before he gently lowered the
dead German to the ground. Within a minute a bullet from
Anderson's .45 fired from close range, penetrated the skull of
the other sentry. The two men then hurriedly laid the charges in
the tunnel and retired to a vantage point to survey their
handiwork. Sure enough the train was heading for the tunnel. 'It
was a terrible mess after the explosion,' recalls Hull. 'The train
was not, as we thought, carrying soldiers to the front, but
German wounded.'

Hull and Anderson returned to Chelmsford after the raid and
Hull's performance was enough to convince Paddy Mayne that
Hull was the man he needed. Maybe Mayne also knew that he
shared a similar humour with Hull and that Billy was also a man

who knew when to keep his mouth shut and when to talk to his Colonel.

Billy Hull's secondment as Paddy Mayne's driver was good news which, alas, was overshadowed by the death of his Royal Ulster Rifles comrades. While they were both walking through Chelmsford, two days later, Paddy stopped to watch a group of German POWs who were repairing a roadway. He turned to Hull and said: 'I bet you'd just love to see some of those bastards make a break for it.'

At Chelmsford, Hull waited for orders to go into action. The Colonel had one job which he knew would provide his corporal with a much-needed distraction. He asked him to go into the town of Chelmsford and pick up a vehicle from a signwriter's premises. When Hull arrived at the shop he was led to a yard at the rear. To his astonishment, Hull found a jeep with the bonnet decorated with an Ulster flag, ringed with shamrock.

In the days that followed, Billy Hull got to know Mayne and his 'peculiar temperament'. He also established a good rapport with his Colonel's batman, Trooper 'Paddy' Williams.

Billy remembers Mayne talking to him about Newtownards and its people, and he was forcibly struck by Mayne's shyness. 'When he was speaking to you he was forever blinking,' Billy says. 'I thought to myself, "How could that man make a solicitor when he's so shy and soft-spoken, low voiced almost."' The tougher side of his character was also obvious, adds Hull: 'After drinkin' his eyes almost popped out. He became talkative and, if riled, his voice was loud and threatening.' One thing which brought Mayne and Hull closer was their common skill at boxing. Hull remembers winning a fight at Chelmsford and afterwards being congratulated by Mayne, who revealed that he had won some money from his fellow officers by placing a bet on Billy.

Later he invited Billy and some friends back to his quarters. He gave them the key to his room and told them to help themselves to drinks until he arrived. Billy recalls that the room was filled with cases of champagne and bottles of every conceivable liquor. 'The place was coming down with loot,' says Hull. Billy and his friends decided the opportunity to drink champagne could not be ignored. They opened a bottle and filled three glasses. 'We were about to lower the stuff down our throats when Big Blair arrived,' says Billy Hull. "Put that stuff away. That's auld women's drink," shouted Mayne. The champagne was discarded, and the Colonel filled the champagne glasses to the brim with whiskey. As the four became merrier, one of Hull's companions, Paddy Dunne from Tipperary, began to sing an Irish ballad in the knowledge that the Colonel liked Irish songs. Mayne rounded on him and said he would have no 'New York ditties'. He walked from the company, reached under his bed and pulled out a wind-up gramophone. For the next two hours he played his guests recordings of songs such as 'Mother Macree' and 'The Mountains of Mourne'. Hull and his friends were 'bored to tears' but didn't dare comment. The drinking spree ended with Mayne removing Hull's two drunken companions to the hallway. Billy remembers waking the next morning and being presented with breakfast. Mayne's bed was empty and Billy was in a bed belonging to the Colonel's second-in-command, Major Poat. Billy learned later that he had collapsed on the floor of the room and was promptly put to bed by Mayne, who instructed his second-in-command to sleep in Billy's bed alongside the other ranks.

Paddy Mayne's closeness to his men and the respect he freely received from them is best illustrated by a story Hull tells of his time at Chelmsford after news reached the base that one of the survivors of the Garstin 'stick' was recovering in hospital. The survivor in question was Corporal 'Ginger' Jones who had escaped with Vaculik. When Paddy Mayne learned that the hospital was not a great distance from his HQ, he advised his men to visit Jones to 'cheer him up' and find out what he required 'in the way of luxuries'. Hull says visitors to the patient returned with the unanimous view that 'Ginger' detested hospital conditions and as a result his health was deteriorating. This was conveyed to Mayne who decided to pay Jones a visit to 'investigate the matter'. Hull says the Colonel was sympathetic to 'Ginger's' view of hospital life, and his desire to return to Chelmsford where he could be of use to the regiment. The Colonel promptly asked the hospital authorities for permission to return Jones to his base, but the request was denied. Mayne returned to his HQ and called a meeting of his officers and NCOs and briefed them about his visit to Jones, and his lack of progress in persuading the hospital administrators that life at the base would be a better form of treatment for their patient. 'This requires delicate handling,' Paddy Mayne told the meeting. Within twenty-four hours a small SAS party discreetly removed Jones from his hospital bed in the early hours without arousing suspicion. Jones recovered quickly at Chelmsford, the hospital was free of a patient, and a confrontation with the hospital authorities was happily avoided.

During the first week of April 1945 when Paddy left Chelmsford and drove straight through to Germany without stopping, his Signals corporal was David Danger, who recalls: 'He directed me to fix a public address system to his staff car with the aim of broadcasting rude words to the retreating Germans. We also fitted his gramophone to the back of the jeep, and all the way up through Holland we played John MacCormack, greatly to the astonishment of the convoys.'

17

The Fourth DSO

WHEN we began researching this book we tended, like others who had written about Paddy Mayne, to accept the official records. In most respects we had no cause to doubt their accuracy although we usually found it valuable to seek other opinions. We had to take into account that the records had a greater claim to authenticity and detail because they were, in the main, written at the time from eyewitness accounts. Forty years on, few if any, of the men who fought with Mayne would have been in any position, or would have wished to dispute the citations for Mayne's DSO or any reports made about him in dispatches. So, when it came to investigating the circumstances surrounding the award of his fourth DSO, we initially accepted the official citation. We also spoke to the two men who produced the draft documents from eyewitness reports. Those men were Major Mike Blackman and Captain Derrick Harrison. The citation reads as follows:

On Monday, April 9, 1945, Lt-Col. Mayne was ordered by the General Officer Commanding Canadian 4 Armoured Division to lead his Regiment, then consisting of two Armoured Jeep Squadrons, through the German lines. His general axis of advance was north-east through the city of Oldenburg with the special task to clear a path for the Canadian armoured cars and tanks and to cause alarm and disorganisation behind the enemy lines. As subsequent events proved, the task of Lt-Col. Mayne's forces was entirely and completely successful. This success, however, was solely due to the brilliant leadership of Lt-Col. Mayne who, by a single act of supreme bravery, drove the enemy from a strongly held key village, thereby breaking the crust of the enemy defences in the whole of this sector.

The following is a detailed account of the Colonel's individual action which called for unsurpassed heroism and cool, clear-sighted military knowledge.

Lt-Col. Mayne, on receiving a wireless message from the leading Squadron reporting that it was heavily engaged by enemy fire and that the Squadron Commander had been killed, immediately drove forward to the scene of the action. From the time of his arrival until the end of the action, Lt-Col. Mayne was in full view of the enemy and exposed to fire from small-arms, machine-guns and snipers' rifles. On arrival he summed up the situation in a matter of seconds and entered the nearest house alone and ensured that the enemy here had either withdrawn or been killed. He then seized a bren-gun and magazine and, singlehanded, fired burst after burst into the second house killing and wounding all the enemy here and also opening fire on the woods.

He then ordered a jeep to come forward and take over his fire position, he himself returning to the forward section where he disposed the men to best advantage and ordered another jeep to come forward. He got in the jeep and with another officer as rear gunner, drove past the position where the Squadron Commander had been killed a few minutes previously and continued to a point a hundred yards ahead where a further section of jeeps were halted by intense and accurate enemy fire. This section had suffered casualties in killed and wounded owing to the heavy enemy fire and the survivors were unable at the time to influence the action in any way until the arrival of Lt-Col. Mayne. The Col. continued along the road all the time engaging the enemy with fire from his own jeep. Having swept the area very thoroughly with close-range fire he turned his jeep round and drove back down the road still in full view of the enemy.

By this time the enemy had suffered heavy casualties, and were starting to withdraw. Nevertheless, they maintained an accurate fire on the road and it appeared almost impossible to extricate the wounded who were in the ditch near the forward jeep. Any attempt at rescuing these men under these conditions appeared virtually suicidal owing to the highly concentrated and accurate fire of the Germans. Though he fully realised the risk he was taking, Col. Mayne turned his jeep round once again and returned to try and rescue these wounded. Then by superlative determination and by displaying gallantry of the very highest degree and in the face of intense enemy machine-gun fire, he lifted the wounded one by one, into the jeep, turned round and drove back to the main body.

The entire enemy position had been wiped out. The majority of the enemy had been killed or wounded leaving a very small remnant who were now in full retreat. The Squadron, having suffered no further casualties, were able to continue their advance and drive deeper behind the enemy lines to complete their task of sabotage and destruction of the enemy. Finally, they reached a point, twenty miles ahead of the advance guard of the advancing Canadian Division, thus threatening the rear of the Germans, who finally withdrew. From the time of the arrival of Col. Mayne, his cool and determined action and his complete command of the situation, together with his unsurpassed gallantry, inspired all ranks. Not only did he save the lives of the wounded, but also completely defeated and destroyed the enemy.

The Squadron Commander mentioned in the citation was Major Dick Bond. It appears that Paddy Mayne was fond of Dick Bond and considered him to be a brave and committed SAS Squadron Commander. In January 1945 the second-in-command, Major Harry Poat, wrote from Chelmsford to Paddy who was home on leave at Newtownards that they were having problems with the Command of 'B' Squadron. According to Poat, Major Tommy Langton, who had been with the SAS since North Africa, had said that 'He was completely played out, had piles and was generally unfit for the job.' Poat also reported to Paddy that Dick Bond had arrived at Croydon only a couple of hours previously and both Tony Marsh and Langton spoke highly of him. Their consensus of opinion, according to Poat, was that Bond should replace Langton who, according to Poat: 'In his frame of mind he is not doing any good to the troops under his command and Bond should replace him.' To reinforce this view, Poat pointed out that Langton also had said: 'The men must come home at once because they are totally unfit, bodily and mentally.' Poat further states that Langton's view was that if he was asked to operate with the men of 'B' Squadron, he (Langton) would be 'obliged to refuse'. This is pertinent when we consider the role played by Bond and these same men during this 'fourth DSO' action.

The citation was written, within forty-eight hours of the action, by Blackman and Harrison and was then forwarded to Brigadier Mike Calvert. Calvert passed it to the Canadians and from there it undoubtedly found its way to London. Calvert, Blackman and Harrison are all convinced that, for this action, Mayne should have been awarded a VC. Blackman and Harrison compiled the citation from accounts provided by, and after discussion with, Lieutenant David Surrey Dane (later a Fellow of the Royal College of Physicians) and another of the subalterns present. Through their eyes, and those of Billy Hull, each of whom witnessed the action near Oldenburg in different ways, a new picture emerges.

There is new eyewitness evidence from Lieutenant Philip Schlee who was in the ditch referred to in the citation. While there is no doubt that the citation contains much of what is true about the episode, it also contains inaccuracies. The inaccuracies do not detract from the heroism displayed by Mayne, though there was another display of bravery a couple of days later, which, for reasons we shall outline later, was not included in the citation.

Of the citation, David Surrey Dane says: 'That's not how it was. It was a wonderful, magical little action but the citation was not an accurate description of what happened. I remember being asked to write an account of the action as it happened. I also remember that I did not approve of the way in which my account was "polished" by well-meaning superior officers. I can remember what I saw and heard of this action more clearly than I can remember the part I played in writing the citation. I think I was approached by Major Blackman and perhaps also by Captain Harrison and asked with another of those present – I cannot recall who it was – to write a description of the action so that Paddy could be recommended for the VC.'

David Surrey Dane says it was unlikely that the other person was John Scott, because he was too closely involved in the action and he, Surrey Dane, believed at the time that Scott would be recommended for a medal for his part in the action. Surrey Dane is sure, however, that he depended on John Scott for some details of the action since Scott was close to Mayne during part of the event. Scott is the 'rear gunner' mentioned in the citation.

'When I had written my description, Major Blackman told me there was a problem,' Surrey Dane recalls. 'Victoria Crosses were usually given for an act of outstanding bravery that helped to turn the course of a battle, or for the rescue of comrades from an impossible situation without regard for personal safety. Our little battle had obviously not contributed any more or less to the advance of 21 Army Group in northern Germany than many other actions elsewhere on the same day and, therefore, the rescue side of the action would have to be given more emphasis.

'My account was accordingly altered and I signed whatever I was asked or told to sign. If I complained, it was only to my subaltern friends.

'We all thought Paddy should have been awarded a VC, but I thought not for this one action. He had been so outstandingly brave and so brilliantly effective as a leader so many times that a VC seemed the most appropriate way in which this could be recognised. DSOs, when given to Lieutenant-Colonels, often reflected the courage and success of the units they led, rather than any particular act of bravery on their part. I can remember Paddy telling me that he would have preferred a MC to a fourth DSO for this reason, though of course he knew that MCs were not usually given to Lieutenant-Colonels. Did not Group Captain Leonard Cheshire of the RAF win the VC for repeated

courage in accomplishing an unusually large number of hazardous missions? Perhaps Paddy's recommendation should have
been on this cumulative basis.'

There is little doubt that, towards the end of the war, the view
within the SAS was that, for all their bravery and courage, they
were still resented for being irregulars. The episode on the road
to Oldenburg is significant both in the way it illustrated the
fierce loyalty of the men of 1 SAS to their commander and the
resentment they felt towards the authorities for not, as they
would put it, properly recognising the contribution of Paddy
Mayne throughout all the phases of the war, by the award of a
VC. Until now this matter has remained a secret within the
ranks of those veterans who fought with Mayne. The real story
of the action which led to the fourth DSO has never been told.

This in no way questions the integrity of the authors of the
citation, or the dedication of Major Blackman and Captain
Harrison. They acted with loyalty towards their commander
whose bravery they personally witnessed on many occasions.
They were also in a war zone. Nevertheless, the record can now
be put straight and, apart from the discrepancies in the citation,
Mayne's heroism on this occasion, if considered in relation to
his other acts of bravery, may well have been sufficient to have
guaranteed him the Victoria Cross. With the assistance, therefore, of David Surrey Dane, Philip Schlee, John Scott, Mike
Blackman and Derrick Harrison, the authors can now present
an account of the episode which encompasses many of the
elements of the citation, but dispenses with others.

Major Blackman says that the plan which Mayne was being
asked to fulfil on the morning of 9 April was a difficult one and
he, Blackman, doubted whether it could work. In essence the
two squadrons were to fan out along two parallel roads leading
to Oldenburg and provide a path for the Canadians whose
objective was the U-boat base at Wilhelmshaven. Gordon
Davidson, who joined 1 SAS from the Gordon Highlanders,
remembers the ground: 'It was unfamiliar terrain for all of us.
Not the clean clarity of the Desert where Arthurian and
Siegfried legend could clash in open conflict to Queensberry
Rules, but a vast unknown in which lurked not only a skilled

professional enemy, but desperate civilians for whom arms and transport were a natural magnet. It was as though our Maquis role in France was reversed. To the Canadians, it was equally strange, and the small swift jeeps had soon lost the heavy Canadian tanks.'

Philip Schlee remembers being given a briefing that morning by Major Mike Blackman: 'And very brief it was,' says Schlee. According to him, Blackman said there would be 'next to no opposition' except, that is, for the German equivalent of the Home Guard.

Schlee says that Blackman told them they would all meet up that night in a forest seventy miles to the north. As it turned out, it took the Allied armies two weeks to reach that point. Schlee says: 'As far as I remember, 1 SAS Regiment had no particular objective in this instance. It was an operation to give the regiment some employment; to act in an ordinary support role on the flank of the Canadian Army and "swan around".

'Each squadron was to advance up a different road. My squadron was commanded by Major Dick Bond who told me I was the officer in charge of Number 1 Section, with three new armoured jeeps, and I would be leading with my column of jeeps all day. Paddy and his HQ jeeps were around supporting all the columns.'

Mayne was certainly told that there were likely to be fortified points on the road to Oldenburg, and several men remember Paddy telling them to be careful. Captain Harrison says he was informed that there could be German paratroopers, but he was more aware of the presence of Hitler Youth whom he says were 'wild-eyed kids', who could prove 'lethal'. In fact, very determined opposition was waiting for the SAS. Unknown to the Allied authorities, members of the German 1 Parachute Division, who fought in Crete, were in the vicinity. This was one of the crack German divisions.

Philip Schlee and the rest of the column were only on the road approximately one hour when his section ran into trouble. 'I was leading the column with my three jeeps up a fairly narrow country road,' Schlee says, 'when we came under fire from a house and a small copse or wood. My sergeant, Schofield, was in the first jeep as gunner with "Jig" Eden as driver. I was in the second jeep with Corporal Ralphs as my gunner, and a third jeep was behind us.

'Sergeant Schofield was immediately shot through the top part of his legs, and the rear gunner in my third jeep was also hit. We returned the fire into the wood and the house, but eventually got out of our jeeps with our small arms, bren, tommy-guns etc. and took to the ditch with the wounded. We were pinned down in the ditch by heavy automatic fire.'

The ditch that Schlee and his men crawled into was deep and waterlogged. The firing from house B and the wood was intense, and the Germans were using machine-guns, as well as Panzer-fausts which were similar to American bazookas, hand-held but not consistently accurate.

Meanwhile, the rest of the column was halted on the road to the rear of Schlee's position with the forward jeep broken down. From the column's position, house A was visible but not house B. The main column was shielded from the threat from within house B and from the small wood surrounding it by house A.

Bond decided that rather than drive up the road where Schlee's three jeeps were abandoned and bullet-ridden, he would walk up the road to investigate. He knew he was relatively safe as long as he stayed on the road, south of house A. David Surrey Dane remembers putting some rounds into house A to discourage anyone from hiding in it. When the bullets struck the roof, a German family came out under a white flag and walked to the SAS column. Bond and his driver, a Czech-Jew named Trooper Lewis, proceeded up the road, while the other men in the main column watched the proceedings. Bond had no experience as a fighting front-line soldier. He had joined the SAS from the Auxiliary Units, the cover name for the organisation hurriedly created by Colonel Colin McVean Gubbins in June 1940 to work in the rear of the German invader, harrying his advancing columns and cutting them off from supplies of water, food and petrol.

Bond left the roadway on the right as he approached house A, and clambered into the ditch, hoping to make his way to Schlee

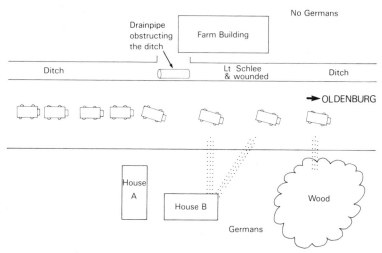

Fig 6 Lt Philip Schlee's map, drawn for the authors, of the scene in which Paddy Blair Mayne gained his fourth DSO

and the wounded (*see map above*). The one obstacle which blocked his way to Schlee was the drainage pipe. He was forced to crawl over it, taking him to road level and leaving him exposed.

At this point, Bond and Lewis made the mistake which cost them their lives. They decided to take a look to estimate the strength of the German position and to establish exactly where the enemy was situated. A German sniper shot each of them in the head, killing them instantly. David Surrey Dane says that when he later looked at the two bodies, there was a clean bullet hole in each forehead and Schlee remembers seeing Bond crawling over the pipe as he was hit. A few minutes later Corporal Ralphs, who was on the south side of the drainage pipe, contacted Schlee to say that the squadron commander and his driver were both dead. Schlee ordered Ralphs to report back to the main column.

As Schlee says: 'This left us without a squadron commander and still in a tricky position, pinned down. We remained in the ditch with our heads down for I don't know how long. There was a tremendous amount of firing including Panzer-faust rockets from the Germans.'

Captain Tim Iredale, who by now had become commander of the leading column, immediately contacted Paddy Mayne by radio. Billy Hull, Mayne's driver, says that when news of Bond's death came over the radio, 'Paddy almost blew-up'. Hull adds: 'Paddy just kept saying, "Poor Dick, poor Dick".' David Surrey Dane recalls Paddy Mayne's jeep 'racing' along the road towards them.

When Mayne arrived at the scene the first man he spoke to was Iredale, who was unable to offer much information on the plight of Schlee and his men. Other personnel in the main column seemed confused about the circumstances of the attack on the jeeps and the death of Bond. Mayne was told that the attack on Schlee's section was swift and decisive but no one was in a position to estimate the enemy strength or his exact position except to say that there was obviously a fortified point somewhere behind house A.

Mayne walked to his jeep and removed the bren and several magazines and began striding up the road. Hull followed him armed with a tommy-gun. 'Mayne was in one of those silent rages,' says Hull. As Mayne approached house A he was fully aware that the only way to change the course of the action was to get a sighting of house B and the nearby wood. He edged his way slowly alongside the side of the house, facing the main column, the bren held at chest height. Hull went inside the building to find some way of bringing fire to bear on the enemy to allow Mayne time to do his 'own thing'. Hull says: 'I went to an upstairs room and fired several bursts towards house B, but the bastards opened up on me and it was all hell let loose. The room I was in was filled with smoke, bullets were ricocheting off the walls and ceiling and in seconds the ceiling was set on fire by tracers.'

Outside, Mayne quickly stepped from the corner of the house and fired short but well-aimed bursts towards house B and the woods. David Surrey Dane says he watched Mayne fire the bren from his shoulder as though it was an automatic rifle. In this short action Paddy Mayne summed up the situation, but it is unlikely that he was in a position to have killed or wounded anyone in house B as mentioned in the citation.

Mayne and Hull left the scene and made for the jeep column.

Mayne had discovered that not only was house B well fortified but there was a rocket team and snipers on the edge of the wood. As Mayne reached the column, men were milling around waiting for his return and still uncertain what to do. Mayne faced them and asked: 'Who wants to have a go?' Several men stepped forward, but Mayne singled out John Scott, who had served with him previously. Schlee says:

'Eventually what do I see but Paddy Mayne coming down the road past me, manning his heavy Browning machine-gun in his jeep, with John Scott as his rear gunner. They were both firing at house B and the wood. He drove straight down the road for quite some way, turned round and came back again firing.'

The man who best knows what happened that morning is John Scott, who was with the SBS and received his Commission in the SAS at the instigation of Paddy Mayne. He says that when Paddy asked for a volunteer, he was probably chosen simply because he was one of the first to step forward. John Scott's version is as follows:

'After Dick Bond was hit, I sent his driver, Trooper Lewis, into the ditch. He was small and I thought he would be able to climb through the drainage pipe and along the ditch. When he was shot I felt very bad about it, since I was the one who ordered him in there. He was a brave man.

'I remember Paddy arriving on the scene racing up the road with his driver and later firing round the side of house A with the bren. He ordered another jeep to come forward for covering fire. He then walked down to the main column and asked the question of us: "Who wants to have a go?" I climbed into the rear of the jeep and Paddy took over the driving. I didn't know what was ahead. There was a coldness about Paddy, and it was that coldness which allowed him to sum things up quickly. Paddy took off up the road and when we passed house A, I began firing the Vickers. I wasn't used to this jeep and the positioning of the weapon and I suppose I was a bit wild with it. Paddy shouted: "The woods – fire at the woods." I turned my attention on the woods. Obviously Paddy was not so concerned about the house. I think he believed there were snipers in the house and they were the ones who got Bond and Lewis, but the major threat was from the area of trees to the side of the house. The Germans must have been more surprised than us. Paddy drove on up the road and turned.

'I jumped into the front of the jeep and grabbed the .50 Browning and Paddy drove back down. I concentrated the Browning on the woods. When we reached Schlee's abandoned jeeps, Paddy stopped our vehicle and jumped out. I did likewise and ran to one of the abandoned jeeps and trained a set of Vickers on the enemy position and began firing. Meanwhile Paddy was lifting people out of the ditch.

'At one stage I shot a German with a very severe stomach wound. This occurred just after Bond had been killed and before Paddy had arrived. I regretted it, but I suppose my nerves were frayed at the time. By the time Paddy got our men out of the ditch, things were quiet and we retreated down the road, some three miles, where we buried Dick Bond and Trooper Lewis at the side of a farmhouse.'

Philip Schlee, David Surrey Dane, Billy Hull and John Scott confirm the circumstances surrounding this episode, but it raises interesting questions about the tactics employed before Paddy Mayne arrived, the calibre of some of the men in that squadron, the advice they were given and the nature of the official citation.

'Major Blackman and Captain Harrison weren't there, but I think they tried to make it something more Hollywood style,' John Scott says. 'I was approached by Derrick Harrison and asked if I would mind if my name wasn't mentioned. I agreed since I didn't think that my part in the action was worth mentioning. I think they wished it to look as if the account was coming from people in higher authority than me.'

John Scott also confirms that the problems which occurred on that morning began in England. He says the regiment was not properly trained for the role given to them in Germany, and there were too many new recruits who were young and inexperienced. Mayne himself was only twenty-nine, but he was a veteran. Both Scott and Surrey Dane say that everyone was of the opinion, as a result of their briefing with Major Blackman, that they were on a 'swan'. Blackman, of course, was only relaying intelligence given him by the Canadians. When Mayne and his men headed along in their sections of jeeps, they were too close together. Scott and Surrey Dane confirm they were both horrified that not only the jeeps but also the sections of jeeps were bunched too closely together for safety and that in the event of a major ambush, they would all have been in mortal danger.

John Scott adds: 'I don't think our objectives were properly outlined. As for the way we were positioned, that morning, I believe the Germans were as surprised as us and that is why only three jeeps were hit. Had the Germans been better prepared, they could have had all of us.'

Dr David Surrey Dane says of the column he was with: 'We were all pretty clueless. We had not much idea of this type of forward reconnaissance work.'

The official citation was written to suggest that Mayne handled the whole matter single-handed, though this was not what was witnessed by Schlee, Surrey Dane and Scott. Hull was not a witness to the final minutes of the action.

Why was Scott asked 'would he mind' if his name was not mentioned? One can only deduce that this was aimed to create the image of Paddy Mayne handling the whole thing on his own with personal danger only to himself. The four witnesses all confirm that the one man who knew exactly how to deal with what was a very difficult situation – one that had not been properly assessed before his arrival on the scene – was Paddy Mayne. His quick thinking, his courage, and what Scott calls his 'coldness' allowed him to make vital decisions with minimum delay. It was a gamble but like everything he did, it was a calculated risk.

Billy Hull talked to Paddy after the war. 'I made the right calculation at the right time,' he told Hull. John Scott, too, talked to him after the event. Scott says: 'He showed me letters from important people about his fourth DSO and then he said, "People think I'm a big mad Irishman but I'm not. I calculate the risks for and against and then have a go."

'What were our chances on that one?' asked Scott. 'Fifty-

fifty,' replied Mayne. 'Christ, I wish you'd told me at the time,' said Scott jokingly.

Certainly many of the men in the main column that morning were new recruits. Also, the recruits were not in the SAS role as it was envisaged before Germany: hit-and-run tactics, sabotage, short-sharp surprise action. They were in the role of ordinary front-line soldiers and as Scott says: 'They really weren't up to that role as they hadn't been trained for it.' Mayne obviously realised that shortcoming when he arrived on the scene to find two men dead – the squadron commander being one of them – and the rest of the column pinned down with others in the ditch and no one capable of reversing the German advantage.

It is ironic that many of the men in the column knew of Mayne before the incident, of his fearsome reputation and his decorations, but had never before seen him in action. David Surrey Dane says: 'Paddy's reputation amongst the younger people was that he was "over the hill" and that he was drinking too much. When he burst into action that day, it was for many a revelation. It was a wonderful demonstration of how the SAS should operate.'

It was this action and the award of the fourth DSO which, because of the nature of the citation, reinforced the view that Paddy Mayne should have been given the VC. Subsequently, many claims were made, whether rightly or wrongly, that this was the supreme example of the prejudice that existed against Mayne.

It is the view of the eyewitnesses, who have talked for the first time, that there was no necessity, whatever the motives, for the citation to be written in such a fashion. Both Scott and Surrey Dane believe that the reality demonstrated once again the sheer soldierly quality and courage of Mayne, reinforcing the claim that he should have been awarded the VC not simply for one action but for the many in which he had been involved.

This was perhaps what Major-General Sir Robert Laycock, then Chief of Combined Operations, was alluding to when he wrote to Paddy Mayne after the war was over:

Combined Operations Headquarters
1A Richmond Terrace
Whitehall SW1

28th August 1945

My Dear Paddy,

I feel I must drop you a line just to tell you how very deeply I appreciate the great honour of being able to address, as my friend, an officer who has succeeded in accomplishing the practically unprecedented task of collecting no less than four DSOs (I am informed that there is another such superman in the Royal Air Force).

You deserve all and more, and, in my opinion, the appropriate authorities do not really know their job. If they did they would have given you a VC as well.

Please do not dream of answering this letter, which brings with it my sincerest admiration and a deep sense of honour in having, at one time, been associated with you.

Yours ever,
Bob Laycock

David Stirling says it was a 'monstrous injustice' that Mayne was not awarded the VC. 'It was the faceless men who didn't want Mayne and the SAS to be given the distinction,' he added.

Paddy would not have seen the citation until some time after the event and his brother, Douglas, has confirmed that Paddy would have preferred a MC rather than a third Bar to his DSO. Others close to him say that he would not have taken issue with the citation simply because he would have wished to avoid embarrassment.

'Then by superlative determination and by displaying gallantry of the very highest degree and in the face of intense enemy machine-gun fire, he lifted the wounded one by one, into the jeep, turned round and drove back to the main body.' It was this last sentence of the penultimate paragraph of the citation which David Surrey Dane finds unacceptable as an account of what happened. He says: 'By the time Paddy hauled Philip Schlee and his men out of the ditch the Germans had been killed or had retreated. By then there appeared to be little danger and there was no machine-gun fire. It would have been stupid and involved unnecessary risks to everyone concerned, if Paddy had attempted the rescue before the Germans were neutralised.

'There is something about this sentence from the citation which smells of bull-shit,' he says. 'I wonder if the assessing officers noticed this? The truth did not need embellishment. It seemed like magic at the time and it still does. I wish some senior officers at the time had pointed out that Paddy was doing this sort of thing all the time in the Western Desert, in Italy and in France over and over again, and that a VC might therefore have been more appropriate than a fourth DSO. It occurs to me that Brigadier Mike Calvert may not have known all that much about Paddy's detailed military past. We knew surprisingly little about his.' At that time Calvert was known as a good soldier, a cheerful, unstuffy brigadier who enjoyed a party in the mess, referred to the Germans as 'Japs' and liked singing a version of 'Bless 'em all' which included the lines: 'Bugger the *Rodney* and bugger the *Hood*, bloody big battleships, no bloody good.' 'I think none of us knew what an outstandingly brave and formidable column commander Mike Calvert had been with Wingate's Chindits.'

Billy Hull had the best opportunity to talk to Mayne about the incident in the years after the war as they lived in the same town and saw each other on occasion for drinks in the British Legion Club. Hull says: 'Paddy never talked much about it, except that he laughed about my predicament. When he told me to go into the house and give covering fire, I knew not to ask any questions. I just listened that morning when he gave me my orders. But when I opened up from the house, Big Blair had the Vickers going. Tracers and rockets hit the house, though I was told that before I arrived some of our lads had fired into the roof. The place was smoking and the ceiling above me was coming to pieces. When I told Blair how quickly I got out of that house, he just laughed. He could always see the funny side of things.'

There is another aspect to the story which, until now, has not been revealed and that concerns an incident involving Blair

Mayne forty-eight hours after the skirmish on the road. David Surrey Dane asked for it to be incorporated in his report for the citation, but it was not used. He says: 'Major Blackman eliminated that from our recommendations [he is referring to himself and John Scott] on the grounds that it was better to concentrate on the one outstanding action. Looking back I wished we had been able to describe it as it occurred.'

The action happened in a forest where Paddy and some men were holding prisoner a large number of German paratroopers. A German sniper had his sights trained on our position and was making life very uncomfortable. The sniper's location was difficult to detect until Paddy moved into action. David Surrey Dane was away making contact with the Canadians at the time of the sniper incident. The story he heard on his return was: 'Bullets hit a mess can and then a tree. Paddy got his Colt .45 out and rose to his feet, crouching. He then began weaving in and out, using the trees for cover, stalking the German sniper. He made the sniper depart. It was a bit like a shoot-out in a Western.'

After that incident Lieutenant Surrey Dane, Captain Iredale, Lance-Corporal Bell and Lieutenant Grierson were returning from a recce through a dense wood of conifer saplings when they were fired on. The man firing at this group was not a German, but one of the SAS men waiting for the recce party to return. Fortunately for Iredale and Grierson, who were shot and wounded, and Surrey Dane and Bell, someone else realised what was happening and discouraged the machine-gunner from continuing.

The incident occurred because the SAS did not have a front line and tended to operate on the basis of very swift reaction. Paddy Mayne was faced with a dilemma. There was no doctor with his party and he was sitting in a wood with German prisoners and having to contend with the Germans, intent on overrunning his group. A decision was required quickly, if Tim Iredale was not to lose a leg and Ronnie Grierson not to bleed to death. Mayne decided that the best course of action was to approach the enemy with a white flag in the hope that they would provide a medic. In typical fashion several men volunteered for the job.

Because Mayne's position in the wood was not the most formidable, he sent Surrey Dane off to find the Canadians and bring back transport for the prisoners he was holding and fuel for the jeeps so that he could make a speedy exit from his position whatever the outcome. Surrey Dane remembers the scene before he left:

'The soldier who had seriously wounded the two officers was very upset at what had happened. It happens in all regiments and in this instance it could well have been fatal. He was filled with remorse and insisted that he drive a jeep with Tim Iredale in it, under a white flag to the German lines. It was a brave thing to do, and he did it.'

As it turned out, the second-in-command of the German unit contacted was a doctor who agreed to return in the jeep to the British lines and also to remove Grierson for medical treatment. When the doctor arrived, he had a look at Grierson and told Mayne that he would see that both wounded would receive medical treatment. Mayne knew what often happened to wounded SAS men at the hands of the Germans and in particular of the SS. The only thing that reassured him was that the German doctor had a rank which placed him in a considerable position of authority. Nonetheless Mayne took him aside and, as only he could do, gave a chilling warning that if either of the wounded men were harmed, he would hunt the doctor down and kill him when the war ended.

There could be an unusual twist to this story. The medical doctor captured by Mayne and his men in the desert is believed to be the doctor who agreed to look after Iredale and Grierson. If this is true, Mayne knew exactly who he was and where he could later be found but made no demonstration to his men of this knowledge. In the official citation the incident of the stalking of the sniper was not mentioned.

One factor, which has yet to be examined, was the aftermath of the events which took place on 9 April after the shooting at the houses A and B. After the event Mayne withdrew the column of jeeps three miles towards the Allied lines. Would he have made this decision if in fact their objective was Oldenburg? We raised this point with John Scott and David Surrey Dane.

They agreed that Mayne was concerned about the fighting potential of the squadron in the role it had been asked to adopt. When Bond was hit, the main column remained static until Mayne arrived. Billy Hull remembers Paddy Mayne expressing anger about the way in which his men were used. Hull will go so far as to say, and so will others, particularly the veterans of the time, that they were really being used as 'cannon fodder', in front of heavy armour, in jeeps not intended for infantry-like assault.

With narrow roads like the one referred to in the citation, jeeps were vulnerable and, as John Scott says, 'a properly laid ambush could have wiped them all out'. Equally important they were ambushed by crack troops after being told that they would simply meet remnants of the Heimwehr (Home Guard). Major Blackman, when compiling his Intelligence Reports on the 9 April action and the wounding of Iredale and Grierson, wrote:

'It now became evident that the enemy opposition was far stronger than had been anticipated by the Staff of 4 Division (Canadian), and also there was no sign of the Canadian armour following closely on the heels of the SAS. Consequently, bearing this in mind, and with the mounting casualties of the Squadron, the Colonel decided to withdraw his force to the British lines and make his report. This was achieved but not without the loss of Trooper Cooper killed and SSM Clarke wounded by snipers.'

As a final consideration of the events of 9 April and the subsequent citation, it must be said that the way in which the citation was written was in response to the way Mike Blackman and Derrick Harrison, and others including David Stirling and Mike Calvert, perceived prejudice towards Paddy Mayne in regard to the award of the Supreme Decoration for Valour.

The war was coming to an end, and Blackman and Harrison may well have seen the 9 April episode as the final opportunity to correct the balance in favour of their Commanding Officer. Derrick Harrison, in particular, whose bravery at Les Ormes and in the Desert was outstanding, would, to this day, say that his contribution was little compared to that made by Paddy Mayne. Another significant factor is the manner in which many citations were written. There was a formula which is evidenced by the following citation written by Paddy Mayne, recommending Tony Marsh for a Military Cross for an action on 10 April 1945. The similarities in structure and style to the citation written by Blackman and Harrison are unmistakable:

> When attacking Esterwegen, the point section of the leading troop drove into the village without enemy interference, but the remainder of the troop was ambushed by severe crossfire from automatic weapons and bazookas from houses on both sides of the road entering the village. An ugly situation developed due to the proximity of the houses to the road and to the lack of cover. Casualties were sustained.
>
> Major Marsh immediately took command of his ambushed forces and at considerable peril to himself, drove up and down the fire-covered stretch of road issuing orders for the counter-attacking of the different enemy strong-points. In this, he was completely successful and finally captured the village, killing 50–60 of the enemy and taking 150 prisoners.
>
> Throughout the action he showed complete disregard for his own safety and his success was directly attributable to his exemplary courage and leadership which inspired and sustained his men in a situation which was highly critical.

18
'Blue-Pencil Idiots'

ON 12 April 1945 Blair Mayne took his men to Lorup, after they had killed approximately 100 Germans and taken 300 prisoner.

He then decided to merge the two squadrons into one under the command of Major Tony Marsh. The intention was to use the one squadron in conjunction with the Canadian Armoured Recce element on the right flank of Canadian 4 Armoured Division. He believed that, because of the nature of the landscape, the stubborn resistance of the enemy, the presence of crack German soldiers and the fact that many roads and bridges were cratered, no deep penetration, as had been initially envisaged, was possible. Consequently, Marsh and his men found themselves operating alongside the tanks and earned themselves the affectionate title: 'Our little friends in the mechanised mess tins'.

The squadron remained in this supportive role to the tanks until it was withdrawn to the area of Divisional HQ, north-east of Friesoythe and three miles south of the Kusten Canal. On 23 April command reverted from Divisional to Corps control and the squadron was placed under an independent Canadian Armoured Brigade with the objective of effecting a breakthrough due north between Leer and Oldenburg, north of the Kusten Canal.

On Sunday 29 April Mayne and his jeeps moved forward to the area of Westerscheps with the Brigade HQ at Osterscheps.

It was here that the squadron, under the control of Tony Marsh, pushed along the road towards Godenshalt. The roads were mined and the men were obliged to operate for some time on foot.

John Scott remembers an episode, involving himself and Marsh, which Paddy Mayne sorted out very quickly and in a fashion which indicated his concern for his men and his awareness of the pressures on them. 'We were in a village close to Oldenburg,' John Scott says. 'I was in a house with Tony Marsh. Pat Riley was also there. We were under sniper fire. Tony Marsh ordered me to take a bunch of young recruits and, on foot, go through the houses of this village one by one and flush out the enemy. I suggested to him that maybe this was a job for more experienced men. Marsh was very insistent. I was exhausted and I was worried about taking a bunch of inexperienced lads into such a situation. Suddenly Paddy Mayne arrived. 'He knew immediately what was happening. He said to me: "John, go sit in the jeep." As I left the house, Paddy looked very angry. I sat in the jeep for some time before Paddy came out. I know he gave Tony Marsh a severe dressing-down. Paddy knew what we had all been through and was obviously not going to allow Tony to push us into an impossible situation. Paddy sent for the Belgian SAS to come forward and assist us.'

The Belgians continued to operate alongside the squadron until the cessation of hostilities on this sector of the Front on 4 May. Of all the SAS-taken prisoners during this push to the Kusten Canal, all were released by the Allies. Lieutenant Gordon Davidson and Sergeant Youngman, who were in a prisoner-of-war camp, escaped and later went back with the Guards Armoured Brigade to release the remainder of the men captured with them.

Major John Tonkin, who was with 'D' Squadron, crossed the Rhine on 26 March and moved up to Brunen. His men faced similar opposition to those under Paddy Mayne. Tonkin later wrote that the OC of a Commando Brigade called the SAS 'blue-pencil idiots' for daring to go into the woods to ferret out Germans without the support of tanks.

On 12 April Tonkin assembled what he called a 'curiosity

party' – composed of himself, Lieutenant Morris, an officer from the Inns of Court Regiment, and Sergeant Tommy Corps. They went into woods to investigate a wrecked train and discovered that it was loaded with V2 rockets. There was also an undamaged chemical factory. After clearing the wood, Tonkin and his squadron headed for a village which was reported to be under the control of the SS. The SAS jeeps advanced in open formation across fields towards the village. They came under considerable sniper fire to which they replied with their Vickers and Brownings. They aimed to set alight a house from which most of the German fire was being directed.

Tonkin's report of the incident ends: 'Eight SS men were brewed up in the house. The Squadron withdrew with no casualties, having taken fifty-two prisoners and killed or wounded twelve of the enemy.'

In the midst of it all, there was always time for humour. On Thursday 12 April John Tonkin filed this report:

This day will go down as being the greatest in the Squadron's history. At 15.00 hrs, alone and without any supporting arms, it captured, at great risk to the personnel involved, a German Baggage. This was an attractive corporal in the Luftwaffe. Sgt Valentine showed great bravery in that he searched her kit. She was removed as rapidly as possible to a prisoner-of-war cage by Squadron Commander. There were no casualties.

In these final weeks of the war Mayne adopted his constant roving role, accompanied frequently by Lance-Corporal Hull and Trooper Williams. During this period there were other episodes for which Hull can no longer supply dates, but his memory of them and the part his commander played are still vivid in his mind. He remembers driving the jeep along a country road early one morning when he was flagged down by two SAS troopers. Mayne was pleased to see the men and it gave him the opportunity of asking them how the battle was developing in their area. The troopers indicated that 'Colonel Mayne might care for some breakfast'. 'I don't know about me,' laughed Mayne, 'but Hull here is ready for food at any time of the day.' They directed Mayne to a nearby farmhouse where two sections of jeeps were parked. In the open were about fifty German prisoners, many of them dishevelled. Mayne stepped from his jeep and went on a quick tour of the farmhouse and outbuildings. He was keen to know about the security of the area and where the section commanders had placed their men. With his arrival there was a marked change of attitude around the farmhouse. Hull noticed that, as soon as Mayne appeared, men were seen to scurry off to pick up weapons that had been left either in jeeps or against the side walls of the farmhouse. Mayne completed his scrutiny of the area by examining a large but empty cattle pen close to the farm outbuildings. Some of the ragged and emaciated German prisoners turned to watch Paddy as he strode into the centre of the cattle pen and proceeded to examine its dimensions. He walked from the pen and summoned one of the section commanders. 'Put the prisoners in there,' he ordered. 'They'll be easier to watch and easier to control if anything happens.' Mayne turned as if to walk away and then looked again at the Germans, 'When they're in the pen, throw them some biscuits,' he said quietly to his subordinate.

Hull and Williams followed Mayne as he made for the farmhouse. Once inside, he turned to a junior officer who was sitting at a rough wooden table drinking tea. 'Have you checked this area? Is it secure? Where have you set the perimeter?' The young officer gulped on his tea. Hull and Williams moved into a corner of the room to watch the proceedings. They were suddenly aware that Paddy Mayne's demeanour had changed. His face bore that heavy threatening look which boded ill for any soldier not living up to Mayne's concept of SAS standards. Another indication of his annoyance was the way he paced up and down the floor, his hands behind his back. The young officer tried to apologise but Mayne was grimly silent. Hull and Williams did not have long to wait for the explosion. Mayne walked to the table and slammed one large fist on it sending crockery spinning on to the stone floor. As the sound of breaking cups and plates ceased, Mayne lowered his huge frame until his head was almost level with that of the young officer. 'That's not good enough,' he roared. There was silence. The young man made to get up but Mayne stretched out, and with controlled force, laid his hand on his shoulder and lowered him back into his chair. 'Make sure those prisoners are secure and send out one of the jeeps on a recce. I have no wish to be surprised by Jerries.' With that he released his grip. 'Yes, sir', the officer was out of the room in seconds. Outside he could be heard bellowing orders to his men. Hull decided that there was a sufficient lull in the proceedings to allow him to confidently approach the fire to prepare a 'brew-up'. Meanwhile Mayne stood at a downstairs window watching events outside. He remained there until a jeep with three men was seen taking off down the lane towards the main road.

Mayne was still not satisfied. He suggested that two other jeeps should be sent in alternative directions. 'It's better to be safe than sorry,' he told the officer in charge. Mayne knew German patrols were scattered widely over the surrounding area. Sitting in an isolated farmhouse with none of the men in an alert role was asking for trouble. As Hull points out, Mayne's behaviour illustrated his sixth sense for danger.

The first jeep that Mayne sent out was winding its way along a narrow road when the driver brought the vehicle to an abrupt halt. His companions asked what was wrong and were told that there was movement in the ditch. The driver drew attention to a ditch at the far side of an open field about sixty yards from their position. The rear gunner surveyed the landscape and said he was unable to detect anything. The front gunner with his hands on the .50 Browning swivelled the large machine-gun until it was pointing directly at the spot.

There was a short debate about whether a few bursts from the Vickers and the Browning might be an appropriate way of deciding if anyone was hiding in the ditch. The driver suggested that it was probably only one man and it might be better if they took him prisoner. As there was no means of driving the jeep into the field because of the deep drain running between the field and the roadway, the three men dismounted from the jeep and decided to proceed across the field. The driver carried a bren, another a tommy-gun, and the third man a pistol. Half-way across the open field, the three debated whether this was at all a sensible venture. There was no movement from the ditch and they were leaving themselves exposed. It was agreed they abort the mission. As they approached the drain which they had to negotiate before they could climb back on to the roadway, they heard messages coming from the jeep radio. They scrambled back on to the road and began replacing their weapons in the jeep.

But as they were boarding the vehicle rifles appeared over the ditch on the other side of the roadway. Before they had time even to consider being heroic a German officer appeared and walked towards the jeep, a Luger pistol in his hand. He was followed by six German paratroopers, some armed with rifles, others with Schmeissers. A smile creased the officer's face. In good English he said: 'You are members of the Special Air Service'. The three men showed no recognition of this use of SAS. 'It's all right, I know who you are. While you were out there I was listening to your messages.' The three SAS men were quickly divested of their weapons and led away. These men were later released, but they were not to know at that time what use was about to be made of their jeep, or the fact that the radio messages had revealed the whereabouts of a SAS Colonel who had once figured in a German document as 'Colonel Kaine'.

Back at the farmhouse, Mayne was treated to a meal prepared by Hull over the open fire. Afterwards, he rested in a chair without exchanging conversation. Now and again he walked to the door and opened it and, after a brief glance outside, he returned to his chair. He even went upstairs and summoned an officer to 'Get a man upstairs to cover the laneway.' Hull knew this was one of those times when it was best to say nothing. He kept himself busy for the next couple of hours, cleaning a bren, a tommy-gun and Mayne's Colt .45, occasionally stopping to make tea. Everything was to change quickly.

Hull had just finished preparing a light lunch when the trooper upstairs shouted that one of the jeeps was on the roadway. Mayne got out of his chair. 'Christ, it's full of Jerries,' came the voice from upstairs. The first person to react was Mayne. He rushed to the side of the fireplace, grabbed a bren and slammed a magazine into it. He bounded up the wooden staircase, his large shoulders banging against the walls. Within seconds it was apparent that the Germans were in no ordinary jeep. They brought a Browning and twin Vickers into action. Bullets tore through the wooden door of the farmhouse, shattered the downstairs windows, ripped chunks out of the walls and ricocheted around the rooms.

The jeep was stationary about half-way along the lane. This afforded a clear view of the farmhouse but not of the other jeeps standing near the outbuildings or the prisoners in the cattle pen. The farmhouse was the main target and the SAS men positioned near the outbuildings were unable to affect the action or determine the strength of the enemy. Downstairs Williams was on the floor and Hull was blindly firing his Thompson raised above his head to the level of one of the windows. Mayne was firing the bren in short bursts, using a favourite technique. He shouted for a box of bren magazines, which Hull dragged across the floor and up the staircase. Mayne kept up a withering fire on the lane. He needed time. He shouted to the men outside to organise and encircle the lane. Three SAS men moved one of their jeeps close to the farmhouse firing into the lane as they positioned the vehicle. Their skill with the Vickers and the Browning was unparalleled and the Germans abandoned the captured jeep and took to the ditch. As they ran for cover, Mayne spotted an officer and four other ranks. The two SAS jeeps on recce arrived at the top of the lane and poured fire into the ditches on both sides of the abandoned jeep. In seconds, a handkerchief attached to a rifle appeared over the top of one ditch. Mayne's voice bellowed from his window: 'Stop firing'.

Mayne handed the bren to the trooper who was with him throughout the action and told him to keep it trained on the German position. He took out his pistol and went downstairs. What was left of the front door he flung open and strode outside, followed by Hull.

'The German officer and his men were being led up the lane by our boys,' Hull remembers. 'Blair waited until they were within yards of him and he then walked up to the Jerry officer and stared at him. Blair held the pistol by his side. He told us to take the newly captured lot into the house and ordered that the other prisoners in the pen be handed over to the Canadians as quickly as possible, because they were too much of a liability. He ordered that two jeeps be kept permanently on standby at the junction of the lane and the roadway.'

Once the German officer and his men were inside the farmhouse, Mayne gesticulated that they should drop their hands and sit on the flagstone floor. The officer made to remonstrate but Mayne reached out, placed a hand on his left shoulder and pushed him gently to the floor. Mayne's first duty was to find out what had happened to his three men who were obviously prisoners; in German he asked the officer if he could speak English and received a negative. An interpreter was sent for. Ironically it turned out to be a member of the SAS who was both German and Jewish. The interpreter conducted a conversation with the German officer while Mayne watched at a discreet distance. Mayne's knowledge of German was not sufficient to allow him to understand the detail of what was being exchanged. After several minutes his tolerance dropped. He walked to the interpreter and laid his hand firmly on his right shoulder.

'Ask the bastard what he's done with my men?' The menace in Mayne's voice conveyed itself to the German officer who removed his gaze from the interpreter to the floor. The interpreter continued to ask questions in a halting fashion. The German continued to stare at the floor never once looking at Mayne. The interpreter turned to Mayne: 'Our lads were taken away for interrogation. This guy says it's nothing to do with him.' Mayne raised himself to his full height and took out his pistol. 'You tell this bastard if he doesn't come up with a better story than that, I'll blow his brains out.' There was silence in the room. Mayne holstered his pistol, walked across the room and sat at a pine dining-table, his gaze firmly fixed on the officer and his men.

The interpreter finally stood up and approached his Colonel. There was tension in the room and no one seemed prepared to move a muscle or even whisper a thought. The interpreter outlined how the three SAS men were captured but pointed out that the German officer was not the one who captured them. He was merely given the jeep. The interpreter continued: 'After our lads were captured they were taken to a Jerry HQ and interrogated. This guy was given the jeep and told to come and get you.'

At that Mayne slammed his Colt .45 on the table. The interpreter sensed disbelief in Paddy Mayne's face. 'In fact, sir,' he continued, 'he knows your name and rank and he even knows that you were a famous rugby player.'

Mayne suddenly looked embarrassed. He withdrew his hand from the handle of the Colt leaving it sitting on the table. He then rose to his feet and to the assembled men in the room said: 'Hold this group here, we'll decide what to do with them later.' As an afterthought he added: 'I hope for their sake that my lads are all right.' He turned and walked out of the room. Billy Hull remembers the look on the faces of the SAS men in the room.

The three captured SAS men under questioning revealed nothing of the whereabouts of the farmhouse. The position of their jeep and the radio messages were sufficient to encourage the Germans to search for others. There can be little doubt that at least one of the messages revealed the identity of Colonel Paddy Mayne, but not perhaps the strength of his position. We will never know the exact thinking of the Germans except that one armoured SAS jeep may well have been considered sufficient to deal with a farmhouse which from the roadway did not seem well defended. Mayne mentioned the episode to Hull later that day. He was surprised that the Germans found him so easily. He left the farmhouse the next morning with orders to hand the German prisoners over to the Canadians. Did that happen in respect of the group who set out to kill Mayne? 'Who knows?' says Hull.

Once again Mayne set off on one of his treks through the countryside, checking on the actions and whereabouts of his units. As dawn was breaking he drove away from the farmhouse with Hull and Wiliams in the rear of the jeep. In this and other respects he was unorthodox. He was never one to stand on ceremony or 'pull' rank. He was always willing to do the other man's job even if that was driving a jeep. In Sicily, his men often thought he was too close to the action. They worried that they might lose a brilliant commander for the sake of a task which any of them would gladly have undertaken just to keep him alive. His men demonstrated a protectiveness towards him but rarely expressed it in words.

After a few miles he spotted a deserted farmhouse and suggested to Hull it was time for breakfast. In joking about Billy Hull's appetite, which was huge for a man much smaller than Mayne, what particularly pleased him was Hull's liking for fried eggs. [It is an Ulster trait.] Hull was detailed to go into the farmhouse to light a fire, fry some eggs and make a 'brew-up'. Williams was left to guard the lane while Mayne sat at a table in the farmhouse sending and receiving messages on his radio. Hull remembers the eggs 'sizzling nicely on the pan' when Mayne grabbed a tommy-gun off the table. As he made for the door he looked back momentarily at Hull.

'That glance was enough for me,' says Hull. Mayne got quickly into the driver's seat of the jeep and Hull alongside him. Not a word was exchanged as Mayne hurriedly started the engine. As the jeep moved off Williams chased after it, yelling to the Colonel 'to wait for him'. Mayne slowed enough to allow him to tumble awkwardly into the rear of the vehicle, and then accelerated towards the main road. Hull and Williams said nothing, though it must have been apparent to both of them that Mayne had something very urgent in mind. They could not know it, but one of the radio messages had informed him of the presence of a German convoy. After five minutes he pulled the vehicle sharply off the road and into a wooded area. The jeep negotiated the path to a small clearing which significantly afforded a view of a roadway and in particular of an 'S' bend. Mayne reversed the jeep into a clump of bushes with the .50 Browning on the front of the vehicle pointing towards the bend. 'Get this jeep camouflaged,' he shouted to Williams. 'Hull, get the bren and a box of mags and get yerself on to that rise.'

The 'rise' Mayne was talking about was ten yards from the jeep and it also afforded a clear view of the roadway about seventy-five yards from their position. As Hull removed the bren and the box of mags from the jeep, Mayne turned to him: 'Don't fire until I tell you.' Billy Hull ran to the rise and lined up the gun on the bend. This was another of those times not to ask questions. Mayne was in a determined mood. He helped Williams place branches across the front of the jeep, allowing just enough space for the Browning to move freely when necessary. Hull could see that Mayne was clinically preparing an ambush.

Williams was busy breaking branches in the clearing when the sound of half-tracks was heard in the distance. Hull remembers thinking: 'Jesus, there could be tanks on the way and here's Mayne about t'take them on with a Browning.' Mayne was sitting in the jeep, his large hands on the Browning. Hull recalls seeing Mayne's 'large beaming face' through the foliage surrounding the jeep. Williams was also aware of the approach of the enemy, so he removed a Schmeisser from the jeep and ran to a point not far from Hull. The air was filled with the sound of German soldiers singing. 'It was an eerie sound,' says Hull, 'the singing and the drone of the half-tracks. Mayne looked as though he had been hewn out of County Down granite.' Hull waited, his finger playing nervously with the trigger of the machine-gun. He knew Mayne preferred the bren to be fired in accurate short bursts – no firing off full magazines! The half-tracks were soon in view, open-top vehicles filled with rowdy soldiers. Hull says he and Williams wondered when Mayne would open up, but nothing happened. They both thought that maybe Mayne had fallen asleep. As the leading tracks were almost out of sight and the 'S' bend was tight with vehicles, the .50 Browning came into action. Hull and Williams did not need any signal. The big Browning, with its large ammunition belt winding into the metal box, was tearing through the bullet supply. Mayne was panning his fire backwards and forwards on the 'S' bend. The singing was replaced with the screams and cries of the wounded. German troopers scrambled out of the three-tonners on to the roadway. Dead lay bullet-ridden in the open vehicles and wounded littered the roadway. The suddenness of the attack caused panic.

As Mayne intended, vehicles were wedged on the bend, abandoned by their drivers. Hull reloaded the bren time after time. Germans who escaped into ditches began returning fire. Hull remembers looking towards Mayne who seemed to be smiling and enjoying the power of the Browning as his bullets tore into the German troops.

As the Browning rounds ran out, Mayne shouted to Williams to reverse the jeep and reload the machine-gun. Mayne sprinted across the clearing to Hull's position and took hold of the bren, and Hull crept to where Williams had left the Schmeisser. At least fifty German dead and wounded were sprawled along the roadway in front of the trucks. Some of them were hit as they climbed out of the half-tracks, others while trying to find shelter in the ditches. The survivors were suddenly directing a withering fire into the clearing. Bullets whistled through the trees and tore into the branches, sending splinters in every direction. Williams reversed the jeep and began reloading the Browning. The bren was soon out of ammunition; so was the Schmeisser. Enemy soldiers under covering fire were making their way up the hillside. Mayne knew that, even with the Browning back in action, the element of surprise was now gone and it was only a matter of time before he was surrounded. He shouted to Hull to 'get the hell out of it'. The two of them dodged the bullets and reached the jeep. In minutes they were out of the wood.

As they drove away, Mayne was silent, although Hull and Williams knew from his facial expression that he'd enjoyed the encounter. He was never a man to boast or to spend time analysing an operation after its completion. He drove back to the farmhouse where the Germans had attempted to kill him the previous day.

As the jeep approached the building, he turned to his two companions and with his penchant for brevity remarked: 'I always believed the Germans knew who I was and given half a chance would have a go.' His expression and tone suggested to Hull that he had just exacted his own revenge. At the farmhouse they discovered that the German Jew who had acted as an interpreter two days earlier was badly wounded. He was in a patrol which had been ambushed several miles south of the farm. He pleaded with Mayne not to send him to a German hospital. Mayne ordered a jeep forward and told the driver that at all costs he should get the injured man back to the Canadian lines, even though there was a chance the man might die on the journey, Mayne understood his fear. He never lacked consideration for those who trusted him.

After a meal at the farm Mayne said he would like to take a look at an area several miles north of their position. He added that he had been told by radio that there were several German units in that vicinity with snipers covering the roads. With Mayne at the wheel, everything seemed quiet as they travelled along at a modest pace. Hull and Williams took the opportunity to relax and that meant, as Mayne later put it, 'they dozed off'. Mayne also availed himself of the peacefulness of the countryside. He was to admit later that for him it was 'simply half-asleep'. Hull says he was rudely awakened by the sudden acceleration of the jeep. To the right of the jeep was a German machine-gun posted on a tripod in a ditch and three Germans sitting around it. Hull and Williams 'froze' as did the enemy, but not Mayne. He drove the jeep into the ditch and over the three enemy soldiers.

'I felt the vibrations as the vehicle ploughed over the three Germans,' Hull says. 'Paddy reversed it, the Germans were writhing on the ground. He stopped the jeep, reached across, took hold of the Schmeisser and fired several bursts into the wounded men. There wasn't much left.' Five minutes later he turned to his comrades and with a glint in his eye said: 'In future keep yer eyes open.'

Two hours afterwards they were grateful for that warning. Mayne stopped the jeep on the outskirts of a village and decided to consult his map. He laid the map on the bonnet of the vehicle and began to scrutinise it. Without warning a bullet tore through the map and richocheted off the bonnet. Mayne jumped into the driver's seat and drove the jeep under cover. He took out a pair of binoculars and scoured the village roof-tops for a sniper. He turned to Hull: 'You say you're a good shot. Well, the bastard is in the bell tower of the church so we'll see what you can do.' Hull sat in the jeep and looked at him. Mayne was being mischievous and Hull knew it. Mayne turned the jeep and told Hull to get into the rear and take hold of the Vickers.

Mayne then drove towards the village square keeping to a path which kept the jeep out of the line of fire of the sniper. As the jeep came into the square Mayne shouted to Hull: 'Have a go, Billy.' Mayne kept the jeep moving as Hull fired the twin Vickers. 'You know,' says Billy, 'there wasn't a centimetre left in that steeple for the bastard t'hide. I almost played a tune on the bells. That Jerry bastard must have thought a Spitfire was headin' for him, and all the time big Mayne's just laughin'. There wasn't a cheep from that tower after I'd put nearly a hundred rounds int' it.' Mayne's bout of laughing continued for some time after the incident.

In the evening Mayne told Williams to watch out for a farmhouse where they could spend the night. His request was no sooner made than they turned a bend on the road and came under sniper fire from a two-storey house some seventy yards away. Mayne drove the jeep into a ditch and told the others to find cover. Hull opened up on the windows of the house with his Schmeisser. As he was reloading, Mayne told him: 'You just keep your head down, I'll try to get behind them.' He then turned to Williams: 'Get back to the jeep and give them a piece of the bren.' Mayne crawled off into the undergrowth and the last thing Billy saw was his Colonel armed with a carbine, heading into a wooded area which almost encircled the farmhouse. Shooting from the house ceased after Williams emptied two bren magazines into the downstairs and upstairs windows. A short time later Billy saw the front door of the house open. He levelled his submachine-gun on the doorway. There was still no sign of Paddy Mayne. Out of the house came an old man and woman with a beautiful young girl. Before Billy could rise from his crouched position, Paddy Mayne appeared and walked casually towards the strangers, his carbine by his side. 'It had obviously been Paddy's intention to go through the front door because he was so close to the house,' says Hull. The old woman explained to Paddy Mayne, who had just enough German, albeit with an Ulster brogue, that the German snipers had fled after they were subjected to concentrated fire. The Germans believed they were outnumbered. There had been eight Germans in the house but the accuracy of the fire from

Hull and Williams suggested there there were more than two British soldiers outside.

The woman was agitated and frightened, and the girl clung desperately to her. The old man remained silent. In a rare display of gentleness on the battlefield, Paddy Mayne reached forward and stroked the girl's hair. He spent that night in the house with his men and was well fed.

19

Final Days of the War

WHO DARES WINS

THERE was always a diversion in which there was space for Paddy Mayne's humour to find expression. At 17.00 hrs one day Mayne and his companions were in a clearing. Paddy was deep in thought and Hull was frying eggs. The meagre meal was eaten in silence, and Hull then decided that something was required for dessert; but all he could find were tins of sultana pudding. He informed Paddy of the limited choice and received the reply: 'Rustle it up.' Hull hesitated. 'Sir, I've had this stuff cold, I've had it with milk. What about me frying it?' Mayne laughed and Billy applied himself to the pan. He was merrily frying it when a tracer bullet burned a hole in the tree beside him. 'Jesus, I froze. I looked round quickly and there was no Paddy Mayne. Where do y' think he was? He was lying under the jeep with Williams, laughing his balls off at me. So up goes the pan and the next minute I'm in there beside them.'

The following morning, Hull decided it was safe enough to go into the woods to relieve himself. His telling of the story which follows was to remain a favourite with Mayne in the mess:

'I needed to do something large – right. But I says t' m'self: "That sniper might still be out there somewhere so I'll just take the Schmeisser in case of an emergency." I crept between the trees until I found a good spot. So here's me, the Schmeisser cocked in one hand and me unbuttoning my trousers with the other. Well, I've just done the needful when I hear a rustle overhead. My first thought was: "That's a pigeon." Anyway, I looks up and there above me is this German. He's strapped to the tree and he's holding a rifle. They always strapped themselves in trees to stop them fallin' if they dozed off. Well, I pointed my Schmeisser at that bastard and before he knew it, I had nearly cut him in half. As I was firing, I fell backwards. What do y' think I landed in!?'

On one afternoon towards the end of April, Mayne spotted a ragged German convoy. Much of it was made up of horse-drawn carts loaded with supplies and explosives. Mayne radioed to a jeep in the rear to come forward but did not wait for them to arrive. He drove his own jeep under cover at the side of the road and waited for the Germans to pass. He checked the Browning while Hull waited with the twin Vickers. As the convoy of carts and old lorries passed, Mayne opened up.

'We tore the hell out of them,' says Hull, 'the carts and lorries were explodin'. We ran out of ammunition. They didn't even have time to fire back. They were in disarray. They didn't know what hit them. Big Mayne reversed the jeep out of the action and loaded up, then went back for more. The roadway was a shambles. Bodies all over the place. Other jeeps arrived and took over from us.'

As they drove away from the burning convoy, Mayne handed Hull a cigarette and to Hull's delight it turned out to be a Gallagher's 'Blue' from the Gallagher's tobacco factory in Belfast. Mayne pulled the jeep off the road to allow time for a smoke and parked at the rear of a farmhouse which looked deserted. As they lit their cigarettes Mayne turned to Hull. 'I know what's goin' through your evil mind.' Hull says Mayne was referring to the fact that Billy was always on the look-out for loot and Mayne at this moment suspected that Billy intended searching the farmhouse for booty. With a laugh Mayne got out of the jeep and walked to the farmhouse door and opened it. Hull was behind him, a cigarette in one hand and a Schmeisser held casually in the other. Mayne nonchalantly opened the door. To his astonishment four German paratroopers were seated at a table having a meal. They were as surprised to see Mayne's huge frame as he was to see them. Their weapons were lying about the room. Mayne had his .45 pistol out before any one of them could move off a chair. Hull says he was not so much astonished to see the Germans as much as the food in front of them. On the table was a plentiful supply of wine and roast duck and a variety of cheeses. Mayne was not concerned with the food. He moved further into the room and, in German, ordered the Jerries out of the house. Outside, he lined them up and then asked in German if they had concealed weapons. German paratroopers often kept knives hidden in their clothing. Mayne could not remember the German word for knife and he turned to Hull whose knowledge of German was limited to key words. Sure enough it was one German word which was in Hull's vocabulary: 'Messer'. Mayne turned to Hull and laughed: 'I'm wonderin' which of us has the University education?' The Germans were noncommital about concealed knives. Mayne stepped in front of one of the paratroopers and, with a blow to the chin, floored the man. He then stood over him and said in German: 'That's for telling lies.' The German reached his hand into his boot and withdrew a knife. The ever-watchful Paddy had spotted the outline of the knife on the outside of the leather boot.

Through the campaign in Germany, Mayne lost contact with many of the men who had fought under him, but it shows the concern they had for him that, even in official or personal letters, his name was always included. One of the bravest of men in 1 SAS was Major Harry Poat. In one of his letters at the time, and in the map (*see opp.*) he drew to indicate the actions his men were undertaking, he describes the kind of action very familiar to Paddy Mayne. It took place near Minden on 8 April 1945.

My dear Mike or John,
I do not know which of you is adjutant at the moment; if it is Mike I expect you are still pale, sallow and worn, while our faces are 'brown'.
I am writing this to try and give you an idea of what is happening here, and would like you to forward this letter to Paddy, as I believe he is off in battle, but have no definite news of him or 'C' Squadron, and would like it very much. We are fairly well, and the men are in good form. The

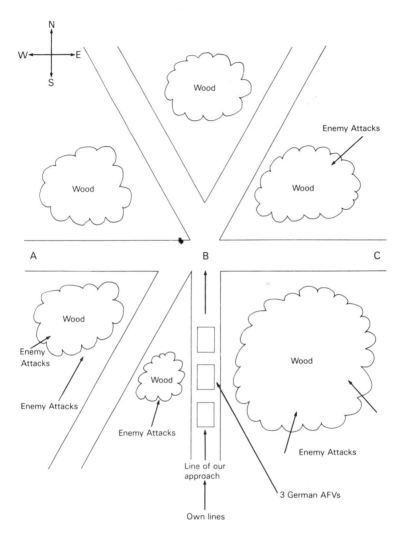

Fig 7 Major Harry Poat's map, sent to Paddy, to indicate the ambush of SAS troops by the Germans on the road to Nienburg, April 1945: map ref. 076421, sheet N3 (Minden), 1/100,000

fighting is very hard and we have mixed it many times with the Hun, and they are all SS, the real thing and no doubt about it, although they no longer have an organised defence, they are fighting cleverly in a guerrilla role and I can assure you they are far better at it than our friends, the Maquis. As you have heard by signal, I hope, we have suffered casualties and on each occasion the chaps have fought magnificently, and killed many SS and captured a large number. Each troop, that is Tonkin, Wellsted and Muirhead, have had three actions each. Wellsted's had a sticky one last Sunday and suffered casualties.

Captain Wellsted: Wounded in both legs below the knees, but very cheerful and I think will be OK. He tried to advance through a hail of bullets to a wounded man. Is now in hospital.

Tpr Owen: A 2 SAS signaller lent to us. Shot through both arms and is now in hospital.

Sgt DuVivier: Wounded in the leg, not very serious, was able to walk about, drove jeep back, is now in hospital.

Tpr Blakeney: Killed, shot through stomach and head.

Tpr Clyde: Killed, German bazooka landed about two yards from his jeep. His head was nearly blown off.

Tpr Davies: Killed, body wound.

Tpr Backhouse: Wounded, he is in hospital.

Tpr Ferguson: Wounded and prisoner, at first believed killed, but later heard of in German hospital, not yet in our hands and wounded in the shoulder. Reported to be in good spirits, as you know he is my batman and it is a great loss to me to have lost him. I hope to get him back when we overrun his hospital. He did a very brave thing, dashed forward to reach a wounded man when two attempts had already failed. I am putting him in for a gong, also the chap who rescued Ian Wellsted.

Four jeeps were lost. We have recaptured three and one is OK. The other two were complete write-offs.

Well, I have drawn a rough sketch of the battle, and will try to explain what happened. Wellsted's troop was sent with one armoured car and two scout cars to act as flank guard on the left and northern flank of the main advance. They advanced through the large wood shown on the sketch, up the track from the south to X-roads B and along west till at A they were fired on by bazookas and heavy SA fire. The enemy had let the AFVs [armoured fighting vehicles] through and a fierce battle lasting ten minutes took place. We lost one jeep and one man killed and took two prisoners. It was absolutely impossible to see the enemy as the woods were so thick.

We were at a terrible disadvantage, standing high up on the road firing our Vickers, while the enemy was lying in the undergrowth. We then, plus the AFVs, withdrew to X-roads B and prepared to make a stand as our line of withdrawal to our own lines was cut off.

The enemy closed in on three sides, his main attack coming from the south. We still could not see him, and were suffering casualties from his SA [small-arms] fire. After fifteen minutes, he launched three AFVs up the track. It was not until the leading vehicle was within fifty yards that it fired and we definitely knew it was enemy. Then I got our armoured car to come up and bolt it with its two-pounder, which it did with great success. It knocked out one and damaged another. The crews baled out into the woods.

The third vehicle turned out to be a troop carrier and a large number of troops got out and into the woods. They tried to close in on us. The chaps fought like devils, firing everything they had. After about ten minutes, I saw we were outnumbered and out-positioned and our casualties were mounting rapidly. I gave the order for all of us to form a body in the jeeps that were serviceable and get the wounded aboard. I ordered that we make a dash for it towards C, then turn right down the track that would bring us down to our own lines.

This was done. I sent Johnny Cooper off first with the wounded at top speed, then made a dash with the rest later. The Jerry was about thirty yards away when we left, and believe me, I never thought the old jeeps were so slow: 50 mph seemed a snail's pace.

The first vehicle we met at our lines was the ambulance and

so we got the wounded straight aboard. I then went and asked for tanks to clear the woods in an attempt to reach Ferguson and Blakeney who had been overrun and captured. This was promised and the time was about 3.00 p.m. The Padre, Sgt Terry Harrison (my signaller), went back to recce the woods and await the tanks. On approaching the woods we met a Polish POW who told us he had just seen approximately 80–100 SS at crossroads B, 5 AFVs and two British wounded being quite well looked after. It was not until about 7.00 p.m. that the tanks arrived, but the Jerry had gone. We recovered the bodies of Blakeney and Clyde and had a burial service the next day. Later when the town of Nienburg fell we reached the hospital and found the body of Davies in a coffin. Nienburg was the SS HQ and it was there we received the news about Ferguson. The lesson learned was not to sit in woods with jeeps, also Tony Trower's armour and windscreen was pierced by German SA. We are now being very cunning about our battles and are refusing to enter woods until we are sure that they are clear. Open country is the only place for us.

Muirhead's troop had a very successful action capturing about 30–44 SS and killing and wounding six with no casualties to ourselves.

Last night Tom Moore sent me a message from Mike Blackman saying Paddy's casualties were two officers wounded, fifteen other ranks and four jeeps missing, but they had taken approximately 200 prisoners. Jolly good. Please have this letter typed and a copy sent to Paddy. To date we have killed approximately 189 enemy, captured 233 and taken much equipment.

Well cheerio for now, let's have your news.

Yours ever,

H. Poat   13 April 1945

During April and, particularly early May, Major Blackman indicated in a dispatch to London that Mayne was impossible to contact. Even so, it has been possible to piece together some of the events of those days.

One afternoon, accompanied by men in two other jeeps, he approached a tiny village in an area close to Belsen. On the outskirts of the village, which looked as though it was not fortified, Mayne told the men to get out of their jeeps. First he advised them to cut all communication lines, then he assembled them and told them to scour the village for enemy soldiers and search the houses for weapons. Mayne, accompanied by Hull and two others, went to the Burgermeister's house. 'It was a large house in the centre of the village and Big Mayne spotted it right away,' says Hull. Mayne hammered the door with the butt of his pistol and waited for the village dignitary to open it.

'Paddy pushed the man into the big room with the .45 at his chest and told him we had the village surrounded. He told him to have all the guns and cameras in the village assembled in that room when he returned in half an hour. We went out and met one of the lads who'd discovered some booze. Big Mayne was bein' cagey. He hoped the head man believed his story about havin' the place surrounded. So he gave him only half an hour to gather up the gear.'

When Mayne returned to the house, the room was full of weapons, some of them vintage pieces and cameras. Hull says Mayne took one or two cameras and told his men to destroy all the other items. Hull remembers helping others to smash 'everything they didn't want'. 'In fact,' he went on, 'I'll never forget this shotgun with two barrels and a rifle barrel on top. It was incredible. I always remembered that, and regretted I didn't take it.'

In another village, Mayne went into the garden of a house and discovered a swastika cut into a boulder. He considered the possibility of blowing up the boulder, but an elderly couple in the house pleaded they were not responsible for the swastika, and that it had been carved into the boulder by Germans who had been billeted in the house. Mayne decided to spend the night there. The woman of the house was unable to speak English and, for devilment, Billy Hull and two other men tried to teach her English words because she was eager to please Paddy Mayne. Unknown to Mayne, the words Hull and the others were adding to her vocabulary were not in the Oxford

Dictionary. At dinner that evening as she served Mayne with potatoes, she pleasantly offered him a part of the female anatomy. Mayne blushed because a Padre was at the table.

The following morning Hull and the others sat in their jeeps waiting for Mayne and the Padre to join them. Before the pranksters left the house, they took the unfortunate German woman aside and gave her their alternative for goodbye. As Mayne left with the Padre, the elderly lady of the house appeared at the door waving and saying 'Fuck off!' As she repeated this Mayne, again highly embarrassed, grabbed the Padre by the arm and hurried him to the jeeps. Hull says Mayne almost smiled as he lifted the Padre into one of the waiting jeeps.

There were many rumours after the war about Paddy Mayne having been involved in looting or encouraging his men to loot. There is little doubt he acquired small things here and there and was always collecting cameras. Taking cameras, alcohol, and, on one occasion a complete darkroom, could certainly be described as acquiring loot, though that is nothing on the scale suggested by the mythology which surrounds his exploits. On one occasion he undoubtedly took a car.

As he arrived at a German farmhouse with Hull, Mayne was surprised at the affluent appearance of the building and the fact that the family had servants. While he searched the interior of the house and questioned the occupants, he ordered Hull to search the farm buildings for weapons.

Hull says he went to the farmyard and, being a man never to miss an opportunity, he bagged a few chickens and placed them in the jeep for the days ahead. One bird persistently avoided his grasp and disappeared into a large haystack. Hull says he couldn't understand how a chicken could disappear in a haystack, and so he 'investigated'. Under the haystack was a car propped up on bricks. Hull removed the hay and to his delight discovered a large and well-maintained Mercedes. The chicken was now far from his thoughts. He rushed back into the farmhouse and informed Mayne, who was a lover of fine cars. From the family in the house, he learned they had hidden the car so that it would not be commandeered as a German staff car.

Mayne demanded to know where they had hidden the wheels and ordered Hull to put the car into working and drivable condition. The car was later sold and Hull received the princely sum of £100 in sterling to account for his share of it and to compensate him for coins which Paddy uncovered in other buildings.

There was also talk of Mayne shooting prisoners in Germany, but there is no evidence to support such allegations. We discovered, however, that members of 1 SAS shot SS guards in the Belsen concentration camp. As John Randall remembers, and he was among the first to go into Belsen, some of the men were given a guided tour of the camp by the Camp Commandant, Kramer, and his assistant, Irma Greese. He describes Kramer as a big 'fearsome-looking' man and Greese as a 'sinister woman dressed in black'. The guards were still arrogant and defiant. 'They just let us drive through the gates. We gave some of them an option to escape. The ones who accepted the offer fled into the woods. We followed them and shot them – probably about six.'

Reg Seekings, who was also at Belsen, remembered a stocky Irishman who was shooting guards for what he claimed the SS had done to his comrades in France. That Irishman was Billy Hull. 'I'll never forget Belsen,' Hull confesses. 'The smell of rotting bodies. The place was an incredible size. I caught a guard beatin' a prisoner behind a hut and I sorted him out. I kept thinking of my friends that the SS executed on the Garstin "stick" in France.

'In a hut I came across five SS guards, three of them women. One of the men began pleading with me and was taking out photographs of his family. As he went to hand them to me, one of the SS women hit him in the mouth. I shot the five of them.'

It has taken Billy Hull over forty years to admit to this, though he adds that another SAS colleague shot a group of captured SS men behind a barn near Belsen. Later when the SAS reached the Kiel Canal, Hull remembers himself and this same colleague watching a line of German prisoners, most of them in Wehrmacht uniform. It was not unusual at that time for the Gestapo or SS to pose as Wehrmacht when the Allies captured towns or villages. On this occasion Hull says that a young girl, wrapped only in a blanket, ran towards him:

'It was bitterly cold and I felt sorry for her. She pointed to a large German who was arrogant-looking and she began shouting that he was SS and not Wehrmacht. We hauled him out of the line of prisoners and he quickly admitted he was SS. We made him strip and gave his clothes to the girl. We then kicked him into the canal and each time he tried to get out, we kicked him back in, until he was no more. I just kept thinkin' of what the bastards had done to my friends.'

The men who trained under Mayne acquitted themselves with valour in north-west Germany. There are innumerable examples of this. The type of warfare may not have been of the kind envisaged in 1 SAS training, but that mattered little when it came to dealing with the enemy.

Captain Alex Muirhead, who was under the command of Major Bill Fraser, recorded in dispatches one episode which shows exactly the speed with which the 2 Troop of 'A' Squadron swung into action and neutralised the Germans. The incident occurred after the failure of a battalion of Canadian paratroops to take a wooded area. 2 Troop was passing through the forward troops when they came upon the Canadians who informed them that they had tried to take a wood but were driven back by heavy Spandau, Panzer-faust and infantry fire. The Canadians lost eight men. Muirhead, in his record of the incident, says the Canadians were considering another attempt by first engaging the wood with mortar and artillery fire. Bill Fraser decided there was a better way.

Fraser told the Canadians he believed he could approach the enemy, without their being aware of his force, by using an area of 'dead ground' on their left flank. The Canadians were intrigued that such a small force should attempt a task which a battalion of paratroops found impossible. Fraser led his twelve jeeps up the left flank of the wood, and approached to within thirty yards of the enemy position before the Germans knew what was happening. A camouflaged Spandau position opened up on Fraser's jeep, driving the vehicle into the ditch and wounding the major in the hand. The rest of the troop, reacting

quickly, fanned out in front of the wood. The section commanded by Lieutenant Pat Riley engaged a German infantry gun
which was swinging into position. Riley's section destroyed it
and its entire crew. Another section under command of Lieutenant Jenson opened up with Vickers and Brownings on the
Panzer-faust and Spandau teams, and destroyed them one by
one. A third section raked a group of houses on the right flank
while Fraser was given first aid.

The whole troop dismounted from the jeeps, leaving men at
the Vickers to give them covering fire, and went into the wood in
search of the enemy and cleared it. The whole action took
merely fifteen minutes and enabled the Allied advance to
proceed a further 2000 yards. During that short battle the small
SAS party killed ten Germans and took thirty prisoners. They
also captured, apart from the infantry gun which was knocked
out, several Panzer-faust and three Spandaus.

It was only a few days after this that, with the taking of Kiel
and the subsequent armistice, the fighting activities of the SAS
in the Second World War were effectively at an end. On 8 May
1945, Churchill wrote to Montgomery: 'At last the goal is
reached. The terrible enemy has unconditionally surrendered.
21 Group of armies, wheeling and striking to the north, had the
honour of liberating Holland, Denmark and of gathering as
captive, in the space of three or four days, upwards of 2 millions
of the once renowned German Army.'

1 SAS was directly involved in that surrender.

20

Norway and Disbandment

IN July 1945 Paddy Blair Mayne, with Brigadier Mike Calvert who, having taken over from Brigadier McLeod in March 1945, was now in charge of 1 SAS, were involved in the capitulation and evacuation of the German troops who were in Norway. In a letter from their headquarters in Bergen to his mother on 18 July, Paddy wrote: 'The Germans are starting to leave here at last, and in a month or so we should possibly be home. I am not terribly fond of the Norwegians. They are uninteresting people and the young men are very jealous of our chaps because the girls prefer them.'

On one occasion when Norwegian police were allegedly harassing SAS troops off duty, Paddy unofficially dispatched a number of his men to deal with the problem. The repercussions of this foray, during which the Norwegian police proved no match for Mayne's men and suffered accordingly, were felt as far afield as the Foreign Office.

As his letter shows, Paddy Mayne was not happy in Norway where for much of the time he was idle. His time in Bergen included, however, an incident which illustrates again how he could explode into violence like a time-bomb, irrespective of who was involved. In some respects it was similar to the fracas which led to his arrest in Egypt. The setting this time was a party in the officers' mess. Present at the function was Brigadier Mike Calvert. Like Mayne he had a considerable reputation as a soldier. He had been in Burma with the Chindits, saw himself as a fighting soldier, and was regarded as being as unorthodox in his methods as the Irishman. Within the SAS, however, there was a semblance of animosity towards him because he was 'not one of us'.

Whether it was this resentment coming to the surface, or perhaps straightforward bravado, Mayne and Calvert found themselves in a physical battle which must have shocked all who witnessed it. Mike Calvert, to this day, is willing to admit the part he played in the fracas, partly because he harboured no resentment in the aftermath and, as a tough soldier, was forced to submit to the physical superiority of his adversary. Calvert was certainly no mean soldier, and a big man. He was a competent boxer, who knew how to take care of himself.

Calvert's version of the story is that he arrived in the mess with one of his subordinates, a general staff officer, Esmond Baring. While Calvert sat down and began drinking, Baring mingled with some of Mayne's close associates. Calvert says that, at some stage, he noticed that Paddy Mayne was assaulting Baring. Calvert felt that Baring was not capable of defending himself: in Calvert's words, 'Baring was a quiet, sensitive chap.' Calvert, of course, knew of Mayne's reputation but that was no deterrent. He got out of his chair and approached Mayne, who at this stage, was remonstrating with Baring. During the mêlée Mayne lifted Baring off the ground with one hand.

'I approached Paddy Mayne,' says Calvert, 'and by a surprise attack I managed to get hold of him and put him on his back.' Mayne threw Calvert off him and got up from the floor. As Calvert got to his feet Mayne took hold of him and, as Mike Calvert vividly recalls: 'He lifted me and threw me over my left shoulder and I first touched down on my forehead, on the fender of a large fireplace. When I eventually got up I had two large bags under my eyes which were filling with blood.' Although Calvert could easily have been killed, no animosity remained between him and Mayne after the event.

Having successfully overseen the disarming of 300,000 German troops in Norway, and with the Japanese surrender on 15 August, the SAS returned to Britain to discover that they were to be disbanded on 1 October. David Stirling, now out of Colditz, had fresh ideas on how the role of the SAS could be developed for future operations. So had Paddy Mayne. But it was not to be.

As Paddy was preparing to return home to Newtownards on leave, he received a letter from Major Bill Cumper suggesting that he should 'do away with the red tape as in the old days' and devise a means of arranging for Cumper to join him in whatever venture Paddy might be planning for the future. Cumper's letter provides also an insight into the mood of the men at that time:

'So the Japs gave it up but they are yellow always. They have done you out of some fine sport I am sure. Never mind, Paddy, it had to end some time so let us bear up.' As an afterthought Cumper touched on the problem he and many others were about to face: 'If you have any books on how to earn an honest living, I would be glad of them.'

Paddy Mayne himself returned to Chelmsford in September 1945, aware that in one month it would all be over. He wrote to his mother:

> I hope everything is well with you and that you are looking after yourself. I am as fit as ever, though with the unit breaking up it is all rather despondent. Saying goodbye is never a pleasant thing. I enclose some photographs of the citation for the last Bar which I thought you would like to see. I have been offered a very interesting job. I will let you know more about it later. I am pretty certain I am going to accept. The more I think of being a solicitor again, the less I like it. Love, Blair.

The 'interesting job' was being offered by the Crown Agents. They were responsible for what was then known as The Falklands Dependency Survey. In September Paddy Mayne, John Tonkin and Mike Sadler saw an opportunity to provide themselves with a professional role after the disbandment of their Regiment. The Crown Agents were advertising for 'able-bodied men, with the ability to survive in difficult conditions and to work with a survey team in the South Atlantic'. An approach was made to the SAS for men of this calibre since they had the type of training which would enable them to live in such isolated conditions. It was really a task for a loner. Paddy Mayne was excited by the prospect of having a job which in any event would require some of the skills he had developed in the SAS. It would also offer him the comradeship of two of the men who had been with him from the Western Desert right through to the end of the war. Paddy was given the job of 'second-in-command' of a survey team which included surveyors and other professionals who would chart the Falklands region. It all sounded grand although Paddy did not take account of two factors: he was experiencing extreme pain in his back; and he was no longer in command.

He had damaged a vertebra in his back while in the Desert, and it had been exacerbated during his drops into France. At no stage did he allow his men to know about it. In France and Germany it was apparent to him that he required medical treatment but he persisted with keeping his disability a carefully guarded secret. In the Falklands, the pain became more acute. He also had to accept the role of subordinate. The man in charge of the Antarctic Expedition was Naval Commander Ted Bingham. From the outset he made it clear to Paddy Mayne: 'Don't do as I do, do as I say.' Bingham was an Ulsterman, too, but even this did not endear him to Paddy. Mike Sadler remembers how Paddy Mayne was 'very restrained', his behaviour, he says, was 'out of character'. He recognised that his former CO was suffering with his back, as well as trying to cope with Bingham whom he did not respect. Sadler was given the job of training dogs, a far cry from navigating in the Western Desert and France. It seems that Paddy Mayne did little but, as Sadler says, 'He had none of his breakouts.' Of his Antarctic experience he did keep a memento, which was discovered among his possessions after his death. It was a doggerel poem, typed on paper headed: Government Telegraph Service/Falkland Islands and Dependencies:

> Ice and snow don't worry me,
> Ice and snow don't worry me,
> Temperatures dangerous to monkeys and brass,
> Frozen John Thomas and piles on yer ass.

For we're saying hello to the south,
We're living each day hand to mouth,
You'll get no promotion or sexual emotion,
Far, far away in the south.

Killer whales waiting for you,
Bloody great sea leopards too,
Fucking great icebergs and snow all around,
There's no dusky maiden has ever been found.

This is my story, this is my song,
We've been out sledging too bloody long,
The more we are sledging, the harder the life,
When I get to Blighty, God help my wife.

Why he should have kept the words of this shanty – some of which would normally have met with his own angry disapproval – is a mystery, unless it was all he ever wished to remember about this unfruitful and disappointing episode. He was, of course, always very fond of ballads and songs, such as those by Percy French, and after the discovery of the above shanty we inquired if there were other songs which he liked to sing. Jim Almonds mentioned 'The Boys of Killyran'. The opening lines have a familiar ring about them when one remembers Paddy's penchant for 'liberating' items such as cameras:

Some they went for glory,
Some they went for pillage,
Pillage was the motto,
Of the boys of Killyran.

David Surrey Dane recalls that during the ceremony at Chelmsford, when the SAS was formally disbanded, Paddy made a speech – typically brief – in which he quoted the above quatrain, adding 'We came for the pillage but maybe we got a wee bit of glory as well.'

The job which Mayne thought would be 'interesting' had turned out to be a nightmare. Within one month he was in hospital in Buenos Aires for an operation on his back and then he was shipped home. He had gone to the Falklands in the belief he would be there for two years or more. Now he was home, disillusioned and, once again, without a job.

21

Home Again

WITHIN two months of his return home Blair Mayne was offered the role of Secretary to the Incorporated Law Society of Northern Ireland, the professional body which serves solicitors. His brother, Dougie, remembers that 'Blair had no intention' of practising law, but this job at least allowed him to make use of his legal training, although it was not a task which would fully tax his mind. It meant also that, in the post-war years, most of his friendships were within the legal fraternity. One of his constant companions was Ambrose McGonigal, brother of Eoin who had been killed in the first abortive parachute raid in the Desert. Paddy Mayne had always been very close to the McGonigal family; and David Stirling confirmed that, 'Eoin McGonigal was the one person who liked Paddy before he became a hero.' There is a letter in the family file from Mrs McGonigal, thanking Blair 'for all his goodness' in the exhaustive attempts he made to find her son's grave. Ambrose, who had won the MC and Bar with the Commandos, was then a barrister, later a High Court Judge. Jack Midgeley, another lawyer and ex-Serviceman, tells of what happened in the Belfast Tramways Club, a less than exclusive watering-hole of those days. 'Mayne, you big ape, I'm not afraid of you,' declared Ambrose. 'Right,' replied Mayne. 'Stand against the wall.' Like William Tell's son, Ambrose, back to the wall, stood unflinchingly while Mayne smashed a succession of tumblers just above his head. Satisfied, Mayne insisted that the entire company drink to Ambrose McGonigal's steadiness under fire. Such were the games they played.

Midgeley also recalls being driven home by Blair Mayne after a night in the Belfast Arts Club. 'He drove on and off the pavement, weaving in and out of the lampposts like a slalom skier.' Mayne had always been a skilful driver, glorying in passing another car on a narrow road and 'taking a coat of paint off him'. But he refused to take part in rallies maintaining that 'it would only wreck' his much-loved 'fire engine', the 2.5 litre red Riley.

Another lawyer, later Sir Robert Porter, a County Court Judge, recalls the gentler side of Mayne. 'Ambrose and he had some kind of row in the Grand Central Hotel in Belfast at a very late hour. Ambrose, well-wined, stalked out, determined to walk home. Blair kerb-crawled after him at a discreet distance, to make sure he got home safely.' On another occasion, at a legal conference in Cambridge, Porter was awakened by Blair Mayne who arrived at about 4 a.m. bearing a bottle and a book of verse from which he proceeded to read extracts for the next hour. Among his books still in the family home are several anthologies of poetry, a favourite being *Other Men's Flowers*, compiled by Field Marshal Lord Wavell. He told Porter once of his habit of going alone to a stretch of the Ards coast near Portaferry where he liked to sit watching the sea and reading verse. His preferred poets were the pessimists, Omar Khayyám, Siegfried Sassoon and A. E. Housman. This was part of Blair Mayne's very private 'inner life'. There are conflicting views of just how articulate Mayne was at times. Porter remembers him at a conference giving a very lucid dissertation on the working of the Law Society, with only the briefest of notes. It emerges that, on a subject he knew, he could speak forcibly, if not perhaps eloquently.

Rough badinage with drinking companions came easily to him. It was in the area of more sophisticated social small-talk that he did not excel, nor wish to. He was more at home with simpler people. Hence his success with those people in what Stirling calls 'the regimental engine-room', the sergeants' mess. He had an instinctive ability to mix, off-duty and even on the most boisterous occasions, while still commanding respect. In the last years of his life those with whom he spent his time, playing bridge or drinking, were none of them sophisticates. Sometimes his old comrades-in-arms would come over from England and Scotland to visit him. Bob Bennett, who had been with him the longest, spent one memorable fortnight.

'I was led into Paddy's office in the Law Courts,' he recalls. 'Paddy was sitting with his feet on the desk. He pulled out a drawer on his right and told me that was his "in drawer" and pulled out another drawer on the left side of the desk and confirmed that this was his "out drawer". He then told his secretary that he would not be back for two weeks and we left for a three-day binge.'

Paddy Mayne was not the only former member of 1 SAS to face the problems of readjusting to civilian life. Jim Brough was what his wife calls a '10 by 10' man. This means that, after the war, Jim drank ten pints by 10 p.m. each day. Jim's wife Dorothy told us that, when her husband returned from Norway, he was 'not a nice man'. Jim says he felt it was so 'unnatural' returning to work as a policeman. As a result of his inability to cope, he found himself unemployed. Dorothy Brough felt that much of this was due to the fact that families were 'pushed into the background' during the war and that men found it impossible to give themselves to family life subsequently when the war was over. When we visited Jim and Dorothy Brough in their home in Liverpool, we found that the couple were frank about the problems their marriage faced in the wake of the disbandment of 1 SAS. Today, they are a happy, successful couple. Likewise, Pat Riley found the readjustment difficult to handle. He became involved in failed business schemes after twice resigning from the police. He admits that he was unsettled for several years. His wife, Kay, admits stoically that life during those years was 'trying'. There were many others in this predicament, some of them with memories of 'awful' events which they were trying desperately to forget. Captain Derrick Harrison, for example, was undergoing psychotherapy. Dorothy Brough revealed that, when her husband realised we were going to visit him in order to discuss the war, he began having nightmares. Like Paddy

Mayne there were many who could not fully accept that it was all over. They missed the comradeship, the frenetic pace of life which was now reduced, in comparison, to a pedestrian crawl. A letter which Paddy Mayne kept in his files from one of his men explains the dilemma that they all faced. It was written by Captain Mike McEwan, the SAS Transport Officer, who joined the regiment before D-Day:

'I was most disappointed when I heard I had missed you, Harry [Poat] and Fraser [McCluskey, the SAS chaplain] in Glasgow, although from Fraser's point of view it was as well, for no doubt between us we should have wrecked his hometown and knocked his reputation about quite a bit. A delightful vision has just arisen. Fraser seated at the organ of some Glasgow kirk playing the hairy tassel and you, me and Harry clutching great pots of beer singing lustily. Yes, such a meeting would have to be staged well away from Fraser McCluskey's home ground, methinks. I was at a complete loss to understand what you said about Harry being cured of pneumonia as he was TT at the time. Surely teetotalism is a more serious complaint? I have had a slight touch of it myself and I can tell you, it is a damned unpleasant thing. I only hope that, as with measles, one cannot catch teetotalism twice in a lifetime.

'I share with you to the full your strange longing for those grand days. Were it not for the steadying influence of Kitty, the dear girl who has been crazy enough to marry me, I should be utterly and completely at a loss. I always dreaded the final break-up and the sense of loss is every bit as acute as I had feared. In my letter to Harry Poat, I was recalling the highlights of those days – Bill Fraser and his stirrup pump, the gaggle of drunken officers supposedly at a conference under old Mike Calvert. The wonderful solo booze-up I had while you lot were parading for some obscure General; the somewhat worrying time when Harry and I offered to attack Clem Attlee's person with a bacon-slicer. Gosh, what a lot of things come back once one starts. Strangely enough too, they don't seem like memories. They seem more like yesterday's happenings. Yes, it's amazing how it all comes back. The difficulty is not to stimulate the memories, it is to stem them. As you say, some of the chaps, a case of beer, a piano, a duck-billed platypus or two and what a grand time we could have. Surely it is not impossible to recapture, in part, some of those times. I cannot close this letter without thanking you for the grand time I had while serving under your command, Paddy. I just wish it had been six years.'

Apart from his job with the Law Society, Blair Mayne now began searching for other projects to occupy his thoughts and energy. He started a chicken farm in the grounds of his house, but this failed. He planted daffodils which remain one of the attractive features of Mount Pleasant to this day. He also felt that he could contribute to helping wayward boys. Jack Clark, who was with the TA, 21 SAS, and was for a time employed as a Housemaster at an establishment in London looking after deprived children, remembers meeting Paddy, who was fascinated by Jack's description of his job. He revealed to Jack Clark that he had applied for several posts as a Borstal Governor as he believed this was the type of work for which he was eminently suited. Clark says Mayne was very disappointed that he was turned down because of his lack of experience.

In the family home Mayne spent much time looking after his invalid mother. Everyone who visited Mount Pleasant noticed the devotion he showed to her. But this was not the full story. He persuaded his sister, Barbara, to leave her job as a nurse to look after their mother. On other occasions he was seen in Belfast in his open-top Riley with his mother in the passenger seat. Dougie also remembers Blair taking their mother on holiday to Donegal. 'He returned unexpectedly in the early hours of a morning,' says Dougie. 'He couldn't cope with the peace and quiet. I was obliged to travel to Donegal to fetch my mother and his car.'

Some people have said that Blair's mother did not know about his drinking bouts but Dougie says that is not true. Dougie saw a lot of his brother in the first couple of years after the war. At that time Blair had much of his frustration and depression under control.

A solicitor, Desmond Marrinan, remembers a golf outing. Blair was a good golfer. He had played the game from his youth and was regarded by others as skilful and a big hitter. Desmond

Marrinan recalls that, at Warrenpoint in County Down, he was chosen to play alongside Blair in a solicitors' team against a team called 'The McCollum Strollers' which was captained by Major McCollum, a resident Belfast Magistrate. 'Blair treated the game with contempt,' says Marrinan, 'he didn't care whether he won or lost. He used a driver off the first tee and also used the same club for his second shot.' Just before midnight that same day, as Marrinan was preparing to set off home, Blair announced that 'they' were going to Dundalk in the Irish Republic for a party and he, Marrinan, was not to interfere with Blair's plan. Desmond Marrinan, showing the better part of valour, did not demur. He knew Paddy Mayne not just by reputation. He knew when the big Newtownards man 'meant business'.

The party which Mayne was assembling for the midnight trip across the Border consisted of Marrinan and two other solicitors. Mayne chose Marrinan's car as the means of transport and the four set off. On reaching Dundalk, Paddy decided they should make for the Imperial Hotel but to his consternation it was shut. That was no great obstacle. He proceeded to smash a window in the premises. He climbed into the building and ordered the others to follow. When the three solicitors clambered over the broken glass they found that Paddy had already raided the bar and was now in the hotel's kitchen preparing what he described as 'army chaw' (bacon and eggs).

As Paddy was practising his culinary talent, the manager of the hotel appeared on the main staircase and started shouting hysterically at Marrinan and his companions. Mayne appeared from the kitchen and offered to pay for any damage he had caused as well as for the 'provisions'. The manager stoutly refused to accept the offer and, in a rage, went off to phone the local police. Marrinan and the others did not waste too much time impressing on Paddy the consequences if the Garda were to arrive. The four made a quick getaway but, instead of making for home, Paddy insisted on heading south because the Garda would expect them to return north. They got under way, after having assured themselves from the safety of a back street that the police cars, with blaring sirens, were elsewhere.

Their route south took them towards Drogheda on the main road to Dublin. En route they stopped a lorry loaded with crates of Guinness. The startled driver was invited to sell some of his wares. The sight of Paddy Mayne was enough to clinch the deal. Fortified with this fresh supply they arrived in Drogheda.

There they managed to find a hotel where they settled down to a few hours' sleep. Later that morning they made the return journey to Northern Ireland. When they reached the Republic of Ireland Customs Post on the Border, the officer in charge demanded to see the vehicle papers for Desmond Marrinan's car which he did not possess. There was an altercation and Paddy knocked the Customs official against a wall. Another official summoned a Garda officer. At this point Desmond Marrinan realised that the arrest of four solicitors would not only prove damaging for them but highly embarrassing for the Northern Ireland Judiciary. As police officers arrived to investigate the assault on the Customs man, Marrinan made a desperate phone call to Major McCollum, the resident magistrate who had been playing golf with them the previous day. McCollum lost no time contacting the Garda Superintendent in Dundalk. The solidarity of the legal profession held firm and the situation was effectively smoothed over and the four were released.

George Matthews was an auctioneer and estate agent with whom Mayne used to spend many hours. Sometimes, according to Mrs Matthews, they would spend days together 'on the blatter', a protracted drinking bout. She, too, remarked on Blair's one-time fascination with hypnotism which he used to practise on his friends. Most, afraid of giving offence, pretended to succumb, and zombie-like, carried out his orders. Others, such as Mrs Matthews, apparently were genuinely subject to the 'influence' and were able to stick pins in their flesh without pain. But from all accounts it is clear that, in this field, Mayne was no Svengali. Was he perhaps seeking to reassert the dominance he exercised in army days? Once he insisted on banishing Mrs Matthews from her own kitchen and on doing all the washing-up himself. Eventually she entered to find all the china and utensils washed but piled together in a shaky pyramid up to the ceiling, ready to collapse at the slightest touch.

In the same household over lunch before a rugby international, James Purcell, a visiting lawyer from Dublin, said something which offended Blair. The next thing they knew Purcell was spouting blood from a gash on his cheek which required six stitches. Blair had struck him with the side of his hand.

There is also the well-documented story of Mayne in Dublin for another rugby international. At a late state in the celebrations he sought to gain entrance to what he believed was the Wanderers Football Club. A man opening the door remonstrated with him and was knocked out with one blow. The owner of the house, thus laid low, was a Senator Quirk in the Dublin Parliament. Mayne was arrested and only high-level representations from the Northern Ireland Judiciary ensured that Colonel Mayne, Secretary of the Law Society, was not publicly convicted of assault. The Northern Ireland Bench was kept quite busy rescuing Blair Mayne.

After the war Paddy began to take an interest in his local football team. He enjoyed standing on the terraces on a Saturday and, as a result, his keen commitment to rugby began to wane. But before long the pain in his back made it impossible for him to stand on the terracing for long periods.

Like rugby, golf, too, increasingly became a casualty. Instead he preferred rugby or golf clubhouses where he was usually found at the bar. His drinking also led him into the kind of company which exploited his potential for violence. As his old friend and former schoolteacher, Ted Griffiths, puts it: 'If he was thwarted he could become awkward.'

On one occasion during his visit to Newtownards, Bob Bennett remembers Paddy taking him to a bar after hours and demanding that the landlord let them in. Once inside Bennett saw that there were two couples in the bar and that he and Paddy were perceived as intruding on an intimate gathering. One of the men who resented this made a sarcastic remark. Paddy hit him a blow on the chin and knocked him down. The unfortunate man was English and he was told by Mayne that Englishmen should not come to Northern Ireland and tell him what to do.

On that same trip, Bennett also noticed his friend's insistence on always returning home, no matter how late the hour and no matter how much alcohol was consumed. Bennett says: 'Once we were out drinking in different bars along the County Down coast and at the end of the night, Paddy took off and drove home without me. I didn't know the geography but I eventually made my way back to Newtownards. Blair didn't mention the episode. I can still remember him driving off and leaving me. The following night he left me lying in a pub and I woke up on the floor of the establishment the following morning. When I arrived at Blair's home it was early morning and he was out chopping wood in the garden. Again, he never made any reference to where I had been or why he had left me in a place which was unknown to me. It made me think that maybe his mother didn't know about his drinking and he was ensuring that he was home for the hour she awakened.' The more likely explanation is that his mother did know, but that he did his best to hide it from her. He certainly never lost the stamina for long bouts of drinking and it was inevitable that during these periods he got into trouble. In bars, Billy Hull remembers him piling glasses one on the other and then smashing them with one blow. His sister, Frances, believes that people took advantage of him, and tried to demonstrate that he was not a hero. 'It was a bit like the Wild West at times,' she says.

Two leading literary figures in Northern Ireland remember Paddy being asked to deal with truculent revellers in the lounge bar of the Belfast Arts Club. Paddy duly agreed, with disturbing consequences. A similar request in a rugby club resulted in Paddy lifting a man by his tie and knocking him out with one blow. There are plenty of other such stories but many of them are apocryphal. The only time Paddy himself felt the power of someone else's punch was during a trip to Dublin with his brother.

'We went to Dublin,' Douglas recounted. 'I was representing Queen's University, Belfast, against a rugby fifteen of ex-servicemen from Trinity College. After the match was over I went drinking in the Shelbourne Hotel. I got very drunk and was attempting to do handstands on a balcony. Now even in sobriety

I would have found such an exercise difficult, but with drink taken I was making a fool of myself. Blair was standing in the lounge bar watching me and he kept remonstrating with me to cease such stupid behaviour. Eventually, I joined him in the lounge. The only other person in the room was a well-dressed elderly lady. Blair grabbed me by the tie and began slapping my face and telling me to behave myself and sober up and that I was a Mayne. The elderly lady took great exception to Blair's behaviour and shouted to him to "leave that young lad alone". Blair was extremely embarrassed and as a consequence he let go of me and stepped back. The elderly lady left the room and Blair turned to me and told me to hit him. I let go at him with this 'hay-maker' of a punch and by chance I caught him flush on the chin and knocked him out. He eventually got up and just laughed. He loved recounting that story. He often told people that his younger brother was the only person who was able to knock him out.'

The closeness between Dougie and Blair evaporated with time. Dougie was married, living away from Mount Pleasant, and his elder brother's erratic behaviour did not make for intimacy between them. Dougie felt that Blair was carelessly wasting his life, and particularly in the last eighteen months of his life.

The part the back injury played in Blair's consumption of alcohol will never be known, though Dougie is convinced that drink was used almost as an anaesthetic. The pain became so intense that he was eventually driven to have an eight-hour operation in which a vertebra was removed but it did not fully eradicate the problem. His sister Frances recalls her mother going to Blair's room early one morning to waken him in the weeks after his operation. She says: 'Mother went into the room and was shocked because the previous night he was still wearing a plaster of Paris round his chest and back. It was gone. She discovered that he had got out of bed in the middle of the night, gone to the garden shed and with a pair of hedge-clippers cut the plaster down the middle and removed it.'

Blair's memories of the war were always with him but rarely surfaced even when he met those who had fought alongside him.

Derrick Harrison saw him at the Special Forces Club in London shortly before his death. Paddy asked him, 'Do you think we could do it all again?' 'I'm sure we could, Paddy.' Paddy replied, 'I don't think so, I don't think we could. These new chaps are much better than we were, they're really good.' Harrison said later: 'I got the feeling that he was deeply depressed, it was almost, with hindsight, like his own epitaph.'

This meeting between the two of them occurred several weeks before Paddy's death. Reg Seekings also met Paddy in England and they both reminisced about their friends and the conversation centred on the fact that many of the veterans were married. Paddy pointed out that his size often led him into trouble, even when he was not inviting it, and he believed the lads hated him for 'all the crap he gave them'. 'Who would want to marry a big ugly bastard like me?' he asked. Seekings tried to reassure him that this was not the case. 'Of course lots of girls would be only too willing to marry you,' replied Seekings. 'Do you really think so?' asked Mayne.

There is little doubt that the hero had no high opinion of himself. The Rev. Fraser McCluskey became good friends with Paddy during his time as SAS Padre and he believes this related in some way to the fact they were both of a similar age. After the war Fraser made a point of visiting his friend in Newtownards. His observations show that, even years after the fighting, Paddy's basic attitudes had not changed very much. 'During the war I knew he was shy and I attributed much of his drinking to this,' says McCluskey. 'He was a man who found difficulty in dealing with personal relationships but at home in Newtownards I could see how much he was attached to his family. He was also very sensitive and easily hurt. In a way, the Regiment became a substitute for his family during the war.'

After the war the Mayne family went their separate ways and Paddy Mayne was left largely alone with his mother who, almost bedridden, now slept in the drawing-room. Fraser McCluskey says that Paddy possessed a 'passionate devotion' to his men. After the war his family did not provide the necessary substitute.

Captain Roy Close, one of his fellow officers, and others were asking a salient question before the war ended: 'How will Paddy ever adapt to civilian life?' This was the man who talked to Close about T. E. Lawrence, who appeared well read and who was already trained for a profession. There were others, few in number, from 1 SAS who were disappointed about the manner in which Mayne saw his life out. Chalky White, who took part in that heroic episode in France, expected his hero to behave differently after the war. 'He was a man without faults during the war, but eventually he let drink get the better of him.' For Chalky White the war should never have ended. To be human, all too human, was not permitted to his hero. For Paddy Mayne it became more and more difficult to live up to the mythology that surrounded him.

'There was nothing he liked better than a good row, a good shoot-up, but after the war he didn't have the opportunity for this and that's why he was so often a frustrated man.' The words are Billy Hull's. He, probably more than most, had the best view of his hero in those later years because they lived in the same town. 'Life was too tedious and quiet for him in Newtownards,' comments Hull, who adds that in some people's eyes Paddy was a 'monster' but not to those who knew him.

Frances remembers her brother explaining why he frequently found himself in conflict with others: 'He told me that people set him up and that because of his physical size, he was unable to go anywhere without being the centre of attention. He said that people tried to provoke him.'

The occasion when he, with two companions, was lured to a party in north Belfast bears out his sister's thesis. On the way he found two cars blocking his path. Seven men got out of the cars. Mayne and his companions had been 'set up'. Single-handed he dispatched four of his assailants while his colleagues dealt with two others and the attackers fled. But it must be said that Paddy Mayne was often the aggressor. It became apparent that it was dangerous to be in his company when he was drunk.

He was known to the Royal Ulster Constabulary in his own neighbourhood and in Belfast. There were not too many policemen who were willing single-handed to answer an SOS call from the landlord of a licensed premises to 'sort out Big Paddy Mayne'. One man, whose father was a Station Sergeant in Belfast, says his father often reminisced about such calls. His response was to send several constables to the scene, but usually they found that Mayne was open to reason and that the origins of the particular trouble lay elsewhere. Landlords were also willing to forget incidents in which Paddy was involved because he was willing to settle the bill for damages.

22

Fish out of Water

WHO DARES WINS

AFTER the war, Blair Mayne was like some great salmon out of water. The last ten years of his life were spent without real purpose, searching for a role. His job as Secretary of the Law Society neither held his interest nor filled his days. He was approached by the Ulster Unionist Party as a prospective parliamentary candidate for Westminster, but he was not interested in politics. He tried poultry breeding like his father before him, and he took a real pride and pleasure in his garden. David Stirling remembers how he loved his roses. Golf he played when his back allowed him to, chess too, and cards. He was good at bridge, better at poker. But on these social evenings, with those who had never served with him, he avoided any reminiscences of his army life. He could never be persuaded to talk about his exploits. His favourite party trick was to take the metal cap off a Guinness bottle – his preferred softer drink – and with finger and thumb bend it in two. Matthews, his auctioneer friend, could recall only one incident involving army experience. They had been talking about the need in war, above all, to stay alive. Paddy brought out his old service revolver and laid it on the table. 'When I come through the door, grab it,' he told Matthews. Matthews did as he was told. But before his hand was even near the table he was looking into the barrel. 'You're dead,' said Paddy. 'It's just a question of moving quicker than the other man.'

To have survived five years of fighting without a scratch

would seem to support the view that Paddy Mayne led a charmed life. But those who fought with him had another explanation. His reaction was instantaneous, quicker than any they ever encountered. Derrick Harrison cites the time in Germany when he and Paddy were crossing a field in the jeep. Paddy was driving, and they were chatting. Suddenly, Harrison was thrown back without warning as the jeep shot forward guns blazing. Paddy had spotted movement where no one else had seen it, and went headlong at the German anti-tank unit hidden in a ditch. 'He went straight from perception to action – not a second's hesitation,' Harrison said. 'He went straight in and cleaned them out.'

But after the war this unique coordination of head and hand was no longer of much value to him. Having drunk delight of battle with his peers, he was left now, like Ulysses, 'to rust unburnished, not to shine in use'.

People who knew him in his latter days could be divided into two categories: those who were proud to be in his company; and those who were afraid to be. For there were two Blair Maynes. On one hand, the gentle giant, soft-spoken, self-effacing, unfailingly considerate and polite; on the other, the touchy, quarrelsome and dangerous human animal which emerged when – as we say in Ireland – drink had been taken.

Like Faust, two souls contended within his breast; the solitary celibate and the loud convivial drinker; the cold methodical killer and the commanding officer who cared deeply for his men – there are countless grateful letters from anxious or bereaved wives, mothers and families to whom he had written with reassurance and genuine sympathy. There was the popular hero who hated adulation and avoided the crowd.

In a study such as this of a man who was a great soldier, it is necessary to probe deeper to try to uncover the hidden springs of a complex human being. What was behind this dual personality? Unfortunately we can only speculate from the superficially extensive, yet in terms of coming to grips with his psychological make-up, very limited data provided by those who knew him best.

His attitude to women was especially interesting. His

antipathy to them, certainly his deep unease in their company, is universally accepted. The exceptions were females outside the zone of sexual attraction, such as his family, the elderly and very young.

There was in him a streak of puritanism – not in the religious sense for he was largely agnostic – which was reflected in his attitude to swearing. The name of the deity was permissible but the four-letter words with erotic connotation, considered indispensable by most soldiers, usually aroused his implacable fury. No one dared say 'fuck' in his presence. It is possible that he considered such language as debasing the feminine ideal, the unsullied image of virginity. He had – as Malcolm Pleydell, the Medical Officer, noted – an almost spiritual relationship with his mother whom he idolised. Did she fulfil an irreplaceable role in his affections, one that no other woman could aspire to? We do not know. There is no evidence that he ever formed a sexual attachment of any kind. For a full-blooded, intensely physical young man that would appear unnatural. Inevitably, there are suggestions that he was drawn towards those of his own sex, but that he kept such inclinations under rigid control. There are two witnesses who assert that such was the case. We do not know. Given the period he was living in, given his family background and his circumstances in the army, the admission of such instincts would have been unthinkable. Such an inner conflict could account for the sudden explosions when, released by alcohol, the repressive lid blows off and the seething frustrations, so conscientiously contained, foam out in violence. There is ample evidence throughout the history of the armed services that many extremely gallant and honourable men shared such inclinations but suppressed them under iron discipline, subjecting themselves in the process to well-nigh intolerable strains.

There is, on the other hand, the word of his brother that, during his days in the desert he had written to a girl in Newtownards proposing marriage but that she turned him down for a merchant seaman. Perhaps his proud sensitive nature, always insecure with women, may have been permanently bruised by such a rebuff causing him to abandon thought of marriage from then on? Which was sad news for the host of eligible young ladies who would no doubt have gladly offered to share their lives with the youthful and handsome war hero. Something he wrote in his schoolboy diary may afford a clue to his lifelong alienation from women. It is a confession of infinite sadness written by a boy of sixteen: 'My education has been so sadly neglected in my youth that I cannot yet write successfully letters of any description from love-letters down. RBM.' His brother has said: 'He never talked to me about getting married. He was terribly fond of children and extremely good to mine. I'm quite certain that, if he had had family life, he would have been happier.'

The real feelings of Blair Mayne will remain part of that 'secret inner life' of which David Stirling has spoken, that region into which, Stirling adds, 'he floated off and would remain incommunicado for days'. Stirling gives another insight into the intensely private thoughts of the man with whom he had whiled away so many waiting hours in the desert. Stirling, a highly intelligent and artistically gifted man, has expressed a view which, on the face of it, seems self-contradictory, but which is worth recording. 'We often talked of the emotional life,' he said, 'and Paddy made it very clear that, inside his mind, he was capable of writing great poetry but, on the other hand, he was quite incapable of putting words to it.'

From all the letters in the files of the Mayne family, from all those received by the authors and from conversations with men who served with Blair Mayne one thing stands out: the supreme confidence he inspired as a leader. There is abundant evidence of the affection and respect in which he was held. But it was his unique ability to convince men, caught in the tightest grip of battle, that all would be well, which shines through. Tough, hardened soldiers, officers and NCOs, have quite independently used the same word: 'No matter how black things looked, once Paddy appeared, it was *magic*.' There is no more to be said about the soldierly genius of Paddy Mayne.

The last twenty-four hours of Paddy Mayne's life began on 14 December 1955. It was an uneventful day and Mayne had only one duty to fulfil. He was to attend a Masonic dinner in his hometown of Newtownards. The nature of such an event did not please him greatly because it was teetotal but he always made an effort to be there. Details of his whereabouts before the meeting are sketchy. His mother saw him as he left Mount Pleasant that evening in his red Riley. For his movements after the meeting, we have to turn to George Matthews who, until 1986, was the only living person who knew of Paddy Mayne's whereabouts that night and into the early hours.

'I was to be at the Masonic Lodge meeting with him, but I couldn't make it,' said George Matthews. 'It was the kind of event where there was no drink and Blair often played bridge when it was over. However, that night he went to a house in Hamilton Road in the nearby town of Bangor and played poker and had some drinks. He arrived at my house at 2.00 a.m. I was in bed and he gave me a lot of abuse for not turning up for the Lodge meeting. He left my house at 4 a.m.'

George Matthews admitted that he gave him drinks. Paddy was known to be a fast driver even under the influence of alcohol, but there is no evidence from our conversations with George Matthews, that when Paddy left the house he was incapable of driving. Matthews was almost correct about the time his visitor left. It was probably 3.55 a.m. because the journey to the spot where he would meet his death would have taken ten minutes at Mayne's usual speed. At 4.05 a.m. he was a few hundred yards from Mount Pleasant when his car struck a lorry parked at the side of the roadway.

At 162 Mill Street, Newtownards, James Alexander was awakened by his wife. The time, he recorded, was 4.05 a.m. His wife complained of hearing a terrific noise outside. He went to the doorway of his house and scanned the street. His attention was first drawn to overhead cables, which were sparking and then to a large Riley car parked on the pavement. Alexander said later that the car engine was running and the headlamps still on and his reaction was that men from the Electricity Service were working at overhead cables, so he went back to bed. That was the evidence he gave at the inquest. Over two hours later on that Wednesday morning, Alexander, who was a bus driver, left his house, joined by two workmates. The car was still there. 'This time,' he told the inquest, 'I saw a car on the pavement which appeared to be damaged. I examined it and saw the body of a man lying in the driver's seat.' That man was Blair Mayne and he was dead.

His car had in fact struck the lorry, mounted the pavement on the opposite side of the road and rammed a pole carrying electricity lines, hence the sparking which James Alexander referred to in his statement to the Coroner. A Constable Elliott, who visited the scene just before 7 a.m., saw Blair Mayne's body being removed from the car. The vehicle was wedged between the telegraph pole and the outside of a house and was badly damaged. Dr William Glover examined the body at 7.15 a.m. in Newtownards Hospital and his conclusion was that death was caused by a fracture at the base of the skull and that death had occurred one to four hours previously.

There has been much speculation over the years. Blair Mayne's car was so well known in the town of Newtownards that could anyone seeing it on a pavement have mistaken it for an Electricity Service vehicle? Did anyone in Mill Street at 4.05 a.m. know that the crashed car contained the body, alive or dead, of Blair Mayne and, if they did, were they frightened to investigate? On this the Coroner's report comes to no conclusion.

The funeral took place on 16 December 1955. The procession that filed behind the coffin was over a mile long and took more than an hour to pass. The army, especially the SAS, the legal profession, the world of rugby were all heavily represented. Along the entire route the blinds in dwelling houses and places of business were drawn as a last tribute to the town's most famous son. The footpaths were lined with crowds standing in places four deep. There was neither fife nor drum, none of the trappings of a military funeral. But the prayers were said by the Right Reverend Fraser McCluskey, once his SAS Padre. Among the mourners was the SAS Regimental Sergeant-Major, Bob Bennett. They laid him to rest in the family grave in Movilla Churchyard, Newtownards.

A road in his native town has been named after him. Yet in

the wider world the most decorated British soldier of the Second World War is virtually unknown.

He was, in the words used by Winston Churchill of Kevin O'Higgins, the young Irish statesman assassinated near Dublin in 1927, 'a figure from the antique, cast in bronze'. War was his element. When it left him, he found himself at odds with an uncongenial and unprofitable world, so stale and out of tune, after the wild annihilating rapture of the one he had known.

He sleeps within the ruined walls of a thirteenth-century abbey in County Down, but the high company of heroes will forever be his Valhalla.

APPENDIX 1

SAS personnel who took part in raids (in which R.B. Mayne participated) on Axis airfields in North Africa, 1941–2

TAMET, 14 December 1941
Lt R.B. Mayne; Sgt McDonald; Pcts* Chesworth, Seekings, White, Hawkins.

TAMET, 27 December 1941
Lt R.B. Mayne; Sgt McDonald; Octs† Bennett, White, Hawkins.

BERKA, 20 March 1942
Lt R.B. Mayne; Cpls Bennett, Rose, Byrne.

BENGHAZI RECCE, 16 June 1942
Maj A.D. Stirling, DSO; Capt R.B. Mayne, DSO; Cpls Seekings, Cooper, Lilley, Warburton, Cohane.

FUKA, 7 July 1942
Maj A.D. Stirling, DSO; Capt R.B. Mayne, DSO; Cpls Seekings, Cooper, Storrie; Pcts Leigh, Adamson, Mullen, Downes.

EL DABA, 9 July 1942
Capt. R.B. Mayne DSO; F/Lt Rawnsley; Cpls Lilley, Storrie, Badger.

SIDI EL HANEISH, 27 July 1942: massed jeep attack
Maj A.D. Stirling, DSO; Capt. R.B. Mayne, DSO; Capt. Jordan; F/O Rawnsley; Lts Bailey, Fraser, Scratchley, Hastings, Mather, Jellicoe, Sadler, Russell, Le Grand, Zirnheld, Martin, Harent, Klein; NCOs

*Parachutists.
†This term was used at first for SAS privates, then abandoned as too narrow.

Seekings, Cooper, Rose, Bennett, Riley, Almonds, Kershaw, White, Tait; Cpls Lilley, Stone, Badger, Lambie, Down, Guegan, Le Gall, Boven, Hurin, Fouquet, Lageze, Boutinop, Leroy.

PERSONNEL IN 'A' SQUADRON RAIDING TRIPOLI/EL AGHEILA
Major Mayne; Capts Fraser, Cumper; Lts Lord Charlesworth, Wiseman, McDermott, Kennedy, Marsh; NCOs Lilley, Philips, Sturmey, Henderson, Maier, Leadbetter, Hindle; Cpls Leigh, Kendall, Downs, O'Reilly, Donoghue, Ward, Allen, Swan, McDiarmid, Belsham, Finlay, Sharman, Adams, Fitch, Kerr, Gladwell, Wall, Wortley; Ptes Moore, O'Dowd, Allen, Sillitoe.

APPENDIX 2

Operation HOWARD Personnel

Nominal Roll of personnel engaged on operations with
Lt-Col Mayne in Germany, 6–29 April 1945

Date of Departure from UK	Number	Rank	Name	Remarks
6.4.45	87306	Lt-Col	Mayne, R.B.	
	71178	Maj	Blackman, M.J.D'A.	
	50968	Maj	Bond, C.F.	KIA 10.4.45
	182297	Maj	Lepine, E.	
	109524	Maj	Marsh, A.	
	184425	Capt	Davis, P.G.	Wounded
	145763	Capt	Harrison, D.I.	
	151191	Capt	Iredale, J.	Wounded, 10.4.45
	325123	Lt	Badger, E.A.	
	301774	Lt	Bryce, T.C.	Injured, 22.4.45
	232606	Lt	Close, R.E.	
	249839	Lt	Davidson, G.C.	Believed PW, 11.4.45
	309000	Lt	Gamblin, J.R.	Wounded, 17.4.45
	249461	Lt	Grierson, R.H.	Wounded, 10.4.45
	284526	Lt	Locket, M.G.	
	302139	Lt	Mycock, E.J.	
	284454	Lt	Oates, C.E.	
	295459	Lt	Richardson, S.M.	
	304695	Lt	Schlee, P.J.	Believed PW, 11.4.45
	245239	Lt	Surrey Dane, D.M.	

Date of Departure from UK	*Number*	*Rank*	*Name*	*Remarks*
6.4.45	333639	Lt	Scott, J.S.	
	308987	Lt	Winterson, M.F.	
	315243	Lt	Tarleton, R.B.	
	312539	Lt	Edwards, N.A.R.	
	80666	SSM	Clarke, J.	Wounded, 11.4.45
	2660913	SSM	Lilley, E.	Injured
	1881793	Sgt	Chappell, A.	
	1641548	Sgt	Cattell, C.	
	2698540	Sgt	Leitch, J.	
	3060979	Sgt	Edwards, J.	
	4126106	Sgt	Schofield, A.	Wounded, 11.4.45
	2886032	Sgt	McSwiggan, D.	
	5774993	Sgt	Youngman, A.	Believed PW
	3597146	Sgt	Storey, J.	
	2695796	Sgt	Downes, G.	
	3711552	Sgt	Higham, R.	Wounded, PW
	2929977	Sgt	Lowson, R.	Wounded, 12.4.45
	802114	Sgt	Mitchell, A.	
	2079918	Sgt	McDougal, R.	
	1488383	Sgt	McInnes, H.	
	2886121	L/Sgt	Davidson, A.	Died of Wounds, 14.4.45
	1531269	L/Sgt	Pitman, G.	
	5949701	L/Sgt	Smith, E.	
	3063766	L/Sgt	Stewart, A.	
	3325421	Cpl	Kent, W.	
	2598882	Cpl	Danger, D.	
	3321353	Cpl	Brown, J.	
	2932428	Cpl	Arnold, D.	
	5574002	Cpl	Burgin, R.	Believed PW
	3656776	Cpl	Ralphs, E.	
	1438601	Cpl	Ransom, T.	
	1428802	Cpl	Jones, W.	
	2938050	Cpl	Little, J.	
	4539369	Cpl	Moore, T.	
	4922374	Cpl	Payne, S.	

Date of Departure from UK	Number	Rank	Name	Remarks
6.4.45	5379566	Cpl	Tilling, C.	
	4130949	Cpl	Wilson, E.	
	2989384	Cpl	Jones, T.	
	6970161	Cpl	Harris, H.	
	3653610	L/C	Myler, R.	
	6468171	L/C	Sanders, R.	
	982396	L/C	Hunt, H.	
	7017936	L/C	Hull, W.	
	6921858	L/C	Davis, R.	
	7626887	L/C	Bell, D.	
	3059224	L/C	Ewing, D.	
	405320	L/C	Hill, L.	
	3189342	L/C	Nixon, J.	
	4544674	L/C	Brearton, A.	
	72461	L/C	Baxendale, C.	
	231198	L/C	Craig, J.	
	5951022	L/C	Cronk, D.	
	14417997	L/C	Harrison, T.	
	64420	L/C	Hine, A.	
	2990061	L/C	Livingstone, E.	Wounded
	14233172	L/C	Milner, A.	
	2992710	L/C	Mitchell, G.	
	5182879	L/C	Rose, B.	
	291944	Tpr	Matthews, W.	
	192816	Tpr	Dryland, A.	
	6019818	Tpr	Wootten, J.	
	14246758	Tpr	Cowe, W.	
	211820	Tpr	Mepham, R.	
	3320111	Tpr	Glover, F.	
	13039921	Tpr	Williams, P.	
	360820	Tpr	Longstaffe, G.	
	843563	Tpr	Gill, F.	
	4398964	Tpr	Hemsworth, C.	
	6407758	Tpr	Harrison, S.	
	5890914	Tpr	Jackson, R.	
	213473	Tpr	Wilmott, R.	
	3718414	Sgmn	Powell, T.	
	880000	Tpr	Reilly, M.	
	14429205	Spr	Goodall, W.	Injured
	2134453	Spr	Wilkins, P.	
	14514028	Spr	Harding, N.	Wounded

Date of Departure from UK	Number	Rank	Name	Remarks
6.4.45	1875757	Spr	Warren, H.	
	2598466	Spr	Baker, D.	
	14427258	Spr	Baker, S.	
	14429007	Spr	Llewellyn, W.	
	5575576	Tpr	Blackwell, L.	
	5575505	Tpr	Blandford, J.	
	5574939	Tpr	Beckford, C.	Believed PW
	2068143	Tpr	Conley, S.	
	3974761	Tpr	Cooper, S.	KIA, 12.4.45
	3310551	Tpr	Dunkerley, D.	
	2933029	Tpr	Eden, B.	Believed PW
	14644277	Tpr	Fraser, A.	Believed PW
	5576991	Tpr	Handford, R.	
	6148301	Tpr	Jeavons, O.	
	14295169	Tpr	Jones, K.	Wounded
	856574	Tpr	McCormack, G.	
	5346584	Tpr	Norris, E.	
	7953448	Tpr	Robertson, J.	
	7938759	Tpr	Rutherford, W.	
	5575601	Tpr	Stoneham, L.	Believed PW
	2880100	Tpr	Valentine, R.	
	67098	Tpr	Straker, J.	
	264571	Tpr	Way, G.	
	3909446	Tpr	Merryweather, A.	Believed PW
	13051348	Tpr	Lewis, M.	KIA, 10.4.45
	3058136	Tpr	Allan, J.	
	14002888	Tpr	Berrie, A.	Wounded, 13.4.45
	14406274	Tpr	Caldwell, E.	Wounded, 13.4.45
	7014058	Tpr	Clarke, F.	
	3063536	Tpr	Crandles, R.	
	3063625	Tpr	Coutts, A.	
	4807469	Tpr	Compton, R.	
	6922990	Tpr	Cowburn, L.	
	7897310	Tpr	Crouch, C.	Wounded, 13.4.45
	6923012	Tpr	Day, A.	
	5126401	Tpr	Gaskin, C.	
	14403606	Tpr	Howes, T.	
	5827088	Tpr	Hugman, H.	

Date of Departure from UK	Number	Rank	Name	Remarks
6.4.45	2763568	Tpr	Hair, J.	
	4806975	Tpr	Hart, K.	
	5949843	Tpr	Jerrom, A.	
	3249119	Tpr	Johnstone, E.	
	1606759	Tpr	Jowet, W.	
	14441328	Tpr	Murray, G.	
	5506755	Tpr	Matt, K.	
	14253436	Tpr	Middleton, G.	
	6460407	Tpr	Norris, S.	
	7952393	Tpr	Pond, J.	
	5622129	Tpr	Bennett-Palmer, N.	
	319429	Tpr	Paynter, A.	
	987448	Tpr	Payne, P.	Believed PW
	7114070	Tpr	McNair, A.	
	2984428	Tpr	McDonald, I.	
	402863	Tpr	Summers, F.	
	772576	Tpr	Squires, W.	
	4976694	Tpr	Tideswell, N.	
	5111086	Tpr	Turner, J.	
	3711202	Tpr	Taylor, R.	
	557904	Tpr	Wilson, C.	
	14334311	Tpr	Woodford, J.	
	974097	Tpr	Josling, F.	
	6913277	Tpr	Wilbourne, R.	
	2931430	Tpr	Stalker, W.	
	1533486	Tpr	Ashurst, E.	Wounded
	6285405	Tpr	Davidson, J.	
10.4.45	138559	Capt	MacEwan, F.W.	
	333683	Capt	Almonds, J.E.	
	(Canadian)	Lt	Ross, H.V.	
	333909	Lt	Deakins, W.A.	
	311007	Lt	Rosborough, C.B.	
	232037	Lt	Neilsen, P.	
	146408	RQMS	Cranford, H.	
	3321290	Sgt	Hatch, D.	
	214964	Cpl	Austen, E.	
	7959279	Tpr	Earle, E.	
	10571395	Tpr	Lea, J.	
	14390407	Tpr	Donaldson, R.	
	221843	Tpr	O'Gorman, B.	

Date of Departure from UK	*Number*	*Rank*	*Name*	*Remarks*
10.4.45	3325313	Tpr	McBride, J.	
	14355535	Tpr	Hayes, S.	
	3321301	Tpr	Whittingham, H.	
	293383	Tpr	Cain, F.	
	5573862	Tpr	Stones, A.	
	3326098	Tpr	Bulleyment, J.	
	6850097	Tpr	Barnard, K.	
	859006	Tpr	Willis, A.	
	7608935	Tpr	Smith, A.	
	14002892	Tpr	Wallace, P.	
	7233971	Sgt	McDiarmid, J.	
	5502535	L/Sgt	Connor, G.	
	4806903	L/C	Chapman, R.	
	3061546	Tpr	Watt, J.	
	14248106	Tpr	Weymouth, K.	
	2880450	Tpr	Byiers, W.	
	320025	Tpr	Kennedy, W.	
	965008	Tpr	Tunstall, J.	
	14410859	Tpr	Primrose, D.	
	4206569	Tpr	Baddeley, H.	
	3325438	Tpr	Glacken, J.	
	14424438	Tpr	Francis, O.	
	889850	Tpr	Arnold, W.	
	1429980	Tpr	Pagan, W.	
	3246895	Sgt	Frame, A.	
	408980	L/C	Logan, H.	
	5950912	L/C	Alcock, R.	
	6023321	Tpr	Angel, M.	
	1807167	Tpr	Hobbs, W.	
	3909490	Tpr	Row, F.	
	14293591	Tpr	Kent, T.	KIA, 29.4.45
	5111040	Cpl	Lewis, N.	
	10603329	L/C	Robinson, T.	
	14215003	Tpr	Collison, G.	
	3530972	Tpr	Gaffney, M.	
	14432369	Tpr	Cutting, C.	Injured
	3187240	Tpr	Palmer, T.	
	14614352	Tpr	Crane, E.	
	7615873	Sgt	Page, C.V.	
	7592344	Cpl	Whitley, A.	
	70453	Pte	Bowles, F.	

Date of Departure from UK	Number	Rank	Name	Remarks
10.4.45	7592682	L/C	Simmonds, L.	
	36096	L/C	Vauthier, J.	PW, 1.5.45
	36355	Cpl	Barongelle, M.	
29.4.45	132513	Maj	Fraser, W.	
	132868	Lt	Shute, L.A.J.	
	6287451	Sgt	Hadlow, J.	
	2875165	Cpl	Brown, A.	
	14509636	Tpr	Mulhall, L.	
	3977106	Tpr	Roberts, B.	
	6210634	Tpr	Kirby, E.	
	5890914	Tpr	Jackson, R.	
	1470461	Tpr	McClements, T.	
	5335827	Tpr	Corner, F.	
	10685693	Tpr	Grierson, J.	
	14498652	Tpr	Bednall, D.	
	11423291	Tpr	Turnbull, J.	
	7962730	Tpr	Greener, W.	
	907631	Tpr	Cargill, D.	
	7888628	Tpr	Stewart, J.	
	5345495	Tpr	Percival, A.	
	3245070	Tpr	Kennedy, D.	
	1948605	Spr	Ovenden, T.	
	1077893	Tpr	Johnstone, G.	

Selected Bibliography

Cowles, Virginia, *The Phantom Major: The Story of David Stirling and the SAS Regiment*, Wm Collins, 1958.

Farran, Roy, *Winged Dagger: Adventures on Special Service*, Wm Collins, 1948.

Geraghty, Tony, *This is the SAS: Pictorial History of the Special Air Service Regiment*, Arms & Armour Press, 1982.

Harrison, Derrick, *These Men are Dangerous: The Special Air Service at War*, Cassell, 1957.

James, [Pleydell], Malcolm, *Born of the Desert*, Wm Collins, 1945.

Keyes, Elizabeth, *Geoffrey Keyes, VC: of the Rommel Raid*, George Newnes, 1956.

Ladd, James D., *Special Air Service Operations*, Robert Hale, 1986.

Lloyd Owen, David, *The Desert My Dwelling Place*, Cassell, 1957.

Providence Their Guide, Harrap, 1980.

McClusky, Fraser, *Parachute Padre*, SCM Press, 1951.

Maclean, Fitzroy, *Eastern Approaches*, Jonathan Cape, 1949.

Montgomery, Field Marshal the Viscount, *Memoirs*, Wm Collins, 1958.

Seymour, William, *British Special Forces*, Sidgwick & Jackson, 1985.

Strawson, John, *A History of the SAS Regiment*, Secker & Warburg, 1984.

Warner, Philip, *The Special Air Service*, Wm Kimber, 1971.

Woollcombe, Richard, *The Campaigns of Wavell, 1939–43*, Cassell, 1959.

* * *

The Official Reports and Operational Records of the SAS, now de-classified and made available by courtesy of the SAS Regimental Association.

Index

Aillont-sur Tholen
  Maquis base, 127
Albert, Capt
  Lorris camp, 123
Alexander, Gen
  Italian invasion, 81
  role of SAS, 60
Allen, Pte
  Matruh, 64
Allied Expeditionary Force of
    Inquiry
  German murders, 139
Almonds, Sgt Jim
  Benghazi ambush, 59
  Op GAIN, 121
Anderson, Capt
  drop in France, 155–9
Anderson, Lt
  Op HOUNDSWORTH,
    136
ARCHWAY, 149
Auchinleck, FM Sir Claude John
    Eyre
  SAS formation, 27
  North Africa, 47–8
Augusta
  raid, 76–80
Auxiliary Units, 170
AVALANCHE, 181

Bagnara
  capture, 81–3
  tribute from Gen Dempsey, 90
Bagnold, Maj Ralph
  formation of LRDG, 33–4
Bagush/Fuka airfield raids, 48
Ball,Ooly
  Op HOUNDSWORTH, 132
Baring, Esmond
  Paddy's outburst at, 211
Bateman, Leslie C.
  Maquis liaison, 123–4, 125
Beauvais
  executions by Gestapo, 112
Belfast Arts Club, 217
Belfast Tramways Club, 216–17
Belgian SAS, 148–9, 184
Belsen
  Paddy's arrival at, 205
Benghazi
  harbour raid, 40
  second assault planned, 57
Bennett, RSM Bob
  attitude to killings, 50
  Augusta raid, 77
  Baron von Lutteroti, 56–7, 180
  Benghazi raid, 40
  first SAS recruits, 28
  jeep design, 150–1

post-war visit to Paddy, 218
SAS 'raid' on NZ camp, 29
Tamet and Sirte raids, 39
Tamimi and Gazala raids, 32
Benzedrine, 130
Berge, Georges, xiv
Bergen, 211
Berka Satellite, 40, 43
Berry, Capt, 101
Bingham, Naval Commander Ted
relations with Paddy, 213
Bir Zalten, 66
Bitter Lakes, 21
Blackman, Brig Mike
citation for Paddy's 4th DSO,
163, 168, 169, 175, 181
in Germany, 151, 152, 154, 181
message to Harry Poat, 204
Blair & Vance, Hematite Iron
Works, 10
Blair, Capt Robert
Paddy named after, 8
Blakeney, Tpr, 202, 204
Bond, Maj Dick
death, 162, 171, 173, 174
Germany, 169
joins SAS, 165–6
Oldenburg, 170
Borstal
Paddy applies for Governor's
post, 220
Bouerat
Paddy omitted, 39–40
Bradford, Capt Roy
Op HOUNDSWORTH, 132–3, 134,
135
Brearton, L/Cpl A.
Op KIPLING, 127, 128
BBC news bulletins, 137
Brough, Sgt Jim, 39
description of Desert, 52–3
post-war readjustment to civilian
life, 218
Browning, Gen 'Boy', 144

Brownrigg, Capt
briefs Paddy on drop, 117
Brussels
night in brothel, 148
Bryan, Capt Gerald
billeted at Arran, 20–1
Paddy's training technique, 19
BULBASKET, 103, 105
Byrne, Pte, 40

'cage'
see Fairford airfield
Cairo, 57, 69
Calvert, Brig Mike, 151, 178
Norway, 210–11
Paddy's outburst, 210–11
Camille
Maquis, 129
Canadian Army
Armoured Brigade, 183
4 Armoured Division, 152, 181
HQ at Nijmegen, 151
Cape Murro di Porco
invasion, 71, 72
Carentan
parachute drop, 98
Castellow, Tpr, 111
Chalaux
HOUNDSWORTH base, 140
Chambon
ambush of Maj Fenwick, 118
Château Chamerolles
Gestapo HQ, 123
Château d'Ouchamps, 125
Chelmsford
SAS HQ, 98
Cheshire, G/Capt Leonard
cumulative acts for VC, 168
Chesworth, Pte, 2, 30
Churchill, Randolph, 45, 46, 60
Churchill, Sir Winston
meets David Stirling, 60
German surrender, 209
words on Kevin O'Higgins, 235

WORKSHOP, 21
Close, Capt Roy, 226
Clyde, Tpr, 202, 204
Commando, 11, 'The Scottish',
  embarkation, Lamlash, 21
  glengarry bonnets ('The
    Hackle'), 19
  Paddy accepted by, 17
  training, 18
Cooper, Sgt Johnny, 203
  Berka raid, 44
  first SAS recruits, 28
Corps, Sgt Tommy
  'curiosity party', 185
  Paddy's batman, 83, 117, 118
Cumper, Maj Bill
  Benghazi ambush, 59
  post-war employment, 212
Cunningham, Gen, 36
Cyprus, 22, 23

Dalzell, Cpl C., 76
Danger, Lt-Col David, 162
Darvel, Ayrshire
  SAS training, 92–7
Davidson, Lt Gordon
  escaped POW, 184
  Germany, 168
Davies, Tpr
  killed, 202, 204
Dawson, Tpr
  Carentan drop, 98, 103
Deakins, Sgt W.A., 78
Dempsey, Gen Miles
  orders capture of Bagnara, 81
  SAS training, 70
  Termoli visit, 87
  tribute to SRS, 90
Desert
  description, 52–3
  training, 21
Devine, Tpr
  Op HOUNDSWORTH, 132,
    133

Diary, Official SAS, 40–1
  Augusta raid, 76
  Bagnara raid, 83
  Cape Murro di Porco raid, 75
  Matruh railway, 63
  Termoli raid, 88
Diffley, Sean
  describes Paddy, 14–15
Dimbleby, Richard
  Paddy's grudge against, 69
Djebel Akhdar, 40
  rendezvous, 58
Dourdan
  Op GAIN, 115
dropping zones
  diagram, 109
  selection, 103–4
Dublin
  Shelbourne Hotel, 224
Duffy, Cpl
  capture and escape, 119–21
Duhamel family, 125
Dundalk
  Imperial Hotel, 221
Dunera, HMS, 71
Dunkley, Cpl
  capture and release, 119, 121
Dunne, Paddy, 161
Duvivier, Sgt Jeff
  injuries, 202
  Op HOUNDSWORTH, 132

Eden, 'Jig', 170
Edouard, M. Le Duc, 100, 103
Eisenhower, Gen Dwight D.
  strategic planning of SAS,
    92
  writes about SAS, 144
El Agheila, 1
El Daba, 48, 51
Elliott, Constable
  Paddy's death, 234
Essex, L/Cpl
  Op GAIN, 124

Fairford airfield, Glos
  'cage', 98, 126
Falklands Dependency Survey,
  212–15
Fauchois (French SAS)
  Op KIPLING, 127, 129
Fenwick, Maj Ian
  ambush, 118
  death, 117, 119
  Op GAIN, 115
Ferguson, Tpr, 202, 204
5 Light Anti-Artillery Territorial
  Regt, 16
Fontainebleau
  camp betrayed by Maquis, 117
  Forêt de, Op GAIN, 115
Forêt des Dames, 132
Fowles, Lt
  Carentan drop, 98, 100, 101,
    102
Frame, L/Sgt A.,
  awarded MM, 76
Franks, Col Brian
  re-establishes 21 SAS, xiv
Fraser, Maj Bill, 73
  Germany, 208
  Op KIPLING, 129
  Tamimi and Gazala raids, 32
  Termoli raid, 84
French, Percy
  songs by, 87, 118
Friesoythe, 183
Fuka
  raid, 51

GAIN, Operation, 103, 107, 115–25
Garstin, Capt Pat
  execution, 112
  murderers of, 139
  'stick', 108, 111, 138
Gazala
  SAS raid, 31
Geneifa
  recruiting for SAS, 28

George, Lt
  recce to Meursault, 143
Gestapo
  executions, 112
  infiltrating agents, 104
  interrogation, 125
  posing as Wehrmacht, 208
Glover, William
  Paddy's death, 234
Goddard, Lt 'Monty'
  reclaims trailer and dies, 140–3
Godenshalt, 184
Greese, Irma
  Belsen, 207
Grierson, Lt R.H., 179
Griffiths, Ted, 117
  Christmas leave (1945), 146–7
  Paddy's army application, 16
  Paddy's violence, 223
  teacher and friend, 12–13
Gubbins, Col Colin McVean, 170
Guingand, Brig Freddy de, 61
Gulf of Aqaba
  training, 70
Gunn, Phil
  Paddy's Molfetta outburst, 89
  Termoli raid, 84, 85
Gurdon, Robin, 46

Hackett, Gen Sir John (Shan), 60
HAFT, 103
HAGGARD, 103
Haig, Sir Douglas
  Douglas Mayne named after, 8
Hall, L/Cpl Jimmy 'Curly'
  death, 129
  Op KIPLING, 127–8
Hanbury, Mrs Christine, 146
Harrison, Capt Derrick, 69, 140
  Cape Murro di Porco raid, 74
  co-author of citation of Paddy's
    4th DSO, 163, 168, 175, 181
  KIPLING, 126–31
  MC, 127

Oldenburg, 169
Paddy's Molfetta outburst, 89
Paddy's reactions, 230
readjustment to civilian life, 218, 226
training in Palestine, 70
training in Scotland, 93
Hastings, Stephen
  lost in desert, 55
Herold, Maj
  murder of SAS men, 139
Hicks, Brig, 73
Hitler Youth, 169
Holliman, Capt, 37
horses
  SAS training, 70
Hotel Morvandelle, 143
HOUNDSWORTH, 103, 132, 140
Housman A.E., 217
Howards Cairn, 64–5
Hull, L/Cpl William (Billy)
  ambush, 192–7
  Belsen, 207
  cannon fodder, 181
  drop in France, 155–9
  German attack on Paddy, 191, 192
  Germany, 155, 185, 186, 187
  Oldenburg, 172, 174
  Paddy's driver, 159
  Paddy's 4th DSO citation, 166
Hurst, Tpr
  Carentan drop, 98, 102, 103
Hylands, Chelmsford, 146

Ion, Tpr
  recce parties and death, 123
Iredale, Capt Tim, 172, 179
Italy
  invasion, 81–90

Jackson, Sgt 'Jacko'
  Tamet raid, 6–7
Jedburg transmitters, 105

jeeps
  design, 150–1
  Paddy's decorated, 160
  Paddy's gramophone, 162
  Paddy's PA system, 162
  stolen and used by Germans, 188–9
Jellicoe, Lord George
  Baron von Lutteroti, 57
Jones, Cpl 'Ginger'
  escapes execution, 112
  hospital, 161–2
Jones, L/Cpl T.
  awarded MM, 76

Kabrit, 21
  SAS base, 28
Kahane, Karl
  Berka raid, 44
Kaine
  German spelling of Maine, 153, 188
Keevil airfield
  Garstin 'stick', 108
Kershaw, Sgt Dave, 90
  Tamimi and Gazala raids, 32
Kesselring, Field Marshal, 47
Keyes, Col Geoffrey
  appointed CO Commandos, 23–4
  attacked by Paddy, 24
Keyes, Lord, Admiral of the Fleet,
  WORKSHOP, 21
Kiel, 149
  taking of, 209
Kiel Canal, 207
KIPLING, 103, 126–31
Kramer, Camp Commandant (Belsen), 207
Kubale, Hauptmann, 123
Kufra Oasis base, 58, 61
Kusten Canal, 183

La Ferté Alais, 110

Lac des Settons, 143
Lamlash, *see* 11 Commando
Langton, Maj Tommy, 165–6
Laycock, Maj-Gen Sir Robert, 22
  letter to Paddy about VC, 177
Layforce, 22
Le Mans, 125, 126
leg-bags
  parachuting, 93
Les Ormes
  SS executions, 127–9
letters
  from Paddy to men's families,
    140
  see also under individually named
    recipients
Lewes, Jock
  co-founder SAS, xiv
  death, 39
  SAS training at Kabrit, 29
  Tamet raid, 4
  Tamimi and Gazala raids, 32
Lewis, Tpr M.
  death, 171, 173, 174
  Oldenburg, 170
Lilley, Cpl E.
  Berka raid, 44, 45
  first SAS recruits, 28
Litani River
  raid, 22
Lloyd Owen, Maj-Gen David
  LRDG Commander, 33, 34
  witnesses Paddy's outburst, 69
Long Range Desert Group
    (LRDG)
  formation, 33–4
  partnership with SAS, 33
  Tamet raid, 3, 6
  Tamimi and Gazala raids, 31
loot/booty, 199, 206–7
  Augusta raid, 77–8
  Matruh railway, 64
Lorris
  Maquis camp, 123

Lorup, 183
Lovat, Lord, 26
Lucy-sur-Yonne, 133
Lutteroti, Baron von
  escaped prisoner, 56–7, 180
Lutton, L/Cpl, 111

MCR I receivers, 105
McCluskey, Rt Rev Fraser
  greeted by Paddy, 96
  Paddy's funeral, 234
  post-war meeting with Paddy,
    219, 226
McCollum, Maj, 221–2
McCollum Strollers, 221
McDonald, Sgt, 32
  Tamet and Sirte raids, 39
McEwan, Capt Mike
  letter to Paddy, 219–20
McGinn, Sgt 'Maggie'
  Op HOUNDSWORTH, 132–3
McGonigal, Ambrose
  friend of Paddy, 216
McGonigal, Eoin
  death, 32, 216
  joins 11 Commando, 19
  Litani River raid, 23
  Paddy's outburst, 21
  SAS recruits, 28
McGonigal, Mrs, 216
McGunn, Lt R.
  Litani River raid, 23
Maclean, Fitzroy, 46
  Benghazi ambush, 59
McLeod, Brig R.W., 210
  command of SAS, 92
  TITANIC, 98–9
MacPherson, Col Tommy
  Commando training, 19–20
Malta, 47
Manfredonia, 83
Maquis, 104
  Aillant base, 127
  assessment, 138

Camille, 129
Forêt d'Orléans, poor
    organisation, 117
Jean, 132
Lorris camp, 123
Paddy's suspicions, 106–7
Marigny
    dropping zone, 98
Marrinan, Desmond, 220–1
Marschler, Rittmeister, 123
Marsh, Maj Tony
    Belgian SAS, 148–9
    citation for MC, 182
    commands merged squadrons,
        183
    dressing down by Paddy, 184
    favours appointment of Maj Dick
        Bond, 166
    HOUNDSWORTH base, 140
    Mersa Matruh, 64–5
    Paddy's outburst, 71–2
Matthews, George, 222
    Paddy's death, 233
    Paddy's reactions, 229–30
Matruh railway, 62–3
    Mayne, Barbara (sister), 9
    comments on decorations, 63
    letter from Paddy: Sicilian
        invasion, 78–9
    letter from Paddy: Termoli raid,
        87
    looks after mother, 220
Mayne, Douglas (brother)
    birth, 8, 9
    grows away from Paddy, 225
    KOs Paddy, 225
    letters from Paddy: Benghazi
        raid, 41, 43–4, 45
    Paddy's preference for an MC,
        167
Mayne, Frances (sister), 9, 224
    childhood, 11
    letter from Paddy after death of
        Eoin McGonigal, 32

letter from Paddy: Tamet/Sirte
    raids, 39
Mayne, Margaret Boyle, née Vance
    (mother), 10
    letter from Paddy: Falklands
        Dependency Survey, 212
    letter from Paddy: Machrie Bay,
        18
    letter from Paddy: Norway, 210
    Paddy's relationship with, 11,
        220, 231
Mayne, Molly (sister), 9
Mayne, Lt-Col Robert ('Paddy')
    Blair
    back injury/operation, 213–15,
        223, 225
    birth and childhood, 8–15
    boxing, Irish Universities'
        Heavyweight Champion, 13
    cameras, interest in, 86
    11 Commando, 'The Scottish',
        accepted by, 17
    death and funeral, 233–5
    decorations: DSO, 38; 1st Bar, 76,
        79, 80; 2nd Bar, 144; 3rd Bar,
        163–82; Croix de Guerre, 144
    drinking, 72, 220–2, 224, 225
    humour, 144–5, 198–9
    hypnotism, interest in, 222
    Incorporated Law Society of
        Northern Ireland, appointed
        Secretary, 216, 229
    inner secret life, 232
    killing, attitude to, 50
    leadership, 232
    music/singing, tastes in, 87, 214
    Parliamentary candidacy, offered
        postwar, 229
    poetry, tastes in, 213–14, 217
    prisoners, treatment of, 113–14,
        207
    Queen's University Officer
        Training Corps, joins, 16
    Riley, 2.5 litre, 217, 233

Royal Cameronians, volunteers
    for, 17
Royal Ulster Rifles, transfers to,
    17
rugby, achievements, 13–14
swearing, dislike of, 231
violence, 20–1, 23, 24, 62, 69,
    71–2, 89, 210–11, 216–17,
    223
women, attitude to, 15, 89–90,
    230–1
Mayne, Thomas (brother), 9
    death, 11
Mayne, William (father), 9
    death, 69
    letter from Paddy: Cyprus, 22
Mayne, William (brother), 9
Melot, Maj Bob
    Benghazi raid, 58
    HOUNDSWORTH base, 140
Menginou, L/Cpl, 119
Merryweather, Tpr A.
    Carentan drop, 98, 102, 103
Mersa Matruh, 65
Meursault
    recce, 143
Midgeley, Jack, 216, 217
Milice, 117, 138
Militia, 138
Minden, 200–1
Molfetta
    relaxation, 89–90
Montgomery of Alamein, Bernard
    Law, Viscount
    acceptance of SAS, 66
    appointed Commander 8 Army,
        57
    Italian invasion, 81
    letter from Churchill on
        surrender, 209
    refuses extra men, 60–1
    strategic planning of SAS,
        92
    tribute to SRS, 90

Montrose, Duke of
    provides venison, 21
Moore, Cpl Tom
    Matruh, 64–5
    message from Mike Blackman
        for H. Poat, 204
Morkel family
    describe Paddy, 14
Morran drop, 132
Morris, Lt
    'curiosity party', 185
Morrison, Tpr
    Garstin 'stick', 110
Morvillier, Jacques
    Op HOUNDSWORTH, 132, 134
Mount Pleasant, Newtownards
    origins, 9
Movilla Churchyard, 234
Movilla House, 10
Muirhead, Capt Alex, 78, 204
    Cape Murro di Porco raid,
        74
    Germany, 208
    letter from Paddy to his mother,
        140
    Termoli raid, 84
Muller, Pte, 48

Nienburg
    fall of, 204
Nijmegen
    Canadian Army HQ, 151
Noble, Sgt J.
    awarded MM, 76
    Op HOUNDSWORTH, 137
Norman, Tpr
    Garstin 'stick' 108, 110
Norway
    SAS role, 210–11

O'Dowd, Pte
    Matruh, 64–5
Oldenburg, 149
Osterscheps, 183

Other Men's Flowers, (Wavell) 217
Ouzouer-sur-Loire, 125
Owen, Tpr, 202

Packman, Tpr, 123
Palestine
    training, 70
Pantelleria, 21
parachuting
    dummies, 98–9
    Scottish training, 93
    see also dropping zones
Paris
    Liberation, 144
Patton, Gen, 126, 130
Pedder, Lt-Col Richard
    killed, 22
    Paddy steals Mess drinks, 20–1
Phantom Signals Group, 149
pigeons
    Carentan drop, 101
    food, 158
    messages, 105
Pleydell, Malcolm
    Baron von Lutteroti, 56–7
    Paddy and killings, 50
    Paddy's relationship with mother,
        11, 231
Poat, Maj Harry, 150
    bravery, 200
    favours appointment of Maj Dick
        Bond, 165–6
    MC, 76
    map, 201
    Paddy's No 2, 93
    post-war, 219
    SAS graves, 112
Poole, Lt
    Carentan drop, 98, 100, 101, 102
Porter, Sir Robert, 217
Prendergast, Guy
    formation of LRDG, 33
Psychological Warfare Branch
    treatment of prisoners, 113–14

Purcell, James, 223

Quattara depression, 48, 51–2
Quirk, Senator
    Paddy knocks out, 223

Ralphs, Cpl E.
    Oldenburg, 170, 171
Randall, Lt John, 149
    Belsen, 207
ration packs, 105–6
Reggio
    invasion, 81
Richardson, Lt Stewart
    Op KIPLING, 127, 128
    prisoners, 139
Riding, Capt C.L.
    Op GAIN, 118, 121
Riley, Lt Pat, 184
    Bagnara invasion, 82–3
    Germany, 209
    readjusting to civilian life,
        218
    restrains Paddy, 71–2
    Termoli raid, 84, 87
Ritchie, Gen, 27, 36
Rommel, F.M. Erwin
    disturbed by SAS, 67
    El Agheila, 66
Rose, Cpl, 46
    first SAS recruits, 28
    Benghazi raid, 40
    Cape Murro di Porco raid, 75
Rotterdam
    disembarkation, 151

'S' phone, 105
SS
    posing as Wehrmacht, 208
Sadler, Capt Mike, 37, 117
    Falklands Dependency Survey,
        212–13
    grenade episode, 144–5
    LRDG, 34

Op GAIN, 121
SAS graves, 112
Tamet raid, 6
Sidi Haneish raid, 53–4
Salerno
landing (AVALANCHE), 81
Sand Sea
Kufra base, 61
Sangro River
raid considered, 88
Saunders, Tpr
Carentan drop, 98
Schlee, Lt Philip, 152, 166, 168–9,
171, 174, 175
Schofield, Sgt
Oldenburg, 169, 170
Scot, Lt John, 167, 168, 173, 174,
175, 181, 184
Scratchley, Maj Sandy, 52, 62–3
Seekings, Sgt Reg
Belsen, 207
Berka raid, 44, 45, 46
Cape Murro di Porco raid, 74–5
Djebel rendezvous, 58
Gen Dempsey's address, 70
lost in desert, 55
MM, 76
post-war reminiscences, 226
Sangro River raid, 88
Tamet raid, 2, 3, 4, 5, 6
Tamimi and Gazala raids, 32
Termoli raid, 84
Wesel raid, 149
Sicily
invasion plans, 71
Sidi Barrani
SAS raids, 48
Sidi Haneish
raid, 53–4
Sillito, L/Sgt John
awarded MM, 76
simulators, 99
Sinai
training, 70

Sirte
Operation, 37–40
ski training, Lebanon, 68
Skinner, Pte A.
awarded MM, 76
Smuts, Field Marshal, 60
Special Air Service (SAS)
badge, design, iv
correct role for, 59, 92
disbandment, 212
formation, 26
German regard for, 152–4
HQ, Chelmsford, 98
ideal qualities, 126
'L' Detachment, founding of, xiv
partnership with LRDG, 33
special raiding squadron, 69,
70–80
21 Regt re-established, xiv
22 Regt created, xiv
Special Forces Club, 225
Stephens, Lt, murdered by
Germans, 139
Stirling, Bill
letter from Paddy, 64
resigns command, 92
Stirling, Col David
artistic leanings, xii
attitude to killing, 50
Blitzwagon, 46, 48, 51
captured, 67
CO Commandos, 25–36
competition with Paddy, 43
Eoin McGonigal, 216
future of SAS, 212
lost in Desert, 55
meets Winston Churchill, 60
Paddy's secret inner life, 232
Paddy and a VC, 177
promoted to Captain, 28
promoted Lt-Col, 60
relations with Paddy, 63
Sirte raids, 37–9
Tamet raid, 6, 37–9

Stirling Lines
  opening of new barracks at
  Hereford, xiv
Stirling, Peter, 26
Storrie, Capt
  Bagush raid, 48
Street, Vivian
  'B' Squadron, SAS, 66
SUPERCHARGE, 63
Surrey Dane, Lt David
  Oldenburg, 170, 172, 174
  Paddy's 4th DSO citation, 166–7,
    168, 175
  Paddy and a VC, 176
  SAS disbandment, 214
Swansea Hotel, 15
Syria
  Litani River raid, 22

Tamet
  Operation, 37–40
  Paddy in raid, 1–7
Tamimi
  SAS raid, 31
  tensions, operational, 129–30
Termoli
  invasion, 83–8
  tribute from Gen Dempsey, 90
Tilbury, embarkation, 151
TITANIC
  assessment, 98, 103
TITANIC IV, 98
Tobruk
  fall, 47
Trower, Tony, 204
Tonkin, Maj John
  'curiosity party', 184–5
  Falklands Dependency Survey,
    212–13
  German agents in Maquis,
    105–6

Ulster Monarch, HMS, 71, 76

Vaculik, Cpl, 112
Valentine, Sgt
  capture of female German
    Corporal, 185

Walker, Sammy, 14, 112
WALLACE, 144
Warburton, Cpl, 44
Warrenpoint, 220
Watson, Lt J.M.
  Op GAIN, 115, 118
Wavell, Archibald, FM Lord, 217
Weihe, Lt
  Garstin 'stick', 108, 110, 111,
    113
Wellsted, Capt Ian, 136–7
  bravery of 'Chalky' White, 132–5
  injuries, 202
White, Sgt Frederick 'Chalky'
  humane killing of a prisoner, 84
  Op HOUNDSWORTH, 133–5
  post-war, 227
  Tamet and Sirte raids, 2, 39
Williams, Tpr Paddy
  ambush, 192–7
  German attack on Paddy, 191–2
  Germany, 155, 185, 186, 187
  Paddy's batman, 160
Wilson, Cpl R.
  Op GAIN, 124
Wiseman, Capt Johnny, 62, 138
  Augusta raid, 77
  Bagnara invasion, 82
  Cape Murro di Porco raid, 75
  loot, 77
  MC, 76
  'shaved' by Paddy, 62
  Termoli, 83, 87
Woodhouse, Lt-Col John
  creates 22 SAS Regt, xiv
WORKSHOP, 21

Youngman, Sgt A., 184